A HUMAN TRAFFICK

S L A V E

Lucy,
Thank you

A MEMOIR

JABALI SMITH

SLAVE: A HUMAN TRAFFICKING SURVIVOR FINDS LIFE
Jabali Ornelas Smith

TitleTown Publishing
P.O. Box 12093 | Green Bay, WI 54307-12093
920.737.8051 | www.titletownpublishing.com

Edited by Kylie Shannon, Judy Mandel & Jackie Gay Wilson
Cover design by Mark Karis
Design & Layout Editor | Erika Block
Interior design and layout by Euan Monaghan

Some names and identifying details have been changed to protect the privacy of individuals.

Contact Publisher Tracy Ertl for all review, media, reprint inquires at
(920) 737–8051 | tracy@titletownpublishing.com

Represented for Film and Television by Intellectual Property Group
Office of Joel Gotler | (310) 402–5154 | joel@ipglm.com 10585 Santa
Monica Blvd., Suite 140, Los Angeles, CA 90025

PUBLISHER'S CATALOGING-IN-PUBLICATION DATA

Smith, Jabali.
SLAVE: A Human Trafficking Survivor Finds Life / Jabali O. Smith.
– 1st edition. Green Bay, WI : TitleTown Pub., c2017.

ISBN: 978-09-96295-14-7

Proudly printed in the USA by Ken Cook Co.
www.kencook.com

10 9 8 7 6 5 4 3 2 1

DEDICATION

This book is dedicated to my son, Aché Durrani Smith.
Believe in yourself and all your dreams will come true!

TABLE OF CONTENTS

ACKNOWLEDGMENTS

Piero Amadeo Infante – Thank you for the wise council.
Jesse Bradish – Thank you for your help and for believing in me.
Randy Peyser – Thank you from the bottom of my heart.
Without you, we would not be here.
Amber Espinosa-Jones – Thank you for all your hard work.
Tracy Ertl – For your kindness, authenticity, and faith in me.
Judy Mandel – For your patience and fantastic work.
© Jackie Gay Wilson – Photo credit

Prologue

The warm, blue waters crashed softly against the glistening white sand. I watched my 12-year-old son Aché frolic in the waves with his friends under the hot Mexican sun. His joyful screams brought unconditional love racing to my chest. Sipping a cool piña colada, decorated with a slice of pineapple and a small pink umbrella, I was delighted to be able to provide this experience for my only son and our friends. My waiter was dressed in an all-white, bellman-like outfit. His cotton shorts and shirt did little to help with the heat.

"Would chu like sontin else?" he asked in broken English.

"No, gracias," I replied. Our tables and chairs were positioned under large umbrellas alongside other vacationers. The sounds of young college kids echoed in the background, mixed with a crying baby, and a trio of brothers having a sand fight before their mother snapped at them, all filling my ears as the mariachi band did a rendition of "Bamboleo" in perfect harmony. In the middle of his beach play, Aché looked up at me, waved, and smiled. His golden brown skin made his teeth appear extra white. Again, I was present to my love for him. Our table was full of half-eaten burgers, fries, tacos, and freshly cooked shrimp on large skewers. There was an array of different drinks, partially consumed beers, juices, and bottled water.

My attention was suddenly stolen by a child no more than five years old. Her hair was matted and disheveled. Her green-and-pink-striped shirt was old and dirty, and her once-white skirt was torn and frayed on the bottom. Snot had collected on the rim of her nose and the sweat from her little head dripped down the side of her cheek, mixed with the tears of her predicament. The dirt of a long day's work made a muddy mess on her otherwise beautiful, innocent face. I looked up to see who was caring for this sad and heartbroken child. A few feet away stood an old, equally sad-looking woman who appeared to be her grandmother. As my eyes found hers, she quickly looked away, forcing me to look back into the eyes of this desperate child.

Her big brown eyes looked through me, as though she had looked into the face of a thousand people that day. With hopeless despair, she held up a small box with an assortment of multi-colored packets of Mexican gum – red, pink, blue, green, and white. "Chicklets," she said in a monotone voice. Her inclination was to turn and walk away almost before I could respond, assuming I would ignore her or shoo her away like those before me and presumably those after me.

My heart was touched by the sad reality of her plight. It had been 37 years since I was last in the town of Puerto Vallarta, Mexico. Returning turned out to be an unexpected encounter with the ghosts of my childhood – brought on by the innocence and pain of this infant human being.

A rush of emotions filled my body as I reached into my pocket to retrieve a 100 peso note. I handed it to her expecting a smile or some outward expression of appreciation, as this amount was many times the value of the entire box. But there was none. As she accepted the bill, she took a double take, wondering if I didn't know the value. I smiled reassuringly, a smile I had cultivated over many years to hide what I felt inside. She waited for me to pick the ones I wanted, but, to her mild surprise, I took the entire box and set it on the table. She looked back at her caretaker, waiting for a signal, which she got in the form of a small nod of her head. The old woman turned to walk away, equally unimpressed with the size of my contribution. The little girl managed to mumble out "gracias," then stumbled through the hot sand in pursuit of her *abuela* (grandmother).

I could only hope that my gesture would provide the little girl with some moments of rest and maybe a snack before she had to get back into the blistering sun. However, this was not the case. This child got no rest. The old lady reached into her knapsack and handed her another box. I watched them cross the endless crowd of vacationers, stopping momentarily, raising the box in offering, then lowering it after receiving a dismissive gesture from an uninterested old man.

The sounds of the crashing waves and the mariachi band had now faded into silence. My thoughts were pulled back into history, back to the ashes of my childhood when I was a child slave, an early victim of human trafficking in this very town.

***

The year was 1979 …

I could see myself sitting on the floor of a small, stuffy, and humid motel room in Puerto Vallarta, Mexico. Incense and the breath of three adults absorbed all the clean air. The walls were white, with heavy brown stains from water that had leaked in over the years. The brown trim that surrounded the bathroom doorway matched the worn curtains that kept the room dark despite the early morning sun.

The squeaking of the loosening bolts on the bed frame made a sound similar to that of an old passenger train, not unlike the one I had ridden into Mexico City a few months earlier. I listened to that, along with the low baritone humming of a large black man, whose sweaty chest and broad shoulders blended into the shadows of Room Number 7, giving me a sickening but familiar sensation. His humming matched that of old Tibetan monks far away in a mountain temple. He was accompanied by a tall, slender brunette whose sweaty wet hair stuck to the side of her face even as she gyrated aggressively, pushing her backside against the abdomen of her humming cohort. Both were blissfully unaware of the third member of the trio, another brunette whose fully naked, short, plump body earned her a distant second place in this pornographic ceremony.

I sat with my back against the wall at the foot of the bed watching, but wishing I could go outside to the beautiful white sand beach. In my mind's eye, I would walk the two blocks across the small cobblestone streets, passing all the vendors and restaurants until I arrived at the beautiful blue ocean. I wanted to get away, but I knew my only way out was through my imagination – or until I heard him call out … "OM!!!" … in climactic ecstasy. The thought of the vastness of the great blue ocean brought me a sense of peace until I drifted off to sleep.

Awakened by the gentle touch of the slender brunette, I was happy to have slept past the climax and cleanup. It was only the two of us, and the musty funk of their bodies and breath had now been washed away with a warm tropical breeze from the open window. The shadows had been burned away by the light and heat of the sun.

Mildly bewildered, I followed her instruction to take a shower and get dressed. Soon we were walking amongst the crowds of tourists shopping and taking pictures of their happy lives. On the corners, in the alleys, and sprinkled about in the crowds, I saw the real people of Puerto Vallarta. They were poor and hungry, many of them begging for help. I was keenly aware of the disparity between all of us. We'd finally made it to the beach, and I was excited to get in the water. As we walked along the promenade, I was impressed with the restaurants that sat facing the ocean and the tropical decor that decorated each one. Open patios with a variety of white-clothed tables could accommodate any size group. They were accented with palm trees and tiki torches not yet lit. Waiters scurried around helping the mostly American and European guests. The beach was filled with families and couples enjoying their vacations.

I saw the hopeless and forgotten making their way through the hot sand, selling different handmade toys, wooden puppets, and fruits. Why were some so happy and rich while others suffered and starved? And, amidst all of it, there was me, 1800 miles from home – scared, empty, and ashamed. No one knew that I was a victim – beaten, broken, and abused – who wanted to whisper to tell anyone who would listen: "I don't belong here; this woman is not my mother."

Between the two restaurants was a creek that ran down from the tropical hills above the beach. The promenade walkway built over it created a mild incline and bridge, allowing the water to make a natural connection to its mother, the ocean. As we walked across the bridge, below I saw a desperate and hungry-looking family cooling off and resting from a hard day's work in the shade of the bridge. I was perplexed by my predicament: to my left was the opulence and leisure of rich people who were laughing and carrying on. To my right, below them, in what was something just short of the gutter, a family crouched on the brink of life and death.

***

"Dad … Dad!" I was pulled back from history as Aché waved and called for my attention. I waved back in acknowledgement. "Are you ready to go?" he asked as he and his friends approached. I knew his question meant they were ready to go.

"Yes," I replied, happy to break away from this painful recollection.

We gathered our belongings and headed back to our villa, which sat high above the beach, nestled on the hillside overlooking the Puerto Vallarta coast. My memories lay heavy on my mind. As I began to pay closer attention to my surroundings, I realized we were staying in the same part of town and walking through the same streets and in the same neighborhood where I had been forced to beg all those years ago.

What were the chances that, of all the places in Puerto Vallarta where my friends could have booked us, it would be here? We made our way through the cobblestone streets of vendors and tourists, and I realized that I was now one of the "rich" people who I had envied so much as a child.

I remembered how jealous I'd been of the kids who had laughed and had no cares, as they trailed behind their parents who window-shopped. They had even had the luxury of being able to eat at a restaurant. Now, it was my child who was blissfully unaware of the hungry children in his midst, as Aché complained about the long walk back.

After several requests for a treat, we stopped in a small store. Entering the store, a bright orange and black package caught my eye and with it came a strong flashback from of a lifetime long ago. It was Gansito, a Twinkie-like pastry. I recognized it, not because I read it, as I couldn't read then. Rather, it was the image of a smiling baby duck that peered over the name that caught my eye. The duck was surrounded by a blue outline and a pink backdrop. Below it was a delicious-looking chocolate frosted cake, layered with a touch of white cream. A soft, gooey drip of cherry filling spilled over the white cake.

I made an immediate move to the small end shelf on which it sat along with many other pastries. Aché noticed my attention being grabbed and followed. I picked up one of the Gansitos and examined it thoroughly.

"What's that, Dad?" he asked, looking over my shoulder. I couldn't respond immediately – the weight of my memory had left me at a loss for words. This was the pastry I had longed to eat all those years ago, but, like all candy products and sweets, they were forbidden to me by my captors. If I got caught eating anything of the sort, it meant a stripping, a cold shower, a whipping with a belt, and then a week in the closet – naked, with only water and one small meal every other day. That was the punishment I received for eating a piece of candy without permission, and it kept me from ever getting my fingers on a Gansito. It was my forbidden fruit. I saw it everywhere we went and always wondered how it's creamy, gooey filling tasted.

My lethargic response was too slow for Aché's attention span. He walked off, looking for his own treat. When I fully returned from my flashback seconds later, I felt compelled to honor the little boy in me that longed for, and suffered over, this simple pleasure. I picked up a dozen, shocking Aché and all our friends.

"Oh my God, Dad, why are you getting so many?" The kids looked back and forth at each other smiling, "Can I have one? Can I have one?"

"Of course, they're for everyone," I responded.

Hiding my eagerness to try one, I reached into the bag and took one out, then handed the entire bag and all of the contents to Aché, much to his dismay.

"I have to carry it?" he blurted.

"Boy!" I snapped back in calm irritation in response to his laziness.

I walked off on my own in a mild haze. Each second before my fingers tore past the smiling duck, I grew a comfort I did not know had been absent. I felt happy to experience the cathartic closing of this small but significant piece of my past. As I took each slow and mindful bite, I thoroughly appreciated the creamy goodness of the cherry cream cake in my hands. Then I ate the lion's share of the dozen. Perhaps my life will be filled with a rich and creamy goodness after all …

***

However, the cruelty and brutality I experienced as a young trafficking victim were only equaled by the mystery of how I wound up in the clutches of a messianic, doomsday sex cult to begin with.

My name is Jabali Ornelas Smith and this is my story. I want to invite you on this journey to witness my life, so that you may understand what really happens to child victims who are trafficked. It is my intention to provide healing through the Well Child Foundation and increase awareness so that we can all help to put an end to the suffering of the world's youngest and most innocent beings.

ONE

Love and Poverty

After the summer of love came the winter of fatherless children.

— PIERO AMADEO INFANTE

I was born across the street from the Black Panther Party headquarters on the border of Oakland and Berkeley, California on March 26th, 1971. My mother was a revolutionary, an intellectual, a Buddhist, hippie, an occultist with a love for black men. My father was Stephen Smith. He was a conservative, light-skinned black man from a small town in Texas. He, like many of the black men in that area at that time, "hit it and quit it." Not wanting a relationship with the likes of my mother, he found a lovely Jewish woman, and, together, they dedicated their lives to the cult of the Jehovah's Witnesses. My father gave me my first name, Jabali. My middle name was the name of my mother's first husband, a Cuban Mexican named Ralph Ornelas. Since my parents weren't married, I did not get the privilege of carrying on the name of my birth father and his before him. Although it was just a slave name, as are all those given to my people, I thought it should be mine.

I was raised by my mother. She was of Irish descent and from a poor second-generation working class family from Oakland, California. She had three children before me by two different fathers. My brother Pio and sister Isabella were the children of her first and only husband, Ralph. He was a cruel man who hospitalized my mother several times, dislocating her jaw and knocking out most of her teeth. I believe he was the man who first broke her spirit. He died of hepatitis from sharing a dirty needle while shooting heroin when Pio and Isabella were very young.

During the last days of Ralph's life, my mother met a man named Jerry

Weeden. He was a tall, handsome, educated black man who was said to be a descendant of Kunta Kinte. While together, they had my brother Jaci. Four years later, she met my father. According to my mother, they were "just friends." However, four years later, one evening, he dropped by to visit her while she was ill and, nine months later, I was born.

She was a single white woman on welfare with four biracial children living in Berkeley, California during its heyday, and, although we were very poor, I remember feeling loved. But we lived in a world of extremes. It was a time when riots exploded in the streets in protest of an unjust war and crooked, racist cops patrolled the streets. People walked hand in hand believing in *free love*. Music echoed the message of peace and revolution. A handheld calculator and digital watch were cutting-edge technology.

It was a time when it was still dangerous for a black man to walk hand in hand with a white woman. Hippie mothers engaged in acid parties and let their children openly smoke weed. And hitchhiking could get a girl home safely.

I was born into these times. Photos show me as a beautiful little boy: part black, part American Indian and Irish with green eyes and blond hair. Bewildered and amazed at life and all of its possibilities, I felt grounded within the love of an acid-taking, weed-smoking, free-love-practicing, orgy-indulging, revolutionary mother.

I was witness to the bizarre and outright crazy world that our mom inhabited. My siblings shared in all the love and hardships; we stood by each other like baby soldiers, moving from one home to another more times than any of us could remember. We all became resilient and crafty because we had no other choice.

I remember the wonderful smells of mom's black-bean stew made with onion, garlic, salt, parsley, carrots, and spices wafting through the house with a faint scent of incense beneath it. The loud, thunking noise from Pio practicing his nunchucks in the bedroom and the sounds of Marvin Gaye lilting softly, a joint between mom's lips as she cooked. She talked about the day when her children would be part of a new system once these "Nazi pigs" fell from power. Isabella hung in the kitchen with mom, learning the ways of womanhood, while I played games with my brother, Jaci, the "enforcer." Games like "that's my car," a game we played while looking out the kitchen window at the passing cars, or "hot lava," where we'd jump from couch to chair trying to avoid the imaginary lava, which was the newly vacuumed floor. A vacuum borrowed from the neighbors.

Those were the games we had to play because for us there would be no Evel Knievel dolls, no plastic soldiers, no GI Joe with the Kung Fu grip. The simple things in life would be enough for our family then. Welfare checks were not enough to buy toys for a family of five. It was also a time when we were truly a family close like families should be, at least to me. That was the autumn of 1974. We all got chickenpox that year, except for Pio, who was always out somewhere. At 13 years old, he was busy running the streets. Sometimes I would wake up to only Isabella. She was my second mother; she loved me like a mother loves a son. She was 11 years old. We lived in an old pink building set between a car garage and a liquor store on San Pablo Ave, Berkeley. It stood two stories high and was run-down and stinky. The smells of old carpet, alcohol, and garbage reeked from inside each apartment. There was no real place to play so we played in the streets, unaware of the dangers.

Sneaking next door to the liquor store to get candy was my favorite adventure. With a few pennies and a lot of charm, I could get loads of the tooth rotting sweets. When I didn't have pennies, I would eat the old gum off of the sidewalk on San Pablo Avenue.

Going next door to the liquor store was forbidden, which never stopped me. When mom asked, "Jabali, did you go next door and buy candy?" I'd answer, "No."

"Are you sure?"

"Yes."

Unknown to me, my face and tongue were covered with Purple Dye Number 5. She would fall out laughing at me.

"What's so funny?" I thought. I had an incredible sweet tooth that may have been inherited from my father. I once climbed to the top of the kitchen cabinets in pursuit of a can of bright red cherries, only to have it and everything else come crashing down on me. The fall didn't hurt 'cause I was more focused on getting those cherries. I pushed passed all the spices and jars and cans that could have given me a concussion to the can of cherries, only to find a white greasy substance that didn't taste anything like cherries. It was a can of Crisco cooking grease. I was so disappointed, and to add insult to injury, Jaci came in from outside after hearing the crash and laughed at me hysterically. That humiliation brought on the pain of the fall. But Isabella came to my rescue.

"Aw, poor baby, are you ok?"

I loved my big sister.

Life was a struggle, even at the age of three. Hunger and neglect were constant reminders of our place in the world. Aki, another fatherless kid from our old neighborhood by the Black Panther headquarters, was a close friend. He often visited us with his older brother, Hilary. They, too, suffered the sad reality of poverty. It was Aki who showed me how to hump, so I could hump Sierra, a girl of mixed heritage who lived downstairs in #4. I learned how to undress Sierra and myself, lay her on the ground, get on top of her and hump her. Aki got a big kick out of it and tried to spy on us when I finally got her somewhere private. She was the daughter of a white lady I didn't like very much whose husband had run out on them. Sierra's mom had a friend, another fat white lady with arms the size of small dogs. She had mistakenly called Jaci a pig. Innocent and shocked, Jaci told mom. With a screech, and "What?!" she flew down the stairs in what seemed like a single bound, confronted the woman, and began beating her ferociously. She smashed her face into a bike sprocket and slammed her down on a glass coffee table. They were like two giant prehistoric dinosaurs battling to the death. Slap after slap, the two exchanged blows for what seemed like an eternity. Finally, after convincingly beating her senseless, mom returned upstairs, triumphant. She had only one battle scar, plus four bloody, tiger-like claw marks on her cheek.

That Christmas, I met my dad, Stephen, and my grandmother and grandfather, and aunts and uncles for the first time. It took me some time to comprehend that these people were my family, too. I was very excited to have a real daddy, and, when they brought in a Big Wheel, I knew I loved all of these people. I almost forgot about them in my excitement to go ride it. On my first test drive down the balcony, where Pio had once tied Jaci in a sleeping bag and hung him over the side, we found a card that slapped back and forth against the wheel, causing a loud rattle. Mom quickly demanded that it be removed, to everyone's dismay, but especially mine. Still, I was happy to have something other than Sierra's vagina to play with.

That gift meant more to me than any gift I have received since. They only stayed for a short while that night, but I felt a deep connection to them all and felt their love for me. I promised I would come visit them very soon and meant it. Shortly after their visit, we moved again. This time into a garage in the back of our godmother Jackie's house with its cold cement floor, uninsulated walls, cobwebs everywhere, and one dirty window with years of dust collected on it. Mom cleaned it out and made it semi-livable, and we settled in. Jackie, my mom's friend, adopted us as her "god-kids", and, without her help over the years, our lives would have been much rougher. She fed us and gave us shelter when mom's selfish inability prevented her from doing her motherly job. Even though we lived in the garage, it was in a neighborhood and we had a lawn out front, away from the boulevard of hookers and pimps and drug dealers milling around.

Jackie was a friend of Mom, a young white woman who had fled an abusive home as a teenager. She and Mom were pregnant and due on the same day in the same hospital. They were wheeled past each other on their way to the delivery room when I was born. But her baby died at birth. Her husband, the baby's father, was an African American man named Bennie Bowden, who was known as a badass. He was a black belt in karate and I loved watching him demonstrate his kicks. I remember the day I overheard mom saying he was found dead in a bathtub up the street from our house. His death was a mystery.

My best friend was a boy named "Hippo," another mixed boy. Unlike most of us, his father Lucky was present in his life consistently. They lived up the street along with his mom, Nancy, in a hippie commune that served as a center point for many families like ours. Lucky was an eccentric man, a Korean War veteran. He knocked all the interior walls out of the two-story home. Hippo and I watched his father beat his mom on occasion. They were at the tail end of their relationship at that time and both of them began to see other people. One man Nancy brought home was a man named James Lewis. A tall, black man with a big Afro, he was curiously nice. James played and laughed with us the whole day, making a great impression me. Having no real male figure in my life, I wanted to get him home to meet mom, so I asked him to walk me home.

"Ok, where do you live?"

"Down the street," I told him. "Let me show you."

It was dark out, but I knew my way at four years old. He offered to give me a ride in his van. It was a passenger van he got from work, as a driver for senior citizens. I loved his van, and ran up and down the aisles to his dismay until we arrived at my house three blocks away. When we got there, I invited him to come inside to meet my mother. He agreed, came in, and spent the next 20 years with her. None of the other children loved him the way I did. But that never stopped him from being kind. He was a gentle and loving father figure to us, especially to me. James was on his way to becoming a great jazz musician, and, like them all, he had an addiction. His was whiskey. His alcoholism didn't bother me like it did mom. She would abuse him while he was drunk, and, although it was unhealthy for me to witness, it was par for the course to me.

We moved again, and this time James came with us. It was a nasty, depressing, filthy house in a horrible neighborhood in west Oakland. There was no electricity, and the sewer pipes were broken, which created a disgusting smell. Mom was often gone and James was often drunk, leaving me to find comfort where lonely children do – in their imagination. Sometimes mom wouldn't come back until late. That was the worst because I was hungry, James was drunk, and it was dark. The only lights that illuminated the house were the small red light from the tiny battery-operated radio James had tuned to the jazz station and the red cherry from his cigarettes. James was so dark-skinned I couldn't even see him; I only heard his low baritone voice instruct me to listen to the music and come sit on his lap until mom got home.

It was a sad and lonely time. Pio and Isabella didn't even come around. They were old enough and smart enough to stay with friends. Jaci and I, however, had to endure the squalor and disgust. One day, Isabella did come to visit. We played together lovingly, and, while swinging me around in circles, she accidentally dropped me face first on the concrete, knocking out my four front teeth. This added to the misery of that horrible house.

Hippo came to visit with our friends, Johnny and his brother Lion – another pair of mixed kids whose father was absent. I was amazed that they were able to find our house.

Riding bikes to West Oakland from Berkeley was an astonishing feat for children all younger than age ten. But those were the times and we were the ragtag batch of fatherless, unsupervised, biracial kids who would attempt it.

Finally, after some time, we moved again, this time to a wonderful, clean, upscale neighborhood in North Oakland. It was a beautiful, white, three-bedroom house across the street from a school. The only catch was we had a housemate. A greasy-haired white man who ate raw hamburger meat on burnt toast. Mom ran him off not long after we moved in.

She was an outspoken, independent woman who wasn't afraid to speak her mind or confront someone or something if she didn't agree. Her strength was the backbone for her four fatherless children. I enjoyed this house very much and had fun riding my Big Wheel up and down the beautifully manicured street. I felt no fear of having it be stolen, and had no fear of a bum accidentally hitting me with his discarded bottle of Ripple. Isabella moved back in with us, and, although Pio was still "in the streets," he spent a lot more time with us, too. I even got to have my friend, Dawn, come over. She, too, was a light-skinned, mixed child without a daddy. Dawn, Hippo, and I were very close and loved to play together. She was also one of Jackie's god-kids.

The streets of Berkeley became a huge part of my life. Spending most of my time at the Mediterraneum Cafe on Telegraph Avenue, I was exposed to all the crazy happenings that Berkeley is known for. The nudists, the Black Panther Party, the Hare Krishnas, hippies, the Hells Angels – they were all influencing me and my community of mixed, fatherless children. We were a mischievous band of kids who got into all kinds of trouble. We would run the streets asking for money, playing jokes on Cal students, stealing, throwing rocks, or swimming in the creek on campus. I was free to express myself, free to see what life had to offer, free to meet new people, free in the complete meaning of the word.

One Sunday, after eating a free meal given at the Krishna temple, Hippo, Aki, Hilary, Jaci, and I decided to go to the campus to play in the egg chairs at ASUC. Someone had the clever idea to pee in the soap dispenser and watch people squirt piss on their hands. One by one, they all took turns peeing in it; it took the three of them to fill it up. Then we all sat back and watched as unsuspecting men washed their hands with baby pee. Someone finally realized there was something wrong with five giggling children in a bathroom and chased us out, cursing and screaming. I relished the mischief.

Later that day, Jaci, Aki, and Hilary planned to ditch Hippo and me. We were the youngest at five and six, and too young to keep up.

"Go home!" Jaci said.

"I don't want to."

"Okay go back to the Med."

"No, I want to go with you!"

"You're too little."

The three of them hopped a fence, and, in an instant, the two of us found ourselves ditched. "We don't need them anyway," I shouted after them.

"Hey! Let's go to Codornices Park," Hippo suggested.

"No, it's almost dark, let's go to the Med." Returning to the Med, we found no familiar faces.

"What should we do?" Hippo asked.

"I have a good idea," I said. "Let's go to Jackie's." We walked all the way to Jackie's house on 61st and Shattuck, a little over a mile away, keeping in mind that we were only five and six years old.

Over the next year, the streets of Berkeley and Oakland became my home. Greeting people, known and unknown, up and down Telegraph was my favorite pastime. All the vendors knew my name and gladly looked out for me. I got free falafels from the falafel lady, a free doughnut from the old doughnut man, and free apple juice from the juice stand. Meeting strangers was part of my everyday life and something I enjoyed very much. I simply asked each man, woman or child: "Do you want to be my friend?" That was my line and it worked well.

The older boys always used me to get food, and then they would all have one big bite or two depending on who was the hungriest (mostly Jaci), and they'd leave me the last bite. We were poor, hungry, street kids who found joy in each other and happiness in creating mischief.

When I did get to visit my biological father, it was only for the weekends – a stipulation Mom insisted upon. I was conflicted. I knew he was my dad and I had a connection to him, but he was very strict and unloving and insisted that I pray to Jehovah every time I came to visit, which I hated. He took me to the Kingdom Hall where Jehovah's witnesses pray, and I met all his friends. I got to hang out with his other child, my little brother, Arran, who I loved very much. But my father beat him often and that scared me. Arran was so scared of getting in trouble he would hide the red leather belt our father used to whip him with whenever I came over.

Although he never hit me, I felt if I ever stayed long enough I would be next. Despite the whippings Arran got and having to go to the Kingdom Hall, I liked visiting him. Unlike my house, his was always clean and well kept, and there was always breakfast, lunch, and dinner. I knew I wouldn't go hungry, which was the norm in living with my mother. Occasionally, he even bought me a well-needed pair of pants from JC Penney.

I was always thrilled to see Grandma Vera and Grandpa Amos, Uncle Lance and Aunty Peggy. They all lived together in a cute Craftsman-style house in south Berkeley. Grandma kept her house immaculate. Nothing was ever out of place, never a dish in the sink or a dust ball in a corner, and she forbid Arran and me to touch the fine china she kept in the armoire. As soon as I got to her home, she put me in the tub and washed me from top to bottom. I wasn't used to that kind of care and cried while she soaped me down, but she did so with kindness and told me while she scrubbed my filthy ears that I was loved. When it was over, she gave me sugar-covered strawberries … after dinner. On Saturday mornings, Arran and I watched the *Three Stooges* reruns along with the *Little Rascals* and *Godzilla* movies downstairs in the den.

Sometimes Aunt Peggy and Uncle Lance would take me shopping at the mall. But as soon as I got used to the finer things in life I was whisked away back into the clutches of poverty. In those small moments, though, at least I knew I was loved. We spent the best Christmas of my childhood in that beautiful white house. After having thoroughly destroyed my Big Wheel, I got a new (used) bike, which I didn't know how to ride, but was thrilled at the prospect of learning.

Again we moved, this time back down onto San Pablo Avenue. The two-story duplex was set off the main boulevard between a small used car lot and a storage building. There were no tenants that lived on the bottom floor, so it felt like it was our house.

James had odd jobs; one was teaching music at one of the local city colleges, which I accidentally got him fired from for being a "distraction" to the class on more than one occasion. Mom was still hanging out at the Med every day but had long since made a reputation of being an outspoken spitfire who was known to whip a grown man's ass if he offended her or any of her kids. So I spent the majority of my time on "the Ave."

Life was a struggle, but we scratched by. After James lost his job, he decided to play his flute on the street for money. Mom opened a sandwich stand on the campus, and that helped add to our family's reputation as Telegraph Avenue regulars. Jaci and I were always hungry but were never allowed to eat the sandwiches she sold. We would be famished and beg her, but that just made her angry. She encouraged me to go get one of the other vendors to give me some of their food. Jaci was too old, at age ten, and too ashamed to have to go ask other people for food. We were constantly hungry, except on the 1st and 15th, when a certain payment arrived.

My brother Pio was also making a name for himself as a daredevil. He was a wild child who loved salsa music and who was quick to defend his family's honor. Constantly at the Med, my play dates with Dawn and Hippo started there, and always brought us to the Cal campus.

Every day, the same patch of freaks and weirdoes went to their favorite spots at either the campus entry or by the fountain or gate. They would scream, rant, and rave about all the problems of the era – the Vietnam War, racism, political and social problems, and of course, the doomsday fear mongers were there.

Then there were the students who rallied behind or argued against whomever touched most accurately on the day's hot topic. Suddenly, 25 to 50 Hare Krishnas would come beating up the street singing loudly with a strong rhythmic bass drum, finger cymbals, and bells: HARA KRISHNA HARA KRISHNA KRISHNA KRISHNA HARE HARE, HARE RAMA HARE RAMA RAMA RAMA HARE HARE. I know that song like I know *Happy Birthday*.

Dawn was scared of the Hare Krishna people and their bald heads, with that small sprout of hair on the top and the paint they wore in between their eyes. In fact, they made her tremble with fear. I led my friends under and through the legs of the crowd to the student union where we could play in the egg chairs or on the elevators, and then go to the creek. We had hours of fun and adventure on the Cal campus. Sometimes, the pottery teacher would let us play with clay after the class was over. I was the ringleader of our trio and relished the position.

Before we left, the adults (Mom) gave instructions to all of us, but made sure to give me especially clear instructions as to where we could and couldn't go. I knew the campus well, but Mom knew my adventurous spirit often got us in trouble. One day, we were supposed to go back to the Med at 3 p.m. when we heard the tower bells on campus ring three times. But I had decided we should go to the track and field stadium to dry off on the steam vents after we'd soaked ourselves in the creek, so we never heard the bells. And before we knew it, it was well past three. We didn't see any familiar faces when we got back to the Med, so I figured that we should hitchhike back to Jackie's house.

I had hitchhiked many times with Mom and saw no harm or danger in it at all. So, I led us to the spot on Telegraph where Mom often caught rides, just south of Dwight way. We all knew how to put our thumbs out like Mom did, and we waited. Three wet little kids (the steam vents didn't work very well) stood on the side of the road hitchhiking. A guy who happened to know Mom and recognized me picked us up, and he drove us all the way there. We were in big trouble when we got back, but they were amazed by our fearless stupidity. I was 5 years old.

March 26, 1977 was my sixth birthday. Mom and a friend took me to the movies to see *Silver Streak* with Richard Pryor and Gene Wilder. I didn't understand what people were laughing at, but I acted like I got the jokes, and the audience seemed to get a big kick out of my movie commentary and me.

Returning home, I was very happy to find myself at my very own surprise party. My best friend, Hippo, had recently left the country on a trip to Kathmandu. Our parents didn't arrange for us to say goodbye; one day he was just gone. But Mom was good at throwing parties and did her best to fill it with friends. Yet, without my best buddy and Dawn, it was bittersweet at best. Pio, Jaci, and Isabella were all there to help me ring in a Happy Birthday. James gave me seven silver dollars. The seventh, he said, was one to grow on.

That night, one of Isabella's friends spent the night. I got to sleep with my big sister and her friend. While Isabella was in the bathroom, her friend, in just her panties, began playing with me and rolled on top of me, pressing herself on me sexually. It was thrilling, but, when Isabella came back into the room, she acted like nothing happened. I was very excited and told Mom and James about my experience the next morning.

Mom said, "Cool!! Did you like it?"

"Yes!" I replied enthusiastically to Mom and James's laughter.

***

That night was the last time I felt like we were a family. Shortly after, Mom was about to shatter the lives of her four children on a scale so vast and so shocking that the ripples would span the next four decades ...

TWO

They Came

T he ASUC student union on the campus was a popular place for kids whose parents didn't care where their children played. Before I was born, one day, Najim, who was one of Pio's friends, fell asleep in the student union and was picked up by the campus police and taken to juvenile hall. Pio, being a young revolutionary whom Huey P. Newton would have been proud of, decided to stride up and down Telegraph Avenue, collecting money from everyone so he could bail out his nine-year-old friend. All the locals appreciated Pio's young revolutionary spirit, and he was able to collect forty dollars for Najim's bail.

The next day, Pio went down to free his buddy and was promptly arrested for truancy. Mom heard the word on the street, and, when Pio didn't come home, she went downtown to get him. After battling the Berkeley police department, she ended up in front of a judge, who told her the only way he was not going to force Pio to go to school was if Mom moved out of the country. So, Mom quickly packed up my brothers and my sister and fled to Cuba via Mexico. Mom did not believe in sending her kids to school, and would not be told what to do with her children by anyone, even a judge.

They ended up in Veracruz where she met with the Cuban attaché, seeking asylum, only to be denied and sent back a few months after arriving. Word got out and Mom was thought of as being a brave and courageous revolutionary in the community.

Mom maintained her hatred for public schools, and, as a result, none of us went to school the way normal kids do. No peanut butter and jelly packed lovingly with a side of our favorite treat. No rushing to get out of the house to make it to school on time, no homework assignments.

We learned what the streets had to teach about the harsh truths of hunger, pain, and disappointment, as well as how to navigate socially from the slums to the hills. black, white, Latino, Asian, Jewish, gay, whatever; we learned how to get along with everybody. The streets were our first and only real teachers. There were some alternative schools in Berkeley that my siblings and friends went to whenever they felt like it. Odessa and Kilimanjaro were schools where sex education consisted of letting the kids watch pornography.

I was enrolled just before the end of the previous year, so I got a taste of school life but didn't really like it – although I did have a crush on my kindergarten teacher. Now six years old, I was ready to go back to Kilimanjaro for the coming school year, but Mom discouraged it. I wanted to go simply because Jaci, Aki, Hilary, and the crew went there, and I wanted to be around them.

Jaci went to visit his dad in Seattle, Washington in the summer of 1977. That summer, life remained quiet around our house. Pio was gone as usual, and Isabella was now off with her friend Julia. I never learned how to ride that bike I got for Christmas, with no one to teach me, and now my Big Wheel was gone. So, I found fun playing in the back yard and planting different plants and flowers with Mom, or I'd hang with James on the "Ave" as he played his flute, leaving me to run up and down the streets.

James often had a can of beer in his hand. Amost always. One day, he got very drunk and I dared him to jump over a wall in front of the ASUC. It was about a ten-foot drop. He was too drunk to realize the drop was that far, even though he'd been at that very spot a thousand times. By the time he realized his mistake, it was too late. "Aaaaaahhh!" was all I heard. I think his drunkenness saved him. Otherwise, that kind of fall could have been fatal. I helped him onto the bus, and we limped the three or four blocks it took to get home. Later that night, he went to the hospital. He had broken his ankle.

James and my mom had a very volatile relationship. She didn't like his drinking, and he couldn't stop, nor did he want to – even after she split his eyebrow open by slamming a door on his face. Their fighting made me very sad. I couldn't understand why they always fought so much, and I felt like it was all my fault because I was the one who had introduced them.

After their big fights, Mom would kick James out of the house for varying lengths of time. Right after this incident, they had a fight, Mom kicked James out, and the house felt lonely and deserted. Pio was running the streets and was hardly ever home. Isabella now had a teenage life and was barely around, and Jaci was still visiting his dad. I was watching "Happy Days" on our small 12-inch black and white TV. Clamps were attached to the channel-changing rod where the dial once sat, and a coat hanger replaced the antenna. The Fonz was about to make his historic motorcycle jump, and Mom was cleaning the house. She reminded me that I had to turn the TV off once the show was over. I agreed and anxiously waited for the commercial break to end. When the show resumed, to my dismay, it was a "to-be-continued" episode.

Mom turned the TV off and ran a shower for me. I had recently begun taking showers because I was a "big boy" now. The lights were low and the house was clean. Incense filled the air. I really enjoyed it when the house was clean and I was clean. If there was food, too, well that was a trifecta. A clean house and food made me feel loved and cared for, like I felt at Grandma's house. I was just getting ready for bed when there was a knock at the door.

A beautiful woman stood smiling at the entrance. She was dressed all in white and greeted Mom as if they knew each other. Mom was very excited to see her and opened the door wide to invite her in. The woman paused for a moment, looked behind her, communicating to someone there, and then quickly darted off into the night.

"Who was that, Mom?" I asked, puzzled by her nervous behavior.

"You'll see," she said, with an excited gleam in her eye. Moments later, the woman returned. She led a group of very strange-looking people into our home. They were all dressed in white, some of them had head wraps on, while others wore shawls lightly draped over their heads. There were men and women of different ethnicities. Children of varying ages accompanied some of the women. A couple of boys were about my age.

The two boys were introduced to me by one of the women: "This is Omson and Freedom."

We said "hi" like all children do upon meeting other children, with an unenthusiastic and barely audible sound. As the group entered our home, the living room was too small to accommodate everyone, so some began to line the small hallway that led into the kitchen. Many took positions on the floor, after making a very comfortable seat of pillows and blankets for someone at the head of the room who had not yet arrived. Others brought an assortment of small instruments – a tambourine, a pair of shakers, a group of jingle bells, which reminded me of Christmas, and small finger cymbals that sounded like the bells at the Krishna Temple. Some others rustled around the kitchen, asking mom questions, which she happily answered with a smile.

They had a very distinct smell, one I was not familiar with, but also which made me think of the Krishna Temple. Finally, the person whom everyone had been preparing for arrived. He was a tall, black man who was also wearing all white. His big body looked strong and healthy. He had a huge smile on his face, and, when he appeared at the door, everyone got down on their hands and knees and bowed to him, including Mom. He took his place on the pillows. Still smiling, he put his attention on me.

"Hello, Jabali," he said.

"Hello," I replied slowly. I looked at Mom for reassurance. Her ear-to-ear smile let me know she was happy I was meeting this person.

"This is OmGod!" Mom said excitedly.

"God??" I said, and my over-animated shock brought laughter to the group. I thought, God was up in the sky; God was a big white man with a long white beard. Or maybe he was blue with many different faces and arms like Krishna, or a fat bald man like the Chinese Buddha, but not an ordinary black man with two arms, two legs, and two eyes.

"Yep!" Mom said matter-of-factly. After a few cordial comments to me, "OmGod" gestured for me to have a seat. I headed over to the chair that was in the corner, but I was redirected to sit on the floor.

One of the women picked up the bells and began shaking them rhythmically, while another began a slow rhythm on the tambourine that landed in unison with the bells. A soft chant began with one person singing, then another and another joined in until everyone began to chant.

"I AM GOD. I AM THE LORD. I AM GOD. I AM THE LORD."

Although it was all pretty strange to me, "weird and unusual" was not unusual for our family. I sat in a mild kind of shock. After all, I was sitting in a room with God!

When the song was over, Om began to speak to the group, and, as he did, one of the women began to rub his feet, applying oils and lotions from different bottles. I did not understand the words he was speaking – not because they were in another language, but because they were adult words. I struggled with them as their rhythm became hypnotic, and soon I fell asleep.

The next day, everyone was gone except one white lady named Perfection. They all had strange names: Inspiration, Lovelight, Harmony, Devi, and Lady Sunshine.

These women began to show up around our house continually at random times, as if they had a right to our home. Mom was very protective of her home, our home. We all knew who was the boss around the house, even James knew. But, with these people, she was completely different. She let the women come and go as they pleased. She let them not only rearrange our furniture, but allowed them to throw things away. This was very confusing to me. I didn't like those women because they were taking over our house.

One day, Mom brought me over to an apartment on Channing and Fulton in Berkeley. Before we got there, I inquired, "Where are we going, Mom?"

"It's a surprise."

When we got to the "surprise," it was the group's apartment. I was very disappointed. We were greeted by Perfection. Om was there, sitting on the same kind of pillow setup they'd arranged at our house. His eyes were closed. His legs were folded in the meditation position. His index finger touched the tip of his thumb. The rest of his fingers spread across his knee.

The house was quiet and all the blinds were closed, which hid the sun's light. There was that distinct smell in the air – their smell. Mom walked me into the bedroom where the two brothers, Omson and Freedom, were playing with two other much younger children; they were about two years old – Triumph and Prosperity. She told me to play with the boys while she talked to the adults.

Omson and his brother Freedom were strange to me. Neither of them was very talkative, nor did they know about or talk about things that boys our age would know and talk about – like Evel Knievel, the Fonz, or the Six Million Dollar Man. As I discovered we had very little in common, I grew tired of them. When I came out of the room, Mom was gone. She had left me there and didn't tell me she was leaving; I was very angry and ran out the door after her. I spotted her halfway up the block.

I screamed "MOM!" and ran towards her, crying and very upset.

"Why did you leave me?"

"I thought you were having fun with your friends."

"Those are not my friends; they're weird."

She was very dismissive of my feelings and told me to stop whining.

Jaci finally came back from his dad's in Seattle with stories of adventure and fun. I missed him so much and was ecstatic to see him, but he didn't seem to care at all or miss me in the slightest bit. When I asked him if he wanted to go outside and play, he said, "No," and asked mom if he could go over to Hilary and Aki's house. That hurt my feelings, but I loved him so much I said, "Yeah, let's go over and visit them."

"Not you," he said.

I often felt hurt by Jaci and never knew why he seemed to hate me so much, but my attention span was short and my years few. I told him about meeting God and he laughed. I told him to ask Mom, and when she confirmed, he was in disbelief.

The next thing we knew, the group moved into the apartment below us. We grew to know them as "the Lovers." Mom had been steadily relinquishing her power to them. They threw away most of our furniture and stripped the house down to a bare minimum. I was forced to sit and listen to them sing praises to Om every night and early each morning.

"Mom, can we watch TV?" I'd ask.

"Ask Om," she'd respond.

"Ask Om?" This was very different than the independent, strong-willed, revolutionary woman who had protected her children against anybody who challenged them. We were now forced to get Om's permission for anything and everything we wanted to do. If we wanted to go outside, we had to ask Om. If we wanted to go visit our friends, we had to ask Om.

Jaci always had me ask. He would say, "Jabali, go ask if we can watch TV."

29

"No, you!" I'd respond. But he was able to convince me that I was more likely to get what we wanted. So, I would finally be the one to go downstairs and ask.

"What are you going to watch?" he would counter.

"Some cartoons."

"I suppose it's okay."

Little by little, Mom gave all her power to him, to my bewilderment and the disgust of my siblings. James wasn't around much at the time. He stopped coming around soon after the Om lovers showed up. I only saw him periodically on Telegraph Avenue. Pio hated all of them from the start. Now sixteen, he really wasn't going to listen to these people tell him he had to get up at 6 o'clock in the morning to sing praises to some black dude who claimed to be God.

A short time after they moved in and took over, Pio came by to pick up his belongings. I knew something was wrong with my oldest brother, but I didn't know what. He was very angry, but he didn't explain why.

"I'll see you later," he said, as he grabbed his belongings and stormed out. That was the last time I would see him or be able to speak to him for a very long time.

Life went on and became stranger and stranger every day. One day, I wandered into the downstairs house to play with Omson and Freedom. On entering, I saw a startling picture hanging above a doorway. It was a close-up of a man's black penis inside a white vagina. The glistening, shiny penis and open vagina made me uncomfortable. Having been exposed to sex at a very early age, I was familiar with the act (in theory). I knew the sounds. I knew what a naked woman looked like. I had even poked out a hole in a Playboy centerfold's pic and humped it when I was four years old. But this picture was something my young mind could never have imagined. I went to get Jaci to show him and he was equally amazed. Part of me wanted to look at it for hours. Another part of me was disgusted.

Afterwards, when Jaci saw his beautiful sister getting fucked, it really sent him for a loop. He didn't understand what was going on and asked Mom.

"Why are they here, Mom? What do they want? I saw him doing Isabella the other day!"

"Don't worry, honey, everything will be okay," was Mom's only response.

After a couple of months, the Om lovers had full control over the entire building. Mom often left me with them and would sometimes not even come home at night, which was very unsettling to me – that, and the fact that they had thrown out our TV.

"All things belong to the Lord now, Jabali," explained Inspiration.

"Where is my mom?" I asked.

"She'll be back."

"I want my mommy!"

"She'll be back soon!"

I cried myself to sleep that night, waiting for my mom. The next day, Mom showed up bright-eyed and full of smiles. I was upset with her for having left me alone and for not coming back all night. She gave me a big hug and said, "I'm sorry honey. Would you like to go over and visit Jackie?"

"Yes!" I replied excitedly. I missed Jackie and couldn't wait to go see her. I spent a couple of days with her. She always made me feel safe and loved. But, when I got back to our house, the entire place was packed up. Everything was either gone or in boxes about to go. I was shocked. When I asked Mom what was going on, she told me she a had a great big surprise for me. I had grown weary of those words, but she explained that we were going on a trip on an airplane and it would be very fun.

"Are you coming Mom?"

"Yes, but not right now. I'm going to meet you when you get there."

"Where are we going?"

"To San Diego."

It sounded fun to me, but I knew there was more to it than she was telling me. "Jaci and Isabella are going with you."

"What about Pio?"

"No, Pio's not going."

"I miss Pio, Mom."

"I know sweetie. You'll see him soon."

This was the second of many lies soon to come. It was a sunny, late summer day and all our things were gone. I sat in a Yellow Cab, saying goodbye to Mom. She was leaning into the window. Her multicolored blouse and dangling earrings were accented by her red hair. I sat next to Om, and they were convincing me that I was about to go on an adventure that was going to be super-fun, starting with a plane ride. I looked at our house and at Mom as we drove off. She was smiling as she waved goodbye.

The airplane ride was very exciting. I got to sit by the window and see the earth from high in the sky. I got to eat lots of peanuts and drink juice, and, in the excitement of being on a plane, I had forgotten all about the strangeness of what was happening. When we arrived in San Diego, half of the group had already settled into an apartment in Mission Bay.

Jaci was there waiting. He didn't know where Isabella was, or Mom, or Pio. We were happy to see each other, but we were both perplexed by our situation. We wondered where Isabella was. Adjusting to these people and their way of life was still hard and very confusing. Jaci was especially unhappy to be in this predicament.

THREE

Alone with Strangers

I woke up to Inspiration's smiling face and kind, big brown eyes. Her hand gently touched my belly. "It's time to sing the praises to the Lord."

The small two-bedroom apartment in Mission Bay, San Diego was filled with the smell of their incense smoke. The sun had not yet made its full ascent into the morning sky. Birds sang their songs and the dew melted slowly from the sycamore trees.

I was instructed to go into the "Lord's" room. Still half-asleep, her words did not register with me. She then led me by the hand to his room and had me sit against the wall in meditation position, facing the bed where the "Lord" Om was sitting, also in meditation position. His eyes were closed, his hands sat relaxed on his knees, and his index fingers pressed against his thumbs as before.

The room was small and stuffy, ventilated only by the small, sliding glass window that was partially opened behind him. I sat there, confused, wondering where my mom was and wishing I was somewhere else. The entire room was filled with naked women and children! Everyone sat facing him, some with their children not old enough to sit still. We all sat there in silence for a long time, most everyone's eyes were closed.

Thoughts of Mom ricocheted through my mind. Then a deep baritone voice startled me and broke the silence: "I AM GOD. I AM THE LORD. I AM GOD. I AM THE LORD," he sang with a nursery rhyme-like tone.

After repeating the phrase for several minutes, the women joined in all at once as if it had been rehearsed or like they'd been given some cue that I'd missed. He opened his eyes and smiled at me, encouraging me to join in. The nudity made me extremely uncomfortable, especially seeing his erect penis poking out from between his folded legs.

I tried not to make too much eye contact with anyone, but his incessant gaze coached me into singing the absurd words in their childish tone. As I struggled to sing along and fumbled with the words, the bells and shakers played by the women helped drown out my little voice.

Jaci and Isabella sat on the opposite side of the bed. Isabella's eyes were closed and Jaci's face looked shamed and forlorn. Jaci wore his embarrassment and pain sadly in his eyes – his ten-year-old mind recognizing the severity of our predicament. I looked to him for safety and reassurance in this situation, but received only a spiteful and evil glare back. He rarely ever displayed the kind of brotherly love I hoped for from a big brother – even before the Om lovers showed up. Jaci seemed to always have hated my innocence, and this hatred grew exponentially in our new quandary.

My attention was broken by the two-year-old Triumph, who crawled in front of me. Triumph didn't crawl like most babies, on his hands and knees; he crawled on his hands and feet with his little naked booty pointing to the sky. His playfulness and innocence distracted me from the absurdity of the situation.

I received another smile and nod from the Lord that told me it was okay for me to play with the baby, Triumph. I used this permission as an excuse to follow him out of the room. Perfection was in the kitchen preparing breakfast. I knew Jaci was envious of my being able to exit, and I teased him with a look of my own.

Then Triumph defecated a hard brown clump in the middle of the living room floor. In disgust, I told Perfection, who in turn told me to pick it up – with my bare hands – and put it in the toilet. I was mortified with shock and nausea. Perfection stood over me, and I stood standing over it. I asked her if I could get some toilet paper, and she scoffed at my cleverness. I could tell she didn't like me, my brother, or my sister very much, but as with everyone else, I was determined to win her over. She forced me to pick it up right there, and its warm, slippery texture made me drop it. She then walked away, waving her hand, and begrudgingly allowed me to get some toilet paper. It was still a revolting job, even with the 12 feet of tissue I used.

Perfection left to kneel down at Om's feet and told him with a gesture that breakfast was ready. He acknowledged her with a slow blink and a nod of his head then called out very loudly, "OM!" And like a high school band at rehearsal, the singing and instruments tapered off, then came to a stop. Everyone remained seated until he was served a hot bowl of nine-grain cereal with dates, raisins, and walnuts mixed in to his liking. Then the rest of us were allowed to take turns receiving a bowl of cereal as well.

In the days that followed, Isabella helped prepare the food and was often out with the "ladies," learning the inner workings of daily operations. She was issued an incense-sales quota to return to Om at the end of each day, along with the rest of them. Night and day, Om and the women molested her. I couldn't see or tell all the ways their molestation was affecting her, but it hurt my eyes every time I was forced to watch.

I felt her shame and embarrassment each time she climbed off of him. I could see he whispered things in her ear that intensified and added to the depth of her brainwashing – which came much faster than that of Jaci's or mine.

I was easy to control because I was so young and impressionable, my mind still half in fantasy. But Jaci had the best perspective of the three of us, knowing fantasy from reality and having his virginity still intact. Maybe that's why he appeared to be so much more miserable than Isabella and me. I felt like they were keeping her away from me on purpose, and I wondered why she seemed content to be apart from me. She had always been my strongest supporter, ally, and friend, but now I felt her becoming one of them. Her distance added to my loneliness, combined with Jaci's cruelty and neglect. My innocence was being poisoned by everything and everyone.

When Isabella brought me my bowl of cereal, I felt a renewed hope that she had not forgotten me. Just that small gesture, I took to mean that she still loved me. I did not care for the taste of the cereal, but ate all of it when I was told there would be nothing else served. I tried to interact with Jaci, but he was completely unreceptive. So, I sat with Omson and Freedom.

Each day was entirely structured and centered around Om, in which everyone pleased him and fulfilled his every wish. Women brushed his hair, filed his nails, rubbed his back, feet, and knees, or performed fellatio or whatever other sexual act he wanted that day. Unfortunately, fellatio became Isabella's job. I was not used to that and did not like it, but I thought, *"Maybe that's how you're supposed to treat God."*

One day, when I left to return my bowl to the kitchen, I saw a figure pass outside the living room window that looked onto the balcony. Then I heard a knock at the door.

"Who is it?" Perfection asked. A woman's voice answered and Perfection opened the door.

When I saw who it was, I let out a scream, "Mommy!!" Jaci turned in shock. We both ran to her arms. She gave us a big smile and hugged us, kissing the tops of our heads. She paused momentarily to give Isabella a hug, too, but Isabella's enthusiasm was not present. Then she pressed on and passed us to greet Om.

I was so happy to see her. It had already been a couple of weeks since I had last seen her in Berkeley, and I hoped she was coming to take us back. I had never spent so many days without her. Even when I went to visit Grandma and

Stephen, I only stayed two or three nights tops. The last couple of weeks had seemed like an eternity.

On instruction from Om, Mom shut the bedroom door behind her. I noticed there was often "adult talk" going on around me, which often required me to leave the room. It was a small nuisance that affected me heavily. It was especially bothersome this time, because I had seen my mother for all of 45 seconds before she was inaccessible again. I waited anxiously for the door to open, and, when it finally did, Mom emerged smiling.

We attacked her again with hugs and long-missed childish affection, which she reciprocated happily. Mom took Jaci and me out for ice cream that day. The sun was now high in the late morning sky, and I cherished the warmth of her hand holding mine. We walked slowly towards Mission Beach. The sun caressed us lovingly, and my heart was renewed; I felt safe again. As we walked along the sidewalk, I listened to Jaci articulate our mutual sentiment of loathing and misery. He bombarded her with complaints and questions about our being there, and I seconded his comments with an occasional "Yeah."

Mom always used distraction techniques to trick me and break my train of thought whenever I expressed unhappiness, but Jaci stayed focused on the topic about how unhappy we were. When we got to the ice cream shop, I was ecstatic. The Om people didn't allow me to eat sugar, so it was a wonderful treat to be with Mom and get to have ice cream. I ordered rainbow sherbet, and Jaci got his favorite, Rocky Road. We walked along the beach, forgetting where we really were and whom we were really with. Mom fielded the questions and complaints like a veteran, never admitting guilt. She deflected and reworded our concerns, rather than outright lying to our faces when she got cornered. She was, after all, still our mom, and she was not going to tolerate any "mess" from a ten- and six-year-old. Whenever she was really challenged, she would use bullying or threatening tactics to win. By the time we returned to the apartment later that day, we believed we would be going home "soon."

When we arrived, Isabella was in a back room on one of her assignments and was visibly indifferent to Mom's presence, but respectfully acknowledging. She carried on like the rest of his disciples. We were told to sit on the floor until Om returned. The sweet smell of honeysuckle oil and myrrh filled the air. After some time had passed, everyone joined us on the floor and began chanting. Jaci and I sat on either side of Mom, clinging to her. I sat beside her, pretending to be happy because I thought that would make her happy. She was constantly saying, "*See? You like it here,*" but, inside, I was afraid and deeply unhappy.

Om finally came back. We all had to bow down, put our faces on the floor, stretch our arms out, and then crawl to him and kiss his feet. He was smiling big as usual, making sure to look at me specifically. Then he pointed his index finger at me, which he often did – his way of making me feel special; it worked.

He beckoned everyone into his bedroom, which was now made up like a throne room from the Krishna temple. Tapestries hung from the ceiling. Flowers and candles lined the walls. Matching big purple and orange pillows rested at the head and foot of the bed. Through the small window, I saw a darkening blue sky.

The Lord climbed into the middle of the bed, while most everyone else took their place on the floor. Lovelight sat next to him, Mom took a spot at his left foot, and Inspiration took his right. Devi and Harmony went to the floor and began playing the bells as they hummed a tune. Perfection tended to the kitchen and to the toddlers, Triumph and Prosperity. Isabella came in last and was directed to sit next to him on the opposite side of Lovelight. Jaci sat miserably next to me.

With three loud claps, Om changed the song: "GIVE UP KARMIC LABOR. YIELD ALL FRUITS TO ME. GIVE UP KARMIC LABOR. YIELD ALL FRUITS TO ME ..." and like a chorus, everyone joined in.

Omson and Freedom were on the opposite side of the bed out of my line of sight. At Om's direction, I tried to sing along, again mumbling the words, not knowing the song. Mom took some sage oil from Inspiration and started rubbing Om's foot. Inspiration rubbed his knee. He beckoned Devi over and whispered in her ear. She then scurried around the room, rearranged the candles and blew some of them out. Isabella looked embarrassed and kept her head down while Mom sat in front of her, rubbing Om's foot. Mom maintained an eerie, strange smile on her face.

There was a hierarchy, long since established amongst them, which I was oblivious to at the time but later came to understand in depth. With the entrance of Isabella, Inspiration had been moved down to the Lord's knees, and Lovelight was moved to position #2. Positions #3 and #4 (his feet or another body part) were normally reserved for Perfection and Harmony. Lady Sunshine and Devi were always last on the list. Because Mom was there, she bumped Harmony to the floor, and Perfection was being punished for something, so she was on kitchen duty. Mom sat there rubbing Om's foot with that weird smile on her face as everyone chanted and worshiped him as the Lord, creator of the entire universe.

***

It was all pretty convincing to a six-year-old boy, and maybe to some extent to a 10-year-old, but now I can't even imagine how it was for a 14-year-old girl, like my sister, who was being ritualistically sexually violated.

Looking back now, I wonder how my mother – a strong, independent, powerful figure in the community – could have fallen for this charlatan. This imposter, this Oakland street pimp who'd pocketed two ounces of stolen spiritual insight. And how could she have offered up her children as slaves to this man? Her virginal daughter served up as the main dish to his pedophiliac defiance? How could she have permitted their lies to influence, destroy, and imprison us behind the walls of silence? My questions would not be answered for 35 years.

***

The chanting, incense, bells, and candles were hypnotizing; the sound went on for hours. Finally, Perfection entered the bedroom with a vegetarian dish of something I didn't like, but knew to eat because they were not going to oblige my culinary desires or preferences.

Om called the chanting to an end with the usual calling out of OM. He, of course, was served first. The meals were brought to everyone in a particular order with the children served last. This meal consisted of bland lima beans with no salt, some kind of mushy starch that, if not for the overly strong onion flavor, would have tasted like plain Cream of Wheat, some cabbage with no butter or salt, and beets. Jaci always had a ferocious appetite for almost any kind of food, but even he had to force down every bite. We knew hunger well from living with Mom. But we got to ask for our favorite meals, and most times got them on the 1st and 15th when the welfare checks came. I didn't require as large an amount of food as Jaci, so the torture of this disgusting-tasting meal affected me less.

I tried to convey to Mom that I didn't like the food and hoped she would understand and help somehow, but, like many times since the "Om lovers" showed up in our lives, she relinquished all her maternal power to him. It remained a shocking contrast to the mom I once knew – the woman who was courageous, strong, powerful.

After the "food spirits" – a name Om insisted we use for all meals – Devi and Perfection cleaned up everyone's dishes. Perfection was noticeably upset by her new position in the kitchen and OM mocked her to everyone's amusement. After all the cleaning was completed, everyone was directed to be silent. The silence lasted several minutes and was finally broken when Om began giving an oration. It was as if he was standing on a soapbox like the crazy people did on the Cal campus back home. He was speaking of things my young ears could not comprehend.

He spoke to no one, yet to everyone. His rhythmic pulse and vocal inflection gave me the impression that what he was saying was very important. He did not yell while he was speaking, like the others on the Cal campus. Instead, he spoke enthusiastically yet quietly, hypnotically, and the entire group gazed at him like he was GOD. Even Mom. He made gestures with his hands, opening and closing them as the inflections rolled off his lips with drips of saliva.

I sat in silence wondering when it was all going to be over. I wanted badly to go back to my life on Telegraph, back to "normalcy." His words began to fade as I slipped in and out of consciousness. Suddenly, his voice rose loudly, which brought my full attention back to his face. His eyes gleamed with intensity. I glanced out the window into the night sky and observed the twinkling little stars. A plane crossed the sky with its lights blinking red, blue, and white. I thought back to my first plane ride ever, the one that brought me to San Diego. I woke up to Mom lifting me up and putting me over her shoulder. I cherished the warmth of her arms around me, her voice tender, telling me it was time for bed. All warm and cozy, I looked over her shoulder in my sleepy stupor and was shocked to see a dreadful sight that is forever burned into my memory. My sister, my friend, my confidant, my surrogate mother when there was no mother, was in the midst of a sea of naked bodies undulating and gyrating. Her mouth moved up and down on his member (his "sacred phallus"). The room was still lit by candles and the smell of marijuana reeked heavily over the incense.

It was all too much for a six-year-old to see. I closed my eyes, and, as they shut I caught a glimpse of Om's face. He was looking directly at me. I reopened them in a slow blink to see him smiling at me, and I shut them tight in fear, content to never open them again. Not knowing what was going to happen next, I squeezed Mom tight, feeling safe in her arms, because nowhere else was safe.

The next morning, I woke up to the sound of baby Triumph crying in the far bedroom. Mom sat at the small, round kitchen table talking to Isabella. Jaci was just waking as well. It was much earlier than I liked to get up, but I was happy to see Mom. I expected her to have a cup of hot coffee and be smoking her favorite cigarettes, Camel non-filters, but, instead, she sat there expressionless, fully dressed, listening to Isabella. As I approached her, she turned to me and smiled big without showing her teeth. She opened her arms wide and beckoned me with gestures from her fingers. She kissed me and squeezed me with her strong arms. I smelled her familiar musty organic scent that I loved but did not like. Jaci followed behind me, also craving Mom's affection.

I asked her where Pio was, and she told me he was back in Berkeley making music. I knew Pio loved music, especially salsa and rumba, and I thought of him briefly and wished I could have said goodbye to him before I'd left. The door to Om's bedroom was closed, and, for a brief moment, it was like we were a family again.

"When are we going home Mom?" Jaci asked.

Isabella turned and walked out of the kitchen.

"You're going to stay with Om for a while," she said in a fake and forced happy tone. I immediately heard the distinction between "you're" and "we're" and I hoped she meant Jaci and not me, but her eyes turned to me and that hope was crushed.

"Don't you like playing with Omson and Freedom?"

"Yes, but I want to go home and see James and Pio."

She began to explain why we were going to stay. When I asked her if she was going to stay with us, she said, "Yes."

Although I didn't want to live with "God" anymore, I was happy she was going to be there with us. Jaci didn't want to stay there either and complained under his breath about the decision, but he, too, was pacified by Mom's reassuring words.

We ate 9-grain cereal again, this time with more honey for our liking. Then the door to Om's room opened and we were instructed by Inspiration to greet the "Lord." We all filed in and had to kiss his feet. On the way in, Inspiration informed Mom that no one was to eat before the "Lord" had his meal. Mom nodded in acknowledgement. Om was sitting up straight in meditation position, smiling. He instructed us to sit in the same position as him. Jaci and I were sitting on opposite sides of Mom, facing him at the foot of the bed. Our backs were up against the wall. Still smiling, he pointed his long index finger at Jaci and directed him to sit in another spot on the wall beside the bed. With the same unbroken smile, he used his other index finger to point me to the other side of the bed, opposite Jaci.

I didn't want to leave Mom's side, but when "God" tells you to move, you move.

Mom reassured me with a smile when I squatted down into my new position. Jaci's look told me he hated it there. After a short time of sitting in silence, Om "dismissed" Jaci and me – a term I learned to long for whenever I was in his presence.

In the living room, Perfection and Inspiration were bringing in boxes from the van, along with gallon-sized, square, silver cans and open boxes of small brown bottles. They laid down a big piece of black plastic and began unloading the contents of all the boxes. Lovelight took Prosperity and Triumph out of the house. Harmony was teaching Omson and Freedom how to clean the bathroom. Isabella and Devi had also left. It seemed everyone had something to do, although I hadn't seen Om give any instructions.

Mom closed the door to the bedroom. Inspiration instructed Jaci to help her unload the boxes. One box did not match the others; the corners were frayed, taped, and half torn, held together by a piece of masking tape. Out of it, he pulled a large tin baking bowl, half a dozen paintbrushes, a bunch of old cleaning rags, and a measuring cup. The other five or so boxes appeared brand new; their corners straight and creased, the tops closed and taped with clear packing tape.

A series of numbers ran along the side, followed by writing I could not read, which looked to me like a series of letters. The two women began opening the boxes, using a knife to cut through the tape. They pulled out round bundles of incense sticks wrapped tightly in cellophane.

Inspiration unloaded all the bundles from the first box and folded the cellophane into one flat piece. Perfection began pouring the contents of the tin cans into the measuring cup and then into the tin bowl, followed by the contents of the brown bottles.

Mixing the two liquids together made about a gallon of a sweet, cherry-smelling fluid that reminded me of candy. They sat facing each other with the bowl in the middle, each having opened a bundle of sticks stacked next to them. They dipped the paintbrushes into the bowl and hand-painted all the incense sticks. They divided the sticks into groups of 25, 8 inches apart, followed by two more stacks that ran perpendicular to the first two, until a structure began to form. They built these stacks about a foot-and-a-half high, letting them sit and dry until several stacks were built.

Then they removed a heavy roll of 2-inch wide plastic from the final box. Perfection went to the kitchen and brought back a butter knife, a candle, and some matches. She measured out the plastic in multiple 12-inch pieces. After cutting 50 or so, she folded ¼ inch of each piece of plastic over the butter knife. Then she quickly ran it over the candle flame, sealing one end by melting it together, which created a 2 inch x 11-¾ inch plastic bag for the 25 sticks of cherry scented incense that sat drying, waiting for packaging.

While all the cherry incense was painted, stacked, and drying waiting for packaging, the next batch, this time sandalwood, was being mixed. The process was repeated for each scent: honeysuckle, jasmine, and frankincense.

This was the beginning of their enslavement of Jaci. At first, it was a novelty for him and he seemed to enjoy it. It took his attention off the fact that he, too, was forced to watch Isabella being molested daily. I enjoyed watching the incense-making process and wanted to help, but was still too young to handle the potentially dangerous and flammable liquids.

The feeling around the house was calm and peaceful. When Omson and Freedom returned, we got permission, by my request, to go outside and play. They were both still very strange to me. Relating to them the way I had related to my friends in the past proved to be a struggle, despite having spent the last couple of months under the same roof. They both seemed mildly mentally impaired to me. They didn't even know common children's games, like "hide and go seek" or "freeze tag."

It was late in the afternoon and we were called in by Harmony. Jaci stood against the kitchen sink, washing the contaminants off his hands, while Perfection and Inspiration cleaned the remnants of the day's work. The apartment buzzed with activity. Mom watched Jaci wash his hands while she talked to Inspiration. I came and nuzzled up next to Mom, who gave me a tender kiss and a hug. Still, she maintained that unfamiliar smile on her face the whole day. It wasn't like her to smile so much, and the sight made me feel uneasy. I was too young to process what I was seeing. All I knew was that the look on her face turned my stomach.

***

Looking back, I now know what that look was … it was guilt. Guilt so strong it created a blank, glossy-eyed emptiness that I had never seen in her eyes before. It was as though there was no person inside, just a shell with a ghostly smile, looking through everyone. Especially me.

***

Om came into the living room from the bathroom, smiling big as usual. He held a Prince tennis racquet in his hand and a single ball in the other. He began gently volleying it between his racket and the front door without letting it hit the floor. Everyone watched as if this was some great feat capable only of the SUPREME BEING. After several volleys, he missed it and the ball ricocheted off the edge of his oversized racket head. He didn't look twice to see where it landed. Instead, he nonchalantly turned his attention to Jaci, complimenting him on a job well done with the incense. Jaci smiled nervously, enjoying the recognition of his hard work.

Mom and Om acknowledged each other with a smile, and she stood up and went into Om's room, only to return with her purse. When she told me and Jaci that she had to go on an "assignment," fear and panic consumed me.

"NO!! I don't want you to go, Mom. Please, can we come with you!?!?"

"I'll be back in a little while," she said gently.

Jaci and I clung to her. I began to cry and continued to plead with her not to leave. "I promise I'll be right back."

My siblings and I were accustomed to Mom leaving for the night or for the entire day with the same line, *"I promise I'll be right back,"* but, after this last disappearing trick that had lasted for two or three weeks, I was afraid she wasn't going to come back for another three weeks. Jaci told her he didn't want to stay with them any longer, but Mom reassured us she would be RIGHT BACK. She pulled away from me and walked to the door, blowing us kisses before she shut the door behind her. Her airborne kisses could not stop the tears from racing down my face. Jaci tried in vain to stop his tears from falling, as big boys do.

***

That moment, those tears and that pain burned a self-concept deep into the back of my psyche that I am still working on dismantling to this very day. What was so wrong with me that she would leave me? Jaci and I never again shared a common tear. I stood there weeping for several minutes, not caring that my pain was obvious for all to see.

Om did not allow crying, and that was the last time I was allowed to openly cry without receiving punishment. I was alone with strangers. Isabella, in her shame and embarrassment, distanced herself from me. Jaci already loathed me and found it easy and sadistically enjoyable to hit, belittle, ignore, or mentally abuse me often. Although we continued to interact, a great separation grew between us.

***

Inspiration consoled me that night. Her kind words were tender and reassuring, and her gentle touch helped ease the pain. I sat next to her during chanting but waited anxiously for Mom. Om talked, we ate, and Om talked again. I wanted so badly for Jaci to love me and be my companion, but for reasons unknown to me then he kept up a fresh, unhealthy dose of resentment toward me.

I was "dismissed" from the chanting before the sex began and slept with a single blanket and pillow. Inspiration rubbed my head and sang an unfamiliar song. I wondered where Mom was and tried to stay awake for her return. I could hear Lovelight moaning in the bedroom; she made a distinct sound when it was her turn to "please the LORD." She sounded like a wild hyena that I once heard on Mutual of Omaha's *Wild Kingdom*. Jaci lay on the floor across the living room, no doubt waiting for Mom as well. Isabella was in the bedroom, a victim of some lewd and lascivious act I was happy to be missing. As I fought my imminent sleep, I felt Inspiration's anxiousness to join the "sacred fucking." Loneliness and fear gripped me as I felt her slip away, thinking I had fallen asleep.

I woke up the next morning with the anticipation of seeing Mom. I woke up countless mornings after that hoping to see her, but she never came. I tried to think back as to what I might have done to make her mad at me. I so wanted to be a "good boy" for her, but it was too late.

Most morning rituals involved silence, meditation, chanting, and "sacred fucking." On this particular day, the children were dismissed from witnessing the pornography – the explicit, graphic, sweaty, unadulterated sex of several grown people, along with my 14-year-old sister. I was happy to be dismissed from the agony it brought me, and I'm sure Jaci felt the same.

We all went to the beach that day. The moment we walked out the door, a wonderful fresh feeling of freedom came over me. I followed Jaci's lead as he led us the several blocks it took to get to the water, trying to show Omson and Freedom what life was like in the real world.

I tried to create an "us against them" feeling of camaraderie with Jaci that he only half participated in. His disdain for them was only a hair greater than it was for me, but I didn't care. I was happy to receive any kind of positive attention that I could get from my brother, however short-lived and half-assed it was.

We walked along the beach, splashing in its cool water and watching people surf and toss Frisbees. A couple of joggers ran in front of me and I screamed, "Wanna race?" One of them smiled and said, "Okay," not breaking his stride. I tried my hardest to beat him. He smiled at me again, then turned around and raced me running backwards as his lead quickly grew. The jogger and his friend smiled as he turned to continue on their run.

Jaci caught up to me quickly as I stopped to catch my breath. He swung a long piece of kelp at me, commanding me to jump.

"Jump over it!" He pretended to want to play with me, and encouraged me with big brother enthusiasm. But his real intention was to trip me and watch me fall. After a few times, he was successful; he timed it perfectly and knocked my feet out from under me in midair. My body landed horizontally on the hard wet sand.

Omson and Freedom watched while keeping their distance. They both held concerned and troubled looks on their faces. Jaci covered his tracks by proclaiming my toughness to them and to me. I took the bait and tried to be tough. (Jaci would continue to trick, bully, and torment me, then hide his sadism with fake brotherly encouragement.)

The day proceeded slowly, and the quick games of Frisbee and searching for sand dollars helped me forget where I was, who I was with, and the sadness and longing I felt about missing my mom.

We eventually headed back to the apartment. On the way, we exchanged the sand dollars we found for ice cream cones at the local ice cream store owned by a surfer family. I didn't know what the value of a sand dollar was, or if the owner was just being kind. I was used to strangers liking me, especially from the days on Telegraph Avenue. Back at the apartment, only Devi was there. That meant we still had free time. She was a few years older than Isabella and the last in the hierarchy.

We all knew we could get away with a bit more with her. She was packing the kitchen up, half nude. She wore a very short tennis skirt with no panties and no top. Her large pink areolas were perfectly covered by her long brown hair, and her bare ass showed when she reached for items from out of the cabinets. We all sensed her closeness in age, and all of us looked at her with fantasy in our eyes. She felt our gaze and clumsily carried on with her job. I imagined having sex with her and wondered what my chances were of it actually happening. Jaci read my thoughts and teased me accordingly.

Triumph and Prosperity were sleeping in the bedroom. Slowly the "ladies" started arriving back from the day's assignments. They all had an incense selling quota to meet and returned with stories from their days work. Inspiration was very happy, as she often had an upbeat and cheerful disposition. That and her good looks made her an excellent salesperson and con artist. At the time, unseen to my young eyes, there was a fierce competition between all the ladies that was fueled by Om's masterful manipulation.

When Inspiration came back with news of her record-breaking sales on any given day, Perfection was especially visibly disturbed by it. When Harmony came back after cleaning up in Chinatown, Lovelight made sure to suck his cock just a little better that night.

***

Now, I recognize that Om was running a basic "pimp/hoe" game on all of them, hidden behind a guru's tongue. After everyone had arrived home that evening, all the women sat in a circle on the floor, counting the remaining packs of incense and money. Om took Isabella into the bedroom and closed the door.

All the women, after cashing in, began packing up the house like blind honeybees with one goal in mind: to get everyone out of that apartment. No "food spirits" were served, beds were made in the corner of the living room, and the kids were all sent to sleep. I went to bed hungry, wondering what was going to happen next. *"Maybe we are going back to Berkeley,"* I thought. I started thinking about Pio, James, Aki, Hippo, Dawn, and, most of all, Mom. Maybe that's why she left – to go get our house ready. I thought of Devi and hoped she would come lie next to me. I fantasized about her laying her naked body on top of mine. She had heard Jaci tease me earlier and she'd smiled at me affectionately, as if flattered that she was a twinkle in my eye. I then fell asleep. Soon, she would be making covert trips to my bed late at night, performing fellatio, then disappearing into the dark.

"Time to get up. Time to get up!" a deep voice proclaimed. It was still dark out, and I was confused as to why Om was waking us up.

"Great morning," he said with a smile. He often changed words around to give the feeling that it was his own special language – "food spirits" meant food, "second wake" meant sleep, "alms" meant money, "throne cake" meant dessert, and "dragonflies" were the police.

I still hadn't learned all of his terms and often asked Omson or Freedom to translate for me, which they failed at because they didn't know the correct English words.

"Good morning," I said, rubbing the sleep from my eyes.

"Great morning!" he said, correcting me while slowly grabbing my hand from my eye.

Shocked, I replied, "Great morning," and he gently took my hand and put it down by my side.

The ladies had been packing all night, and, as we all got up, they made several trips in and out of the front door. Jaci was given instructions to help empty the house.

Omson, Freedom, and I were instructed to go downstairs and get into a van. I had never seen it before and felt curious about its origins but did not ask. It was a seven-passenger Ford Econoline with two opening doors on the sides, a big glass windshield, swiveling captain's chairs, and a bench in the back. It had wall-to-wall carpeting and a small table between the captain's chairs and the driver and passenger seats. The ceiling perimeter was lined with small lights that gave it a charming glow.

I was the first one in and claimed the farthest chair. Omson hurriedly got to the second one before Freedom. They were only one year apart, with Omson being the older of the two, so the rivalry was fairer and the fights more evenly matched, compared to Jaci and me, although Omson was the consistent winner. Om followed shortly after. With both arms spread wide holding both the folding doors, he smiled and said, "Stay put," before closing the doors one after the other.

There was another vehicle of some kind parked out of my line of sight. Most of their belongings were being loaded into that other vehicle, which was driven by one of the ladies. Perfection and Inspiration filed into the van followed by Om and Isabella. Inspiration took the front passenger seat, Perfection moved the three of us to the bench seat in the far back, and Isabella sat next to her in a captain's chair.

Perfection brought two blankets and told her sons to share them with me, along with several bags she loaded into the back behind the bench seat. I saw Jaci one last time before leaving. He was carrying a box down the stairs of the apartment. Even though he was always cruel and sadistic to me, I felt sorry for him having to work in the middle of the night. He was my big brother and my heart was still young and untainted, not the stone it would become. I was scared I wouldn't see him again, but I felt safe with Isabella in the car. The rumbling of the motor was hypnotic and quickly put the three of us back to sleep. I woke up to a loud bang. Some of the items that were packed on top of the van had smacked against the entrance of an archway of a small motel parking lot. The noise woke up several tenants and brought the manager out.

Om jumped out of the van to greet the manager and assess the damage. But there was none to either the archway or the van. The manager, a small, brown man yelled in a foreign language, and, from the veil of sleep, I was barely able to recognize its origin; it was Spanish. I had learned a word or two back in Berkeley, and now I wondered why he wasn't speaking English.

Om parked the van while Inspiration secured the loose items. We sat in the van for quite a while as Om and Inspiration negotiated our stay. Eventually, we all filed into a small room that held only two beds, plus a small chair, a side table, and a bathroom that featured pink and green tile. The sun was almost up, but Om was going to sleep, giving everyone some much needed rest. Before I knew it, we were back on the road.

The streets looked different; the roads were only partially paved, and the buildings and homes we passed didn't look like anything I had ever seen.

I asked curiously, "Where are we?" to which Om replied, "Here." I'm sure he thought it was a clever play on words. However, I did not appreciate his response and asked again, "Where?"

Not one to be manipulated by a child's questions, he did not respond. There was a long silence that intimidated me. I shrunk back to the back of the van, still wondering.

The scenery was both shocking and beautiful. At one point, there were broken-down houses made out of cardboard, tin, trash, and horrible junk of every kind. Dirt roads became muddy as we drove through rainstorms. Half-naked kids played in the streets and stared at our van as we drove through. I even saw some dogs fighting each other over some dead animal.

The faces of the kids were solemn and gaunt. Never before had I seen such a sight. I saw what I could only imagine were mothers cooking pots of food over open fires, using iron wires to hold their pots. It made me think of Mom and the black beans she used to cook in her favorite black cast-iron pot. I missed her deeply but was too scared to express it. Not for fear of bodily harm, but out of shame. Now, I felt shame for not being satisfied with "God" as my caregiver.

I turned to Isabella for comfort, which she gave me, but there was something different. I felt a cold, distant, unfamiliar feeling. But my longing for her love and sisterly affection reached her and peeked through for just a moment, and she gave me a loving hug and whispered in my ear, "We're in Mexico."

It was an amazing revelation. I remembered the stories about their trip to Mexico for political asylum in Cuba. So, I had pictures in my mind of what Mexico looked like from the stories brought back by my siblings.

I pictured Mexico as a giant, hot desert wasteland of red, dusty rocks and mountains. It was a shocking discovery to see Mexico as it really was, and

I stared out the window with renewed awe. We arrived sometime later at a two-story duplex somewhere in this foreign land. It was fairly new, cloaked by several other buildings that were under construction. The surrounding neighborhood was dilapidated, neglected, and extremely poor.

All the neighborhood kids watched us drive in and followed the van to its resting spot. It was a pea-green colored building. A large patch of dirt covered the area out front where there should have been grass. The kids bombarded us with smiles and curious stares.

They treated us like celebrities. "You American?" "Shake, shake, shake, you booty!" one kid sang out proudly in a thick accent. I was amused that they knew that song because I had all but forgotten it after all the chanting and "sacred fucking" that was constantly going on around me.

We began unloading the van, as the kids lined up along the Mexican-style fence between the street and the yard of dirt. A crowd of about 15 others watched us as we moved in. Some offered to help with gestures and broken English, which Om kindly refused, but he allowed the three of us the freedom to interact with them.

The most outgoing of the group repeated, smiling, "Che, Che, Che your booday!"

I laughed and nodded in agreement.

"Hey, American boy, c'mon. Te gusta fútbol?"

All I understood was the word football, so I smiled and said yes. He and some other boys and girls were very eager to make friends, which thrilled me. Even though we didn't speak the same language, it was refreshing to engage with normal kids. Communication existed between us that didn't require words; it was an unspoken universal language of children, no matter the race, nationality, gender, or socioeconomic upbringing.

I learned how to relate to people and to a different culture that day. I became a master at it long before I learned to speak their language or even learned to read or write my own.

We were called inside and our introductions came to an end. We had finished unpacking when another truck pulled up in front. Harmony was driving, Jaci was in the middle, and Devi occupied the passenger seat. I was happy to see Jaci and got a mild smile from him. He must have been glad to see us, too.

***

Nothing was ever explained to us. We were never told where we were going, what the plan was, or how it was to unfold. Everything was always a mystery. Part of Om's philosophy was that children should be seen and not heard. Although, up to this point, I hadn't been physically harmed or mistreated, I knew and felt a distinct difference between life before with Mom and life afterwards with "God" and his worshippers.

***

As the second truck was being unloaded, I became ecstatic at what I saw right before my own two eyes. Two brand new, shiny bicycles rolled out from the back of the truck along with several soccer balls, footballs, basketballs, tennis rackets, and clubs. It was as though Santa Claus came to Mexico to reward us for all our chanting. Om was throwing everything out of the truck and the balls went bouncing everywhere.

I thought, *"Wow. Maybe it won't be so bad after all if he went to the trouble to get us all these wonderful toys. Maybe it can be fun here."* I never got a brand new anything back at home.

I headed straight for the smaller of the two bikes, as did Freedom and Omson. None of us knew how to ride, but we were definitely about to try. That's when our real rivalry was born. Perfection, being the bitch that she was, made it clear that the two bikes were intended for Omson and Freedom, but that we could all share them. Jaci was more or less excluded from riding them, and he was the only one who knew how.

***

Looking back, I truly believe that the whole cult was racist against Jaci's blackness, including Om himself, but especially Perfection and the other women. I saw the mistreatment of Jaci by everyone and, even at age six, I intuitively knew that his cruelty towards me was just the misguided hurt of a 10-year-old boy who was like the black sheep of these so-called Enlightened Ones. So, when I made gestures of empathy, he in his anger and shame acted out against me, for I was his only safe outlet.

***

Jaci was happy to have the toys as well. Seeing them meant that not all of our time would be consumed with having to worship Om's "sacred fucking." We slowly settled into the new home, and Om began to methodically indoctrinate us into life as new devotees of his maniacal, self-centered, sociopathic, dissociative, and narcissistic God complex – none of which of course was evident to me at the time.

I thought he was God. He said he was, Mom said he was, and all these grown-up women said he was and treated him like he was.

Every day, I became convinced more and more that he was God through the constant fasting, chanting, and praising of him that lasted for hours and hours on end. I had to listen to him give speech upon speech about Jesus, as if Jesus was Om's son. Om plagiarized scriptures as his own, and I had become accustomed to witnessing all of these women performing daily sexual rituals to satisfy him.

All these activities, although seemingly harmless at the time, grew to have a monstrous effect on my brother and me. For the time being, as a six-year-old, I just lived for each moment, dealing only with whatever was right in front of me. Om gave us enough free time to almost make it seem as though we were not there against our will.

We got to play outside with all of our new balls and bikes, and we were allowed to go down to the beach. In this first year, life wasn't so bad. It was strange and uncomfortable, but not unbearable.

I tried every day, and was allowed to learn how to ride that bike, but I just didn't get it. Eventually, we were allowed to move about the neighborhood. After making trips to the local market with different grownups, some of our neighbors would wave as we drove or walked by.

There was one house whose owners held cockfights, and, if we were lucky, we would have free time to watch the bloody mess. The fights brought out all the kids in the neighborhood, as well as their parents. It was like a block party. They'd bring out food and drinks that consisted of meat, beans, rice, corn tortillas, sweet cakes, and pastries. Horchata and tamarindo were the drinks of choice. Most of the adult men kept the kids away from the actual fighting, but there were some that let me push under their elbows to catch a quick glimpse.

Omson and Freedom lacked the ability to assimilate into their new environment. They were born into the chanting and rituals, so socializing the way normal kids do was foreign to them. Because of my spirit and the fact that I was a poor boy from the streets, I knew how to navigate through different environments with an optimism and fearlessness that set me apart from most kids, even my siblings. I was navigating through the biggest reality shift of my life to date, so making friends and learning how to survive was a skill I honed and perfected.

After visiting several of my new neighborhood friends' homes and eating as much as I could fit in my belly, I thought I'd better check in back at the "Ponderosa." Omson and Freedom were playing in front. I had lost them earlier in the day by no accident and was happy to see that it was still free time.

They both snubbed me as I approached, so I decided to see where Jaci was. I found him in the living room with what looked like a year's supply of incense-making work ahead of him. He looked too heartbroken to even scowl at me like he usually would. There was so much work to be done, he accepted my offer to help.

Isabella sat down with instructions to aid us in the monumental task of transforming what lay before us into a finished product ready to sell. I tried to help, but my youth didn't allow for much effect. It was nice, however, to be in close proximity to my brother and sister. Isabella was no longer a girl, but a wife. I, in essence, was a baby and Jaci was just a boy. The years that once separated us now seemed like generations. Isabella was never the same. Our bond felt broken and forgotten. She tried to treat me like her little baby, but she was now just a shell. The Isabella I once knew was gone.

I fell asleep long before they were done, but first, I had to get permission to fall asleep.

I don't know how long we stayed at that location. Weeks? Months? Time seemed to blend into itself, with no parameter for seconds, minutes, hours, days of the week, or months of the year. These were all kept from me as a teaching. I think it was late 1977.

I hadn't seen Harmony or Lovelight for quite some time but didn't mind. My well-being was never a concern of theirs. They, more or less, looked right through me.

One morning, Om woke the whole house by singing at the top of his lungs. Perfection and Inspiration seemed to already have been up. They were packing the whole house in a speedy emergency fashion. Everyone worked into the mid-afternoon, and, just like our move from San Diego, we were gone in a flash.

We drove for a very long time, broken up into two groups. Om, Isabella, Perfection, and "the boys" as we were called – Omson, Freedom, and me – were in the lead van along with Triumph and Prosperity. Inspiration, Devi, and Jaci followed behind in the truck. The day was drawing to an end, and the excitement of being on the road was gone. We arrived at a checkpoint and were asked to get out of the vehicles. Everyone unloaded and headed to the building. We sat and waited while Om discussed our entry deeper into Mexico.

Ultimately, we were turned away and sent back. Everyone was tired, even "God." So, after a short ride back towards some unknown place, we pulled over and slept. At sunrise, we were back on the road again for only a short distance before we stopped again – this time to go for a hike in a very majestic mountain setting.

The sun was low on the horizon and the desert air was still icy cold as we made our ascent, single file. The elevation gain was maybe 1,000 feet, but looked huge to me. Our entire group hiked up the narrow trail, surrounded by thousands of cactus plants and desert rocks. We reached a point where we couldn't continue, about halfway to the top. The mountain trail had ended, and in front of us lay only jagged rock. We settled there, everyone securing a place to sit. We could see for hundreds and hundreds of miles across the desert floor. A few popcorn clouds drifted over our heads. We were still in the shadow of the mountain, but the sun's early morning rays were giving the mountain top a beautiful orange glow. The air was still and quiet, damp from the cold desert night.

Out of nowhere Om yelled at the top of his lungs ...

OOOOOOOOOMMMMMMMMM!!!!

Two or three seconds later, the sky exploded with a tremendous BOOOMMM!!! The sound crackled across the entire mountain range and rolled out into the open sky, like thunder. We were all flabbergasted. Everyone looked around at each other in amazement. Om kept his cool, appearing as though he had expected it, his poker face unbroken. I was too young to read him then. Later, reading his mood was a skill I would learn and perfect in order to survive.

This was the moment when my child's mind became convinced that I was, in fact, with God. I could not explain it. I did not understand it, but it appeared that Mom and all these adults were telling the truth. I do not have a scientific explanation as to what happened that day (I'm sure there is one), but, for a 6-year-old boy, it was completely convincing evidence that this was God.

We made our way down the mountain after several songs in which we worshipped Om and his divinity. The chanting and singing echoed throughout the mountain range, the intensity of which I had only seen before at the Krishna Temple back in Berkeley. Soon we were on the road once more. We ended up in Ensenada, a small Mexican town south of Tijuana.

This time, we settled into a small apartment nestled somewhere next to nothing. The building was three stories high with a pool in the center courtyard. I liked it there because we were allowed to play outside and interact with the other tenants. I was a very outgoing and friendly boy, and people always seemed to enjoy my company and laugh at my jokes. I always felt like it was easy to win people over and quickly made friends with the neighbors and kids across the street.

Although Om always had a watchful ear and eye on me, I reveled in my interactions with strangers. A couple that lived next door spoke broken English and tried to teach me how to play dominos. The cult was seldom together in public all at one time, for security reasons. Om always kept the big kids with the help of one to three of the women, while the other women and kids would go to some other location.

On this occasion, Isabella had gone along with some of the other "lovers." Jaci, Omson, Freedom, Triumph, Prosperity, and I were all staying at this apartment complex along with Inspiration and Harmony. It was during our stay there that I witnessed, and was forced to participate in, the most egregious and pernicious act against a child I had experienced in my entire life. In the back room of that small apartment, lit only by the small rays of light that shined through the semi-closed blinds, were the stained walls and carpet still stinking of mildew and dirt from the previous tenants. The room was furnished with one small pale green dresser that was attached to the wall. It was missing several knobs. In the middle of the room stood a small, rickety bed that slept only two. A recently placed stick of incense burned in its holder.

The silence was broken by the whimpers of a child. Om had tied Prosperity, who was only four, to the bed with rope. Her hands and feet were tied and spread to the bedposts. She was naked, except for socks that were being used as gloves on her hands. Her black hair was tied in a bun on the top of her head. Her brown skin contrasted with her bare pink feet. She was Asian and black, Harmony and Om's daughter. A beautiful, sweet little girl with a wonderful smile, now gone. Prosperity had some kind of skin disease that made her scratch the joints of her extremities until they bled. Tying her down was Om's way of treating her disease.

She cried and howled in pain. She rolled her head back and forth. Her body would shake violently as she desperately longed to scratch herself. She would writhe in agony until she passed out from exhaustion. Her screams were so unbearable to me that I was ashamed to be relieved when Om ordered the door closed. He would untie her only to use the bathroom, and, if she didn't scratch, she was allowed to remain untied. She inevitably would begin scratching her arm joints and the joints behind her knees until they were open flesh wounds nearly dripping with blood.

Om would then tie her back up, and the horrendous sounds of the innocent little girl would shatter the silence that Om demanded at all times. Once, Om left and took the other boys with him, leaving me to watch over her until he returned. The rest of the group were still off on assignment, so it was just the two of us. Under strict orders not to let her up from the bed, I was to wait until he returned. When she woke up again, her voice was hoarse, her throat sounded sore from her earlier screaming, and, as it warmed up from her discomfort, it got even louder. She called out for anyone to let her up. She also knew when she said she had to use the bathroom she was often let up.

When I opened the door to check in on her, she begged me to scratch her, but I couldn't do it. Her body jolted back and forth so violently I thought she might dislocate her limbs. I tried to comfort her by dabbing a cool rag on her arm but it just made it worse. She became more agitated and upset.

She begged me to scratch her arms again and to let her up so she could use the bathroom. But Om told me not to let her up no matter what. When I reluctantly said that I couldn't, she pleaded with me once more to scratch her legs. Streams of tears rolled down her face as bubbles of snot dripped from her nose. Finally, she peed. I felt so bad I got another rag and wiped her face, then forced a towel under her body to try and keep her dry. I was scared and sad and lonely and confused. I wanted to help her, but scratching her arms or her leg would have meant aggravating her open sores.

The thought of collecting her bloody flesh under my fingernails repulsed me. I felt very ashamed, and I offered her water, which she accepted. I stayed with her until she passed out from exhaustion. Seeing her in so much pain was unbearable. I cried for her and for me.

I was not allowed out of the house, but I had to get away. Just outside and down the hall, a Mexican couple and some friends were playing dominos. Their door was open. Through hand gestures and broken English, they asked me what was going on. I was glad there was a language barrier and pretended not to understand them. I fantasized about telling this family my situation, but I knew they were incapable of helping me. I gladly scarfed down a delicious treat they offered me before I darted back to Hell. It was sad to me that Prosperity had to suffer while other people played games, laughed, and had fun. I felt hopeless even though she was the one who was tied down.

I went back to be with Prosperity, although I wanted to never go back or see her in pain again! Her cries for help disappeared into a half-conscious whisper as I walked into that dark ugly room.

Finally, Harmony appeared, with some kind of ointment that looked like it came from a doctor's office because it had official looking letters on it, which stood out against all the natural herbs, tinctures, and homeopathic concoctions in the home. I hated Harmony for having let her own daughter suffer like that. The guilt and shame of that day stayed with me for many years.

Eventually, Prosperity was let up from the bed as her arms and legs began to heal. Om continued to tie her hands together with rope and covered them with socks, and she stayed like that for some time. She was happy to be up and walking around again, but with her hands still tied together so she couldn't scratch. They kept her hands tied until her rash was completely gone. I will never forget that day. I can still see her pretty little face smiling.

***

The neighbors I befriended were constantly questioning me about Prosperity and our "family." I wanted to tell them everything, how they were sexually molesting my sister, torturing Prosperity, and abusing my brother and me. I wanted to tell them I didn't belong there. It was all a big mistake. I wanted them to save me, but I knew they would never understand the severity of my predicament or the language I spoke. As with the thousands of other people I met on this tragic and painful journey, my longing for help would go unheard for years, and the guilt and shame of that day would stay in my heart for many more.

That Om was wanted by the FBI, that I was being beaten and starved, that none of the children were in school, that Om and the Om lovers were sexually molesting my sister in group orgies – all of the atrocities were to be kept silent. The secrets and the silence began to build the walls of my prison.

***

Unexpectedly, we were on the road again, moving from one small motel to the next. There were far fewer sex rituals and chanting during this leg of the journey. Now, silence was mandatory. We were in a game of cat and mouse with the "dragonflies," a term used for all government agencies, the FBI, and the Mexican authorities.

Om appointed different women to be lookouts. They would be positioned in various places around the motels or were instructed to sit across the street at cafes, just waiting to see if any dragonfly cars were patrolling our motel. He developed a secret knock: 1, 2 … 3, 4 … 5, 6 … 7 that was to be used for us to identify ourselves.

I didn't understand the silence and the sneaking around. Most days, I was quarantined to a small space by the side of Om's bed where I was "encouraged" to sit still and be quiet. Sometimes, we were allowed to play directly in front of wherever we were staying.

The cult was divided into the same groups as before, and I didn't see Jaci for several weeks, if not months. Om continued to resort to his heavy indoctrination techniques to ensure my compliance. "God" told me that time didn't exist. Fasting, chanting praises to him, meditations, sitting in silence while he chanted out loud and hours of long, hypnotic oration were the order of every day. My sense of time and reality had mutated into what I can now only call an extended hypnotic state, a brainwashing.

Inspiration appeared, then disappeared, for several days at a time. She would be replaced by another "lady," either Perfection or Devi. God kept Isabella very close by, tantalized by her refreshing young beauty. After several moves and some evasive maneuvering, we lost the dragonfly Federales. Om proudly bragged about it, which was how I got to partly understand what was happening.

We finally settled back in Tijuana. Om rented an old nightclub that was on a main thoroughfare at the end of town. I think the street was called Agua Caliente. The old, brown wood club had several big bay windows that faced the street. They were tinted, so we could see out but the public couldn't see in. The building had long been abandoned. Crooked old stairs ran parallel with the sidewalk and the small parking lot sprouted an assortment of gangly weeds. At the top of the stairs, two giant wooden doors were locked together by a thick, old rusty chain. The doors opened to reveal one giant room. Structural beams were placed every 20 feet or so.

The building was rectangular. To the left, under the bay windows, ran a short ledge along an elevated stretch of industrial carpet. It ran all the way to the far wall, separating that section from the rest of the floor plan. To the right were five steps that led to an elevated section that looked like it once held a long bar but now just held nothing. In the middle was what looked like a large dance floor, and, against the farthest wall, adjacent to the bay windows, was the remains of the stage, elevated about four feet. In the farthest corner from the entry were the bathrooms. One of the two doors read: "Caballeros" and on the other all that was left was an "S." They were typical club bathroom stalls, three urinals in the men's, the frame of a missing mirror leaning sadly next to an old faded mirror. The toilet area sat farther back than the main wall, creating a very dark corner.

We found the small kitchen at the very end of the bar. The ceiling and floor had been painted the same dark brown as the exterior large structural beams that ran along the ceiling, giving the whole place an almost barn-like feel. Eight circular wooden chandeliers hung from the ceiling; each had 20 to 30 light-bulb sockets that once illuminated the entire cantina. It reeked of dust and 20 years of spilled alcohol. This place was dark and mysterious, sad and lonely.

A massive cleanup job was soon underway. The windows, floors, bathrooms, kitchen, and parking lot had to be scraped and scoured. My job was to scrape the discarded gum off the gray tile dance floor with a screwdriver. It was a daunting task, as there was an enormous amount of gum everywhere.

That was the first time Om was unkind to me. Up until this point, I had avoided his disapproval when he was reprimanding anyone in the cult. But, when I showed how overwhelmed I was with the task at hand, he quickly snatched the screwdriver from my hand and demonstrated angrily how it was to be done. I didn't have the strength needed to get the head under the dirt, alcohol, and grime mixture. Occasionally, I'd get one or two up. The burden was a man's job. In fact, a grown man with the right tool would have taken at least eight hours to complete this gargantuan task, and I was commanded not to leave the area until the assignment was completed.

I was overwhelmed and saddened by my predicament, as well as so shocked by God's anger toward me that I became paralyzed with fear. I gouged reck-lessly at some spots out of anger, and half-heartedly at others out of self-pity. The day dragged on and on with only a few pieces scraped up. After many hours, Perfection gave me permission to stop.

Om had gone somewhere and the day had turned to night. Perfection made a sleeping area under the bay windows, which was the most comfortable spot in the whole place due to the carpet. I fell fast asleep after having spent the long day entirely on my hands and knees.

Suddenly, I was awakened by a pail full of cold water that was being dumped on my face and body. I was drenched from head to toe as was the thin blanket that covered me. I jolted up, gasping for air. Jaci and Omson also awoke from the residue of the splashing liquid. Startled, scared, and unable to see, I heard a deep voice:

"Didn't I tell you to scrape the floor until the assignment was completed?"

God waited for my answer, but I was so confused and scared that I didn't respond. He grabbed both of my shoulders with his large hands and pulled me up off the floor. He stood me up and said, "Finish the assignment!"

I told him Perfection told me that I could stop, to which I received no reply. Candles were glimmering in the dark, positioned sparsely throughout the building. His dark figure walked away, and I followed him through the dark, soaked, to the middle of the dance floor. He left me standing there and returned with a candle. His dark eyes and muscular frame illuminated by the candle frightened me.

He sat the candle down and dropped the screwdriver on the ground, returning moments later with a towel and a can of turpentine from the incense boxes. He demonstrated how I was to hold the towel firmly over the nozzle, overturn the can, and then use the wet part to dab over each piece of gum. The chemical helped loosen the sticky substance, allowing the screwdriver head to more easily slide under the gum. I was unaware of my wet hair and body. My focus was on the turpentine and how relieved I was that there was a method to actually get the gum up. He told me to demonstrate that I understood the process, and I mimicked him, turning the can over with the towel securing the amount of liquid released, dabbed it on a spot of gum, and with a couple of stabs, it slid off.

I was excited that my job was now so much easier. But, after a few moments, the sorrowful reality of my plight roared through my mind and body. After several long and lonely hours, Inspiration told me on her way to the bathroom that I could go to sleep. This time I refused and told her what happened. She assured me that it would be okay if I went to sleep. Receiving conflicting instructions from different adults would later become such a significant issue that I would have to navigate through, that I learned to use it to my advantage.

I was too scared, however, this time to take her word for it, so she got permission for me. I told her that my bed was wet and she let me sleep next to her in the throne bed, an act that I appreciated at the time but later regretted.

The water assault put fear in my heart; the whole night scared me deeply. I knew instinctively I was potentially always in danger, especially when I went to sleep.

The next morning, I woke up to the sound of moaning and grunting. The bed was moving, and the sounds of a female panting heavily began to arouse me. I lay there as still as possible, not wanting to be discovered. Her moans and grunts were becoming more pronounced. Inspiration was gyrating and moving sexually, perhaps waiting for her turn. I couldn't see who was making the sounds. Inspiration adjusted herself into a different position, which allowed me a clear line of vision to see who was making these erotic noises. It was Isabella!

I was disturbed and repulsed. I got out of bed meekly without making eye contact with anyone, but not before I caught an eyeful of the most private parts of my sister's anatomy. I went straight back to finish the gum assignment and found a patch far away from the vile act that had woken me up.

Eventually, the morning rituals began again. I heard the singing and chanting, then the jingling of bells and their rhythmic clatter. The other women's voices began, followed by the other kids'. I kept my head and eyes focused on the task, hoping to be left out of this morning's punctilios.

I was able to keep a low profile until "food spirits" were served. I eagerly ate the hot bowl of 9-grain cereal sweetened with dates. After eating, I went back to finish the job. Finally, I went back to report completion of my duty. Walking over to him was frightening. He was bouncing a basketball loudly and aggressively while speaking harshly to Isabella about something that I didn't know about.

As I got closer, I could see the anger on his face and hear the rage in his voice. He threw the basketball against Isabella's head and asked her a question. Again, he threw the basketball against her head and asked her another question. He told her to go get the ball, and give it back to him. Then he threw it against her head once more, even harder this time, and asked her the same question. He made her retrieve it over and over and keep throwing it against her head. Her face was red and she fought to keep her tears in, now unable to answer. BAM!

Each time he threw it, it was like a two-handed pass, the kind you see in a basketball game. Each throw jolted her head back. The final blow struck her square in the face and knocked her to her ass. I began to cry. A feeling of horrible helplessness consumed me, and I turned and snuck away.

I could not understand why he was treating her that way. In my mind, I thought that he cared for her. Why would he have sex with her and then do that? I was so confused. I had to escape, so I went to the bathroom and silently cried. I hid in a stall, my pants around my ankles, and sat on the toilet.

I wondered why. Why were we here? Where were Mom and Pio and James? Why had they abandoned us? I struggled to make sense of it all. But it made no sense, none of it. I dried my eyes and went back to report the completion of my duty. When I came out, he was there inspecting it. He looked at me with a big smile, the one he always used. The one that said nothing of the water wakeup nor the NBA basketball practice on my sister's face. "You're dismissed."

We spent a long time at the "old club." Christmas came. I was now being sent on incense-selling assignments with Inspiration. The other boys went with their mom or with the other ladies. Another devotee named Lady Sunshine showed up one day. I hadn't seen her since Berkeley. She was a short, dark-skinned, black woman. The only black woman follower I ever met. She was only there a few days before I saw Om rough her up and kick her out in the middle of the night. I had been woken up by a scream, and, through the darkness, I saw Om manhandling her. She pulled away and ran screaming towards the door. Om grabbed a chair and threw it at her. It whizzed past her body as she barely got out the door. I never saw her again.

I hated living in that place. It was dark, lonely, big, and scary. The days that I got to go out and sell incense in Tijuana were my happiest. The streets buzzed with a hum of activity. The roads were made out of dirt, and the cars and buses stirred it up like a stampede of a thousand cattle. Horns blasted angrily at one another, and plumes of black smoke billowed out from exhaust pipes of every kind. Vendors traded goods everywhere.

The people were small in stature, but their hearts were as big as lions'. Little old ladies walked with large bundles of goods balanced on long poles that ran across their shoulders. Little kids younger than I sold Chicklets in the streets at all hours of the night.

We walked and walked and walked even more. We walked everywhere, selling bags of incense. "Quieres comprar incienso?" (Do you want to buy some incense?) was the first sentence I learned in Spanish. We went to shops, restaurants, bars, grocery stores, industrial districts, and to businesses of every kind. On every other block, small newspaper stands sold magazines with the grotesque images of mutilated bodies on the cover, as well as peanuts and dulces. Sometimes, after an 8- to 12-hour day, we would end up far away.

Inspiration would get us on a bus for a restful ride back. She was groped, pinched, and disrespected countless times daily, especially when we rode the bus. The buses were packed like sardine cans; a person had to fight their way on and off the buses. Little kids sang sad love songs in an especially pathetic way with an unforgettable howl in their voices, then asked for compensation in the jam-packed stench of 40 to 50 mostly men.

Inspiration jumped and jerked as a finger found its way to her most private places. Sometimes each man got a feel of her as we exited. We tried different techniques when riding: stay next to the bus driver, fight for the first seat available, stand next to women, nothing worked. But our exhaustion from hours of combing the city kept us riding back home.

Occasionally, a gentleman would offer his seat or begin arguing with those who accosted her. Inspiration wasn't afraid to start screaming and would cause a scene if it helped. If we had a really good day, and the bus ride was too unbearable, and it was raining, we would sometimes take a taxi – but never directly back to our residence because that would be a security breach. She would make the taxi driver drop us off at least several blocks away, nowhere near our location.

Deeply Catholic, Christmas is a big deal to Mexicans. Every shop, restaurant, and place of business was fully decorated in all the Christmas merriment imaginable. Taxi drivers, bus drivers, everyday people, stores, markets, and panaderas (bakeries), all celebrated Jesus' birthday very enthusiastically. When I asked Inspiration what it was all about, she told me to ask Om. Whenever I asked questions about how things were, what was true or false, what happened to my Mom, or about who Jesus was, she always told me to "Save that question for Om. He has all the answers." I could tell she was putting me off, but, for the most part, I enjoyed our time together.

Sometimes, she would grab me, and quickly, out of the blue, make a direction change or speed up almost to a run too fast for my short legs. My heart would begin to race as I looked up at her, her face solemn and stoic. Most times, I could see and feel her fear. When I tried to get a question out, the speed of our escape from whatever the threat was often prevented a clearly audible inquiry. If I was able to get a question out, she quickly and firmly hushed me.

"Don't ask questions, just move!" We would quickly dart into a store or restaurant – any place that could be used to conceal us. Sometimes, we'd drop into a clothing store and she would change her entire outfit, then recklessly slap a cap on my head. I always had to wait until we got back to hear exactly what it was we were so desperately avoiding. Sometimes, it was because the Federales in their unmarked cars were following us.

Even though they were unmarked, they had very distinct looks – one I was eventually trained to spot. Usually, they were Ford sedans with blacked-out windows that had a single giant antenna mounted on the trunk and one or two spotlights mounted outside the driver or passenger door above the side mirror.

The occupants wore plain clothes, usually jeans with dark, windbreaker-style jackets loose enough to conceal a firearm. They wore dark or mirrored glasses like Pancho from CHiPs.

Other times, we were escaping a dangerous situation from civilian threats, like thugs who were plotting to harm or rob us, or men who wanted to violate Inspiration's femininity. We were physically attacked on many occasions. We maintained some safety precautions that were designed at the beginning of our day from Om's early morning direction:

Number One: Transfer money into shoe after three hours of sales.

Number Two: Never keep money in purse.

Number Three: Carry money in multiple places (both shoes and underwear).

Despite our precautions, we were mugged by a man who came running up from behind us and swiped a wicker bag from Inspiration's arms. He was a short, muscular man with black pants and a dark, hooded sweatshirt. We had enjoyed another record-breaking day and had followed the safety rules, so all he got was the bag and a few packs of musk-scented sticks. They were the worst smelling in my opinion. Inspiration and I laughed at his folly, and we immediately left the area as quietly as we had arrived.

We were the best duo of everyone who went out "alms collecting." I savored the positive attention I received for being such a good servant of the Lord. But it was fleeting. No sooner did I receive one compliment than I received two belittling, demoralizing comments.

He didn't want me to feel good about myself, and I didn't. I learned to hate myself and to mistrust my feelings. I depended on him to dictate who I was, what I was capable of and whether I was worthy of his, my own, or anyone else's love and appreciation. Mom didn't love me, Jaci didn't love me, Isabella tried to love me, and I tried to find love by pleasing him.

I wanted so badly for the Lord to love me, to call me son. I tried to do things to win his favor. I'd volunteer to rub his feet or bring him a refreshment as a surprise. I'd find something to clean and hope he would recognize I did it on my own without it being commanded of me. I felt the kind of deep longing that only a child can sustain optimistically in the face of inevitable repudiation. I tried and tried again.

I found some tenderness in Inspiration. She offered a kind hand on my head and often told me how handsome I was. That always made me feel good and helped me to get through the day.

However, each day brought with it fear as well as curiosity. Learning how to sit still or meditate required great discipline, which I had not yet developed. Once, while sitting at the foot of Om's bed in the third or fourth hour of a particularly un-special day, my back began to slouch and my mind fell in and out of consciousness. A booming voice from some dark corner startled me back into perfect lotus position: "Back straight!"

Hunger pains rolled through my body. The thought of the banana I'd spotted in the fruit bowl, but knew better than to touch, made the rumbling even louder. The tap water from the bathroom sink had been my only nourishment so far for that day.

Time dripped by as slowly as the wax on the blood-red candle that illuminated my corner of this dark and lonely place that had become my home. But, a home it was not. It was a prison, and my only escape was through the door of my imagination. There, I played wonderful games with my friends and family. There, my mother loved me. Lavish assortments of all the food and desserts

I could wish for appeared in my mind's eye. There, the sun shined lovingly against my face; I was loved, I was safe, I was free.

I woke up in the middle of the night. Everyone else was asleep. It was the perfect time to sneak into the food area and scarf down an easily consumable item. I grabbed some almond butter and flour tortillas. I was so hungry that my stomach evaporated the fear of ghosts and monsters and every creature that can hide in the mind of every little boy. But, most of all, it was the fear of Him.

My hunger was a formidable opponent to the fear that night. I often found myself powerless against it. It drove me to disobey "God" himself. It forced me to risk pain, humiliation, demoralization, ridicule, and embarrassment. But I eagerly went about paying that price and filled my stomach fast with as many flour tortillas as I could eat without the almond butter. The jar had not yet been open, and I knew better than to risk opening it and being found out. Plain flour tortillas. They were so good that night, so delicious, so rewarding ... so nourishing.

I have a special love for them to this day. I had stumbled upon a means to feed myself, a midnight expedition that entailed dangerous curiosity. I wondered how long I would be able to get away with it. Sometimes, though, I slept through the night and disappointedly missed my date with dinner.

Harmony and Lovelight returned after having not been around for some time. It turned out that they had been arrested and had been put in jail. Then they had escaped and had hitched back to Tijuana. How they found us was a mystery to me. I can only now assume there was a system in place for emergency situations – probably some outside entity that Om kept in touch with via mail that was the contact point for all the lovers. I have often wondered if it was my mom.

Om fucked Lovelight day in and day out for weeks. It made all the other women green with envy. Perfection pouted in her passive-aggressive way. Harmony received a little attention but acted aloof and prideful. Inspiration was not afraid to speak her mind and shared her discontent. Devi was too low on the list to even be noticed, and Isabella must have been glad to finally get a break.

I was still secretly nourishing my young body whenever I was able to wake up. One night, my stomach told me it was time. I got up out of the kids' bed and quietly and methodically made my way across the old dark wooden nightclub to the food area. Om must have favored those flour tortillas as much as I did because there was always a big bag of them. I had become more daring in my midnight pilfering of sustenance.

On this night, I was especially hungry and angry at my quandary, so I decided to use some almond butter and honey, both of which had already been opened. I wasn't a fool! I was inhaling and enjoying not only the sticky buttery goodness, but, more than that, the defiance, the disobedience, my own clever-ness. My mouth watered and endorphins rushed through my body.

"What's that?" I half choked on the bite that was in my mouth. Gulp! I forced it down half-chewed in order to respond. All I could come up with was very un-clever. "Huh?" Gulp! Swallow.

Harmony had stumbled upon me on her way to the bathroom. She peered down at me wickedly, put her fist in my face, rolled out her index finger, and beckoned me like an evil witch to follow her into the darkness. She led me into the bathroom that said "Caballeros" on it. The other one didn't work. She got right up in my face and, knowing the answer, she asked in a whisper whether I had permission to be eating. I fearfully muttered, "No."

She was obviously getting off on dominating me and tried to trick me into lying. She asked me again if I was sure I didn't have permission. I knew better than to lie, on top of my first crime of defying the Lord's wishes.

I shook my head no and quietly told her that I was hungry. She instructed me to wait there. So I stood waiting in the blackness of the bathroom, not knowing what she was going to do. I didn't care about goblins or ghosts. My re-ality was far more frightening. She had left me in there to scare me, hoping the darkness would produce tears, or better yet, she really wanted me to disobey her command to wait. I was too clever for that trick. I sat down on the cold tile floor and outwitted her. She finally returned, her round Asian face, plump nose, and black hair illuminated by a small candle.

I stood up as she entered and she set the candle down on the sink under the faded mirror, which seemed to brighten the room a little more. My eyes had adjusted to the dark while she was gone, so the candlelight shone bright enough for me to see she was holding a 2x4 piece of wood in her other hand. I was terrified now. I didn't know how she planned on using it. I thought she was going to club me over the head with it. She told me to remove my clothes. I was confused and terrified. I wanted to call out, but there was no one that would rescue me. I nervously looked briefly over my shoulder, hopping on her command to disrobe. She stood over me, one hand on her hip, the other resting impatiently on the 2x4 like it was a cane.

"Let's go," she said, as she tapped her weapon intolerantly. My arms felt heavy as I unbuttoned my pants. I lost my balance when I pulled my first leg out, which caused me to stumble. I hopped for a second and got the other pant leg off. Naked, she told me to turn around and put my hands up on the wall – like it might have been done to her in prison. She told me not to make a sound.

I was terrified and felt helpless as my hands felt the cool metal of the old stall wall. She positioned herself like a batter at home plate and swung the 2x4 swiftly against my bare bottom. A sound arose out of me that I'd never heard from a human being before, let alone myself. It was a deep moaning, grunting sound that morphed into a falsetto-ish hyena cry. The utterance of pure pain.

It was so foreign of a sound that she chuckled. My instinct was to block the next hit with my hands, but I thought the blow would break my fingers. My hands instantly came off the wall and tried to console my cheek as I jumped around in too much pain to cry. She told me to put my hands back on the wall.

"No, please," I said.

"Turn around," she commanded me. I slowly turned to face the wall again, and, just as I turned my head to the wall, I heard her body wind up for the next strike. This time, it was harder. It was a pounding, bruising pain, unlike the leather belt which always produced a cutting, stinging pain. I wondered how many more blows I could endure. I thought angrily that the food was not worth it. I let out another animal sound and fell to the floor, hoping it would convince her to stop. Then she callously told me to put my pants back on and go to bed.

The next morning after all the rituals, I hoped not to hear anything further about the night's events. When I accidentally made eye contact with her, it reminded her to tell Om. She tauntingly and sinisterly smirked at me, being the sadistic and vile person that she was. I tried not to look at them and headed to the bathroom to escape whatever was coming next. Maybe that little bit of time out of sight would spare me an immediate beating. But, before I made it out of his sight, I heard my name called.

"Jabali!"

Om had given Jaci and Isabella their new names but had not yet given me one. I'd wondered why. I was the only person in the fold with a worldly name. Worldly meant the outside world and was often called the "old world" in this cult language. It is a term used by the cult of Jehovah's Witnesses and other cults. Jaci had been named Majesty. Isabella was Dharma.

God summoned me over to him and dismissed Harmony, who smirked at me once more as we passed one another. Terrified of what was coming next, my mouth dried until my saliva became like chalk. I couldn't swallow. My heart pounded furiously in its cage. My hands dripped a nervous sweat. I couldn't read his facial expression. He purposely hid his intention; it was a technique he used to confuse and mislead me.

However, when I got within striking distance of his long arms, he smiled and said, "Get dressed. You're going out into the field today." And that was it. It was psychological warfare. He knew I was petrified and used techniques like this to keep me constantly in a heightened state of fear. Slowly, the benevolent and loving calmness in him became quiet and evil loathing. I never knew what to expect, except to expect the unexpected. That place of uncertainty, that place between peace and purgatory, became my home.

It was another regular day out in the streets of Mexico, my escape from home. I asked Inspiration if I could have a share of her bundles since I was learning the language almost faster than she was. I felt confident I could sell. She agreed and told me she would get me a treat at the end of the day if I was able to reach ten bundles.

I eagerly and happily went about showing her that I could do it. We arrived at a grocery store parking lot. It was one that we had visited before and had become a favorite of ours, but couldn't frequent too often for security reasons. Everyone was instructed not to go back to a particular place of business more than once a week in order to not draw attention to ourselves. Still, not drawing attention to ourselves was very hard to do for a five-foot-nine white woman, obviously American, who had a young, yellow-skinned, green-eyed child in tow. We were easy to spot amongst the crowd of Mayan descendants.

I began my sales presentation: "Hola! Quieres comprar incienso, es muy bonita? Tengo muchas aromas, tengo de jazmín, fresa, más y más." (Would you like to buy some incense? It smells really beautiful. There's lots of flavors … jasmine, strawberry, and much more.)

People were often amused by seeing an American child selling incense on the streets. I loved interactions with regular people, and I didn't care about the language barrier. Just being able to engage with them gave me a sense of happiness that was void back at the Ponderosa. When I was out in the world, I developed a sense of self-confidence. A small inner voice let me know that I was charming, smart, and handsome.

People always told me, "Tienes ojos bonitos!" (You have beautiful eyes!), which helped my self-esteem. I easily sold my ten packs, and, at the end of the day, Inspiration complimented me on a job well done and treated me to some ice cream. She also reassured me that she would report to the Lord about what a good job I'd done and how obedient I had been.

One day, I was coming back from a laundry assignment with Devi when I saw Freedom begin his very first pedaling strokes on the bike. I couldn't believe my eyes. He wobbled the handlebars frantically, kept pedaling to maintain his balance, and cruised off down the dirty street.

I wanted so badly to take the bike from him and do it myself. I knew that if he could, I could. I brought the laundry back to the club and got permission to go outside and ride the bike with Freedom. By the time I got back outside, I saw Freedom riding down the hill just as a VW bug turned the corner – and hit him head on. Freedom's momentum flipped him over the entire car. He did a somersault on the bike, never letting go of the handlebars until he was on the backside of the car. Then the bike went flying and he disappeared behind the car.

Two guys jumped out of the VW thinking they'd just killed this kid. I ran all the way down to them, and, to my amazement, I saw Freedom standing up from behind a car. The driver was so shocked that he kept looking back and forth at the point of impact, to where Freedom was standing in the street. The passenger attempted to straighten out the handlebars. Freedom started dusting himself off. His Afro had been brushed up, tied with a rubber band, and sat large and puffy on his little head. When the passenger and driver saw that he was okay, they hopped back into the bug and drove away as if nothing had happened. I couldn't help but laugh at what I just saw. Freedom, however, did not find it amusing and tried not to cry. I asked him if he was okay.

He replied, "You can have the bike."

I stopped laughing as he turned and proceeded up the hill. I walked the bike back to the top of the street, to the flat part, put my leg over the bicycle seat and pushed hard on the pedal. I mimicked Freedom's frantic gyration of the handlebars with a little more poise, and I, too, began my bike-riding career.

We moved out of the old brown wood nightclub shortly after that. I was happy to get out of there, but the mystery of my uncertain future – the where, why, when, what, who, and how – was ever-present and disconcerting.

We arrived at a new location in two groups as usual. Now, we were in a small, dusty town in the middle of nowhere. It reminded me of an old cowboy town whose time had come and gone, and all that remained were tumbleweeds and the poor souls who couldn't get out.

Meanwhile, there was something brewing in the adult world of Om's communication with the ladies. The prison break conjured a lot of adult talk that I was not privy to. But what was going on this time had something to do with Isabella. Some plan had fallen apart while we were in this dusty, nowhere town, and soon we would be gone again.

Apparently, Isabella had failed an assignment, which is what had caused us to leave shortly after arriving. I was somewhat relieved, since it was going to be a miserable stay anyway. However, I had spotted a cute girl, which might have eased my continual despair if I had gotten to know her.

Om made us leave the bicycles back in Tijuana, and now, somehow, Isabella had not returned with the van. So Om broke us up again, taking Omson, Freedom, and me with him on a bus to the train station in Mexicali.

FOUR

Left Again

T he Mexicali train station was abuzz with hundreds and hundreds of people walking, running, screaming, and moving in all directions. The huge building reminded me of a giant church with its incredibly high arching ceilings and entryways. It looked bigger and crazier than anything I had ever seen, but, to the eyes of a child, everything looks big.

We walked to many different counters before Om finally bought the tickets. Seeing all the people hustling and bustling around thrilled me. Some of them looked extremely poor and miserable. Others seemed happy and content. There were vendors everywhere, selling everything from fruits and vegetables to clothes, trinkets, toys, tamales, corn on sticks, and even raw meat. The floor was dirty and the air smelled of sweat and mustiness and animals. I loved every second of it. It was an adventure, and my eyes were overwhelmed with curiosity.

After some time of waiting, Om bought us some corn on a stick, the cob skewered and covered with mayonnaise and cheese, as well as several bananas, mangos, and oranges. Then we headed to another section of the station. We walked through a pair of double doors, and before me was what looked like an old locomotive from the turn of the century. It was packed with people, some of whom had goats and pigs and chickens. Some were caged, some not. Every single person whom we walked past stopped and looked, their heads following us as we passed them. In a sea of people no taller than 5'7" it was understandable. They stared at this tall, black man. His hair was black highlighted with grey, and had been pulled into a tight bun on the top of his head. He never seemed to notice or care about the stares; he just calmly smiled. He didn't engage with me either. He just kindly smiled down at me but would not answer any question I asked of him. I did not like that. I was used to people giving me lots of attention and engaging with me when I was selling on the street. But I knew better than to push him past his smile.

Time was moving fas. He asked a conductor where our train was, not by speaking in Spanish, but by showing his tickets to the man. The conductor, unimpressed with the Lord, gestured down the runway impatiently. Om never broke his smile. We found our car and boarded.

The train was even more crowded than the station. People pushed past each other, eager to find their seats. We made our way behind some goats. That helped with the congestion. Their owner was looking at us like we were from Mars. Babies cried, chickens clucked, and I loved every second of it. Then Om discovered that we had actually boarded the wrong car, so we had to make our way back through the entire car filled with people and animals until we finally got to the right one.

At the end of the car was a small rest area. We passed it and entered our car, and immediately to the left was our cabin. It was far nicer than the previous car. This one allowed us to have a private room that had beds.

With so much action and entertainment, I hadn't really paid attention to the incredibly heavy bag I had lugged through the station until it was time to put it in the overhead compartment, which Om did for me. I wondered desperately where we were headed, but the excitement of being on the move was hypnotic. The "where" weighed in far less than the "how." I had never been on a train before and I marveled at all its mystery. We settled into our cabin, my eyes fixed on the people still hustling around on the platform outside. Kids walked up and down it selling peanuts and Chicklets. Others sold fruit, sandwiches, dolls, or puppets. Some had nothing to sell. Poverty and hunger displayed more in their eyes than on their dirty clothes or un-showered bodies. The sad, heartbroken pleas of mothers, their newborn babies straddled to their backs, with their hands outstretched, burned powerful images into my young mind. I knew hunger and was a friend to loneliness and despair, but seeing these poor, sad faces who depended solely on the generosity of others gave me pause.

It was hard to stare into the face of a child my age begging me for money. I didn't know what to do. Sometimes I shrugged my shoulders and held my hands up to show that I had no money. While that worked sometimes, others still stood with their hands outreached, insisting I had something to give to them. I had to break eye contact and look away. It was an extremely heart-breaking reality for anyone to face, let alone a child.

Then a woman whose age showed in the slow shuffling of her feet and hunched back, with two very young children following behind her, looked up at me sitting in the window and put her hand up, asking for anything. Then she looked back at her kids behind her, as if to say, "Can't you see I have two hungry children? Please help us."

I felt so sorry for her, for all of them. I could not help any of them. I was just a boy.

Om pulled down the blinds, causing an immediate darkness to fill the cabin. He was preparing for a nap, which meant I had to sit there until he woke up or get permission to leave. I asked if I could use the bathroom and he said, "Yes, but come straight back."

Damn! I thought. I wanted to check out the train. Omson and Freedom also came along and that really foiled any chance of me having a leisurely walk through the car.

We quickly returned and settled in, careful not to make too much noise. Adrenalin still coursed through my veins from all the traveling and witnessing. It took a while before my exhaustion finally set in. I wondered where Jaci and Isabella were, wishing I could have shared this experience with them as I dozed off to sleep.

I woke up to Om having returned with some sandwiches and juice. He pulled the blinds up and the bright sunlight helped lift the fog from my dream state. The vast landscape was littered with tin shacks and homes made of cardboard, plastic, wood, anything that could be used for structural support. Filth and garbage replaced lawns and rose bushes of memories past.

Small streams of smoke signaled the cooking of whatever meager meals were being thankfully consumed. Then, suddenly, there was only vast emptiness, brown earth with no signs of humanity. Minutes later, farms, pastures, cows, horses, goats, and small people hunched over in large fields came into view. The people all wore large hats to protect them from the sun's unforgiving heat. Then, in the distance, nothing. The sky was a cloudless pale blue.

Suddenly, I became overwhelmed with fear and despair. I could see that every passing farmer, animal, and blade of grass, I was getting farther and farther away from my home, my mom, my family, and all that I knew. I was terrified – I was never going to go home. I had to face and accept the uncertainty of my future with this person who claimed to be God. He was cruel and malevolent, yet had the ability to turn on a dime and be kind and gentle.

Here I was, on a journey with a so-called spiritual teacher of someone else's choosing, his qualifications unconfirmed, and his intentions unknown. My age was inappropriate for much of the subject matter, and I was far too young to have been splashed with the sweat and juice of two or more adults having sex, let alone that one of them was my barely teenaged sister. Nevertheless, this was my predicament. I had no advocate, and no one in my life had the authority to stop the mistreatment and abuse. I forged on, facing uncertainty and shame every day, and hoping that every day would be the day I went back home.

The novelty of this trip disappeared with a lonely, crushing feeling of desperation for home, for normalcy. The day turned to night, but the train's unwavering commitment roared on. The loud crashing noise of its heavy steel frame against the narrow helpless tracks below reflected the pressure under which it persevered.

Unknown to me, my spirit would carry a far greater load along this treacherous and foreboding path that was yet to be traveled. As the evening grew and the four of us grew restless, Om invited us to take a walk through the train. Our car and the very next one ahead of us towards the engine were far nicer than all the other cars. There were no animals allowed and the people were groomed and clean.

They all still stared at us. I enjoyed it. I liked the attention. Most of it was positive, and the look of shock on their faces thrilled me. I received long stares and smiles by parents and kids alike. Sometimes I got a dirty look or a negative vibe from people, but mostly they stared at Om. I had more or less gotten used to stares from being out in the streets on "assignments." But we drew ten times the attention as we trailed behind him.

Conductors positioned at the doors of these two cars prevented anyone without the proper ticket from boarding. The train was by no means technologically advanced. The suspension felt like it sat on metal poles instead of shocks. The seats were worn and the floor was dirty. The train rocked heavily back and forth, causing me to stumble and reach for any available seat or handle. We walked to the front of the train and finally came to a locked door that was protected by yet another conductor.

Om tried to ask the man questions, but his Spanish was pathetic and his accent even worse.

"Why does God not speak Spanish?" flashed through my mind.

The next morning we pulled into a small station, and the conductor yelled out the stop. We were in the middle of nowhere. Out the window, I saw more poor people selling goods. Men, women, and children happily greeted the train, waving and running alongside, waiting for it to stop. None were allowed on, but people on board disembarked, some happily greeting family members, others stretching and purchasing goods.

Omson and I were instructed to stay in our cabin while God took Freedom with him. Where? I knew better than to ask. I began noticing that he favored Freedom. In and out of station after station, the poor struggling faces began to blend into one giant swarm, and my heart began to harden to them.

On the second day, the sweltering heat inside the train was unforgiving. Each car became a sweatbox of hot breath and body odor of 50 to 70 un-bathed human beings. Mothers fanned their crying babies and men wiped the sweat from their necks and brows. Countless flies found shelter inside from the blistering sun.

The steel rest area at the end of the connecting car was a refuge from the smell, but was even hotter, since the steel conducted the heat like an oven. The train moved at a snail's pace through the desert sun – in reverse – for miles. Then it slowly came to a jerking stop. We sat there, cooking in the desert for quite some time. People got off of the train out of desperation, only to find the natural environment to be equally as grim. Conductors were harassed with barrages of what I could only half-interpret as questions as to the nature of the predicament.

Just as real desperation and panic began to set in and consume men and women for the safety of their children, people were ordered back aboard and the train jerked its start – again in reverse – but this time picking up enough speed to keep the flies from landing for too long, although people didn't seem bothered by them. By this time, a hot blow dryer would have seemed cooler than the temperature of the air.

Eventually, we began our forward progress again. The adventure had become an agonizing campaign deep into Mexico, the destination unknown. The blistering heat started to subside as the sun slowly began its long descent across the Mexican sky. We made yet another stop in an even smaller pueblo. And even in this tiny place, there were children selling goods.

The train line was a lifeline to many. Om bought hot tamales, plenty of water, and popsicle sticks. Once again we were off, this time without a screaming announcement. In the distance, I saw a huge mountain range that crossed the entire horizon.

I asked a conductor on the way back from a filthy, disgusting shit and piss-filled bathroom, "Vamos a las montañas?" (Are we going into the mountains?)

He said, "Si, pero cambiamos primero." (Yes, but we change first.)

I didn't understand anything at the time except for "Si", but that gave me a small sense of where we were headed, at least directionally.

By nightfall we had stopped again. Small lights scattered in the distance were all that illuminated the pitch-black night. I felt the rumbling engine cut off and a quiet fell over the train – a long needed silence and calm.

Being exposed to so much that was going on around me but being disconnected by the language barrier and purposely being kept ignorant about our destination caused a lot of anxiety for me. It was like traveling blind, yet seeing everything and hearing everything, but understanding nothing. It forced my mind, brain, and spirit to work overtime all the time. The conductor yelled out commands that forced Om to check the wheres and whens. Of course, he did not report back to us to let us know what was happening.

That night, God read to us from his manuscript. He told of a supernatural, fantastical, never-ending, omnipotent magical love affair between the Lord of all Creation and his mother, and that, through Immaculate Conception, she had given birth to him. Coming down from Heaven as King and Queen, she had taken human form and lived on Earth long enough to give birth to her King in Heaven, but child on Earth.

Because he read from a book, it made it appear more authentic and believable to my young ears. He said he wrote the Bible, the Quran, the Tao, and the Bhagavad Gita. I had never heard of any of those books except for the Bible. But I knew that it had something to do with God because my dad, the Jehovah's Witness, brought me to the Kingdom Hall every chance he could, as he tried to save me from my hedonistic and occultist mother.

As God read, he glanced over at me, always answering any question I posed that related to him or his book or to his beloved mother/lover, "Grace." I didn't understand how his mom was his wife, but was willing to accept this pronouncement just as I was willing to accept that he was God.

His reading was hypnotic. I grew tired but tried to stay awake out of fear and respect. Freedom eventually dozed off, but I wanted to impress Om with my stamina and attentiveness.

Morning came and with it the feelings of adventure again mixed with sorrow, fear, and mystery. Om was already awake, so I asked for permission to stand in the rest area of the next car. He smiled and, with a rolling gesture of his hand, like a maharajah, he excused me with words I didn't understand the meaning of. So, I repeated my request to which I received the same smile but now a bigger gesture. Concluding I was free to go, I left.

The morning air was pleasant and refreshing. The wind whirled around the open area and the rhythmic motion and speed of the train gave me a simultaneous sense of loneliness and peace.

I enjoyed my solitude for a few moments before I was joined by another passenger, an older man who smiled at me curiously while out for some fresh air and a morning cigarette. It was forbidden for me to talk to anybody outside our group, but my naturally friendly inclination almost always got me in trouble.

I wanted to find the right person and tell them what was happening to me. Clearly, this old man was not that person, but the chance to engage with a normal human being was something I longed for constantly.

He spoke no English and my limited Spanish meant that he posed no threat in case Om should come check on me. Still, our broken conversation made me feel good. I could hear the tenderness in his voice and saw a spark of a love for children in his eyes. I gathered that he was a grandpa of four and that he was going to visit them in some town, probably like one of the many we had passed on this trip. I stuck my head out of the rest area to see what it looked like behind us. The old man screamed and grabbed me, dropping his cigarette.

In a panic, he showed me with concerned desperation that I could lose my head if I stuck it out there. And, as if the universe had sent him to protect me, a telephone pole passed us right at that moment, close enough to be fatal. Both of our eyes lit up in surprise, then his surprise turned to wisdom and mine to youthful embarrassment. There was a moment of silence, an unspoken appreciation of what had just happened on both our parts. He finished his cigarette, and, with an experienced smile, said goodbye. A moment later, Om and the boys appeared.

We made our way into yet another small pueblo where we switched trains and began our ascent into the mountains. It was midday and the green terrain of trees, plants, bushes, and foliage helped give the air a semi-tropical feel.

This train felt older and tougher than the first one had. The toilets opened up right onto the tracks, and I could see the ground passing beneath the train. The passage through the mountains was incredibly rough and extremely serpentine in its meandering journey high into the mountains. I could see both the front of the train and the back simultaneously, as well as the narrow path that it rode on. We were so close to the mountain face, I felt like if I reached out I could touch it. Looking down, there were only endless miles of sheer mountain rock. There were no guard rails.

I marveled at how anyone could have built this terrifying path into the mountains so high up. The lay of the tracks made it look like we were just mere inches from death. I couldn't look outside for too long before vertigo set in. I was afraid that if everyone onboard were to gather on that side of the train, it would tip over and we would all fall to our deaths.

I feared tremendously that I would never return home, and, finally, I mustered the courage to ask when and if we would ever go back to Berkeley.

Om replied, "Yes." He told me I could go back whenever I wanted to, but he wanted to know if I really wanted to go back to the "Old World" where all would be destroyed in Armageddon. He asked me if I wanted to be by his side to help him rule the earth, to which I felt honored and privileged.

Through his series of questions and many more, I slowly forgot my sorrow and began focusing on living on a paradise earth in which I would help the Lord and his mother/wife rule all the world. I remembered how he'd made the thunder roar through the valley that day and remained both confused and convinced at his proclamation of being the Creator of All.

The long, slow, and arduous passage through the high mountain range kept my mind ricocheting. Where was I going? Where was I from? What would the future be like? My thoughts were mixed with the fantasy, mystery, and awe of a young boy traveling to a distant land. It was 1978.

After many hours, we arrived at our destination. We disembarked and caught a cab to a small motel. This was no small town but a huge metropolis. The air smelled stale and stuffy, combined with the powerful odor of exhaust.

It was sometime after midnight, but the city still hummed with activity. We checked in, and we all fell right to sleep.

Two days passed before Inspiration and Perfection showed up. Omson and Freedom were happy to see their mom. I was disappointed that Jaci and Isabella were not with them, but Inspiration assured me that they were on their way.

The next day we moved to a quiet country town outside of the city of Satélite, to a medium-sized white house that sat at the end of a long curved driveway. High, golden-brown grass led up to the front door. A tall, white wall created its boundaries. On the side of the house was a tennis court with no net. The surrounding area was made up of huge sugar cane fields, and some other houses like ours, but mostly there was just farmland.

We quickly settled in and began the now-accustomed rituals. Jaci showed up with Harmony and Lovelight, but there was no sign of Isabella. I asked Jaci, but he didn't know why she wasn't around. My need to know was too strong to second-guess whether or not I would get a straight answer. I approached Harmony after Jaci, then Devi, then Lovelight. I gathered that something was amiss.

Finally, Om reassured me I would see her soon. Om instructed Harmony to make a net for the court, since she was a seamstress. Harmony put together a makeshift net with squares large enough for balls to fit through. Om was not happy with it. One day, the gas stove blew up in Jaci's face, which singed off his eyebrows and seemed to render him blind. I sensed he was faking his injury but couldn't blame him for trying to get out of work and chores.

The women played nude tennis, and, somehow, the word spread to the neighborhood kids. Soon after that, if a ball could be heard being hit back and forth, the top of the wall would be lined with the heads of every boy in the area. Then, as if they weren't seen, they would drop their heads out of sight whenever there was a pause in play. What could be better to a young, Catholic farm boy than watching naked American women play tennis?

During our brief stay, Om, with the help of Lovelight and Inspiration, organized a sex party/orgy with some Mexican people I had never met. I wondered how he knew them. There were three men and four women. Their arrival was pleasantly surprising for me, since any contact with the outside world made me very happy. New people meant a welcomed change of dynamics. Instantly, the energy amongst everyone in the cult was different, lighter, more playful. It was a facade for sure, but I enjoyed it.

They started by playing naked tennis, a doubles match. Jaci was still pretending to be blind, so he had to stay inside with his eyes covered. Omson, Freedom, and I were the ball boys. And, of course, we had the audience of 15 to 20 boys lined up at the top of the wall.

The adults rotated partners at the end of each set. Drinks and food were also served throughout the day. At one point during the women's doubles match, Om and two of the men shooed away the neighborhood boys for continuously making cat calls at the women as they played. But, as soon as Om left, the boys were back. It got so bad, they stopped playing at the request of one of the female guests. I was ordered to clean up the food and dishes. I took the opportunity to get permission to play tennis with Omson after I cleaned up.

One of the guests stood out more than the rest, a man named Ricardo. He was an outgoing, friendly man with long, curly hair that he pulled back into a ponytail. His infectious smile and playful, inquisitive personality won my affection. We became friends that day when he took the time to play tennis with me for a few minutes and praised me for my ability. His words and his seemingly caring nature touched me and made me like him even more. I missed approval and encouragement, and I longed for it. Ricardo's words felt like nourishing rain after a long drought.

Evening was fast approaching and Om moved the "party" into the large living room that was his quarters. The vast meal had been prepared and served. Omson, Freedom, and I were ordered to once again clean up, then go straight to bed. During the cleaning, Om read out of his book, this time in Spanish, to an amused group of strangers. The women smiled at his pronouncements. The men sat in bored disbelief.

Ricardo left the room to help us clean the kitchen. He rolled his eyes. With a confused frown on his face and a gesture with his thumb, he pointed back, as if to say, "What the hell is he talking about?"

I nervously acknowledged this look that he instinctively gave only to me. Lovelight followed him into the kitchen and requested his return. In adult talk, she told him that, if he wanted to have her, he would have to sit through the sermon. He returned with Lovelight but looked back at me with a huge smile. I couldn't blame him, I wanted her too.

We finished cleaning and headed for bed. On our way, I saw Inspiration and one of the other men putting a large mattress across the entrance to the living room. I wondered why they attempted to conceal what they were about to do. I would have gone straight to sleep as ordered, but my curiosity was piqued. That inquisitiveness kept me awake past the other kids, and ultimately, indelibly, changed me forever.

I snuck out of bed, and, ever-so-cautiously, walked back towards the living room. The house was dark except for the light that glowed from behind the bed. It offered a partially blocked view into his quarters. Incense drifted through the sleepy house, along with the gentle intermittent sound of the jingling bells.

Then the singing began: "Om is the basis of sacred fucking … Om is the basis of sacred fucking … Meet in Om's new temple … Take off all your clothes … Hypocrisy … unfolds …"

I got closer to the darkness on my side of the mattress. There was enough space between the wall for me to see the room. Om was at the back of the room behind a woman who faced him; the shadows of her vertebrae descended into the top of her buttocks. Her head was tilted backwards. On the floor to the left was Inspiration on her knees. Her legs were spread wide. She was facing in my direction as she aggressively gyrated backwards. The small, bearded man behind her adjusted the glasses on his nose.

The singing stopped and Inspiration began chanting, "Om potency, Om potency ..." It seemed she intended to conjure up an erection. Meanwhile, I could hear Lovelight's distinct moans and the grunting of a man who I secretly hoped was Ricardo. The others were out of sight to my right.

One of the Mexican women got up from out of my line of sight and crossed the room. On her return, she caught my eye and smiled. It startled me. I tried to lean back into the darkness. She seemed amused and sauntered over to the corner where my voyeurism was discovered. I retreated, got up from my squatting position and backed up into the darkness. She crunched down and squeezed through the opening between the bed and the wall: I was busted.

She put her finger to her lips, suggesting quiet and walked past me to the kitchen. Still stunned, I stood there watching her naked body glide through the dark as she retrieved some juice from the refrigerator. She walked back to me and drank another sip. Both of her hands clasped the libation. She offered me some. I took it. Juice was a rare commodity for me.

She smiled and put her hand on my head, playing gently with my curls. Her naked body stood before me, almost touching me. Her nipples floated in front of my eyes. I felt her warm breath blow across my eyelashes. She took the glass from my stunned but curious hands. In the same motion she took my hand and put it on her breast. Her eyes looked deep into mine with a tenderness, maturity, and seductiveness that hypnotized me.

She led me into the small room where Prosperity and Triumph were sleeping just off the living room area. I thought to myself, *"It's about to happen."* She laid me down on the floor a couple of feet away from Triumph. She kept looking at me with that same look. I remembered earlier in the day of having tried to make eye contact with her, and her not having given me the acknowledgment I wanted.

Now, I was the object of her undivided attention. She slid my pants off in one motion. I felt her inner thigh glide atop both my legs, her pubic hairs slightly damp on my hip. Lying on her side, she propped her head up with her hand. Her black, shoulder-length hair dropped behind her hand. Her look told me that I was beautiful. She leaned down and kissed me with her open, soft, wet lips. With her other hand, she gently pulled my chin down, which opened my mouth slightly. Then she tenderly pressed her wet mouth against mine and faintly moaned in my mouth. Her hand drifted slowly down my torso, feeling my erection. I felt her pelvis press hard against my hip.

Her hand rose back to my face, her leg rising up to my stomach. She pressed past my scrotum and penis, opening her wet vagina onto the top of my thigh. Then she rolled on top of me, put her top leg on the far side of my body, and straddled me. I was extremely aroused and also a little scared. She agilely pressed her entire body against mine. Her nipples were hard as they pressed into me. Her face was beside mine, cheek to cheek. Then she pushed both her knees high up alongside my underarms, causing my arms to rise. I slowly put them on her shoulder blades, which caused another quiet moan and intense muscle contractions in her whole body. Her vagina was gliding back and forth on my penis, pressing hard, grinding up and down and in circles.

She reached under her stomach and took my penis between her fingers and gyrated it speedily in a very particular place on her vagina then quickly slid her whole body down. She put my penis in her mouth, then licked all around the whole area, as well as the joints between my torso and legs. She then pulled one leg over, spreading my legs, and put her tongue on my anus and licked all the way up past my scrotum to the top of my penis. The sensations caused me to jump nervously, but I quickly calmed down with a gentle touch of her hand on my chest.

Sensing that was too much for me, she came back up my body and put her tongue deep inside my mouth. I could taste a hint of Jumex mango juice in her mouth and wondered if she did, too. I felt so insecure. I had no idea what to do. She felt my body tense. I liked it, but I didn't like it at the same time. I liked that she wanted me enough to be with me, but her wet vagina gave me shivers. She pulled away, but I pulled her back down. I didn't want her to leave me. She seemed to sigh in relief when I pulled her back to me.

She continued grinding her spot on me, then used her hand as she kissed my cheek. She moaned three distinct high pitched moans in my ear, which reminded me of Lovelight. Then slowly, she relaxed her body and laid next to me, breathing heavily. She seemed very relaxed. I wondered if it was over. She softly stroked my chest and face, looked at me in the eyes with "that look," then put her finger to her mouth. Now, it was more than quiet that we were keeping. She kissed me on my lips one last time and left, never uttering a single word.

I lay there shocked and amazed, wondering if she was coming back. I felt exhilarated. My heart was pumping. I was proud. I felt loved. I felt like someone cared for me, like I was special. She gave me what all these women gave Him – attention, focus, and love; I was worthy. I was good enough for someone to appreciate and give their love to. In her perversion, and in a single night of what was to become years of loneliness, neglect, sadness, and abuse, I found a sense of self-worth.

On the move again, we landed in a nice apartment in Mexico City. It was a one-bedroom on the fourth floor of an older, middle-class neighborhood. Half of us had to sneak in and out because there was no way the landlord was going to let 13 people move into their one-bedroom. We came and went in shifts, hoping not to raise suspicion.

Shortly after arriving, I was allowed to go with Inspiration to meet Devi and Isabella at a cafe a few blocks away. I was ecstatic to finally see my sister after what seemed like forever. We were to meet them at 3 p.m.

Arriving a little early, we took seats at the long counter. I happily hopped up onto one of the green swiveling stools and began turning myself in circles. The other customers looked at us strangely, but I was used to it. After a few rotations, Inspiration moved us to a booth where we ordered some hotcakes and waited for them. And waited. And waited.

Finally, Devi walked through the door. She immediately spotted us and made her way over. Before she could sit down, I blurted out, "Where is Isabella?" She did not answer. Instead, she greeted Inspiration with the customary, "Om Eternal," while putting her hand in front of her chest and making the official hand sign – index finger touching the thumb, exactly like the "okay" sign. The signal had recently been deemed a security violation because it identified the cult to the dragonflies. Devi constantly made mistakes like that. Inspiration mildly reprimanded her and reminded her to be less conspicuous.

"Where is Isabella?" I said again, expecting her to walk in.

Devi overlooked my question again, obviously hiding the answer. She looked to Inspiration, a blank look of confusion on her face. Inspiration, mildly irritated, also inquired about Isabella's whereabouts. This required Devi to divulge that she didn't know, that Isabella had failed to meet Devi at the agreed place.

My stomach sank to my feet. The green and white checkered floor that matched the green tables, that matched the green swiveling chairs, that matched the white walls, made the hotcakes in my stomach feel green. My mouth went dry. The sunlight glared through the blinds, white hot as it brightened the smoke-filled room. The chattering of people's conversations around me, the clanging of dishes, and the frying of bacon, all went silent.

It was slow motion time. I watched as Inspiration put her hand on my head, but I didn't feel it there. Her mouth hung open in mid-sentence. Buzzing flies froze, suspended in midair. The white clock on the wall above the door remained unreadable, its green hands moved at lightning speed around and around.

Time did exist and I wanted to be able to understand how it worked. How much time had elapsed from the beginning of this nightmare when Mom had walked out that door? And how much time was yet to pass before this nightmare would be over? When would I be able to see her again?

I knew Isabella was never coming back. In that moment of suspended time, our lives together replayed in my head. I saw my beautiful sister, who she was to me from my earliest memories of the joy and love we shared to the shame and horror of when we last made eye contact. My protector was gone.

We hurried down the street, pushing back to the apartment to report the news. Careful not to be followed, we used the standard operating procedure. Upon returning from being outside, we walked into a small store, waited five minutes, and watched the door to see if a clean-cut, casually dressed, 25 to 50 year-old man or woman, usually wearing glasses, would walk in behind us. Whether they did or not, we doubled back the way we came, watching for any unmarked cars with large antennas and tinted windows. After zigzagging 2 to 3 blocks, finally, we'd walk around the corner to our building.

Inspiration sent Devi first. We followed shortly thereafter. Jaci had been out all day. He had discovered where Om kept all the cash and had been secretly stealing money. He pretended to be out selling incense, which masked the fact that the money he brought back as earnings from his sales was, in fact, money he had taken earlier while Om was in the shower.

He learned much earlier than I did that this man who called himself the Creator of All was only a mere mortal. In order to fend for himself, he had decided to learn the language, adapt to his environment, and make it work for him the best he could. When he arrived home that night, I rushed to tell him of Isabella's disappearance. He acted casually and remained nonchalant about the news. His disinterest in me and the important information I had just shared with him made me feel even more alone than ever.

I yearned for Jaci's love. I loved him so much. But his heart was broken, his faith spent, his hope shattered. He had long ago retreated into the "safety" of his reality. It sounded fun to me, but I knew there was more to it than she was telling me. "Jaci and Isabella are going with you."

I witnessed and experienced the changes in Om's actions immediately after Isabella disappeared. The morning sex stopped. The sex was replaced with mandatory silence. Quotas were raised. Devi got slapped for every little mistake she made. Jaci was forced to make all the incense by himself. Everyone was forced to fast, but I knew Harmony was eating outside somewhere because she was too fat to be fasting. The smiles from the Lord turned into empty stares.

One day, while everyone chanted and adorned him with love, sang to him, gave him foot rubs and brushed his hair, the house shook violently, sending dishes, lamps, books, and everything else crashing to the ground. We all looked around in amazement, not quite sure what to do. Om sat still, unnerved. A huge earthquake had rocked the entire city, the first earthquake I had ever experienced. The quake was scary and exciting at the same time. It created a buzz amongst the women, but Om made it seem like no big deal.

Soon after, life went back to being horrible, strange, confusing, lonely, and scary. Jaci became more withdrawn than ever. After spending countless hours in the closet where he was forced to sit and make everyone's incense, he would leave for the day and not come back until late at night. But Om couldn't get mad at him because he was making (stealing) his quota.

By this time, I accepted that Om was God and that He had a divine purpose for all humanity, especially for me. I understood why Isabella left, but was simultaneously confused. Nothing was normal. I spent week upon week locked up in that apartment with only Om's constant lecturing for hours and hours every single day. Then silence. "No talking" all day, day after day after day.

If I goofed and spoke, I was punished with a belt, a cold shower, isolation in a closet, *and* starvation. This punishment was exclusively tailored for me. I loved to talk. I loved to tell Omson and Freedom stories about my life before I knew them and about all the fun I used to have. I wasn't obedient enough and that made Him extremely angry. But there was some aspect of my personality that he enjoyed over his own two sons.

Perfection gave birth to a baby boy Om named Marvel. He was so ugly that, when they brought him home from the hospital, I thought he was deformed. Lovelight was also pregnant, just a few months behind. As the shock of Isabella's escape wore off, and as everyone continued achieving their new quotas, Om started up the sex again. He even invited Ricardo over.

I was very happy to see him again but was not allowed to talk to him. When we saw each other for the first time, he gave me a hug and asked how I had been, but I could not answer. I wanted so badly to speak to him, but knew if I did I would be sent to the closet. So, I signaled to him by opening and closing my hand like a puppet then gestured, "No." He understood and rubbed the top of my head.

Without saying a word, he looked at Inspiration with a frown, as if to say, "What's going on with this?"

That afternoon, he brought Om and the ladies to a hotel called the Camino Real and showed them how to use the facilities without paying. Soon after, Om allowed us boys to go on occasion, to swim and play tennis. However, not long after it became our personal hotel and resort, the hotel security began to recognize us and forbade us from returning.

For a short time I got to pretend to be a normal kid. The days in the pool, in which I made friends with the other kids and watched how the world outside operated without me, were bittersweet. One day, I made friends with some other American kids. Finding English-speaking people in a foreign country and from behind the wall of secrecy in which I lived was what I longed for desperately. They taught me to play Marco Polo and shared their lunches with me. I wished with my whole heart that they would take me with them.

Om began beating the ladies whenever they displeased him. Inspiration was the main recipient of his abuse. She always talked back to him and he constantly kicked her ass. Next was Lovelight. She was a bona fide nymphomaniac who often got in trouble for her addiction. Although most of the conversations around why any of them received beatings was above my head, I was able to glean some things despite my youth. On many occasions, Om would kick Inspiration out of the house and she would be gone for weeks. Other times it was Lovelight. Perfection, Devi, and Harmony didn't really talk back, and, if they did, he beat them into submission. Lovelight got sent away for something and I didn't see her for the rest of our stay in Mexico City. I think it was because she was fucking Ricardo behind Om's back while she was pregnant.

As the weeks turned into months, Jaci secretly planned his escape, having familiarized himself with the culture, language, and environment. Inside and outside of our silent prison, he had gathered an unbelievably immense amount of courage. This inner strength had been forged out of the hate, spite, and injustice to which he was subjected. And, on an early rainy morning in Mexico City, two thousand miles away from a home, our paths crossed one last time. I don't know how or why I happened to be up that morning. Was it destiny or luck? For whatever reason, here he was, in a black and grey tennis jump suit, a bag strapped over his shoulder, and he was making his way out the front door. He looked over at me, mildly shocked to see someone.

I asked him where he was going. He put his fingers to his lips, instructing me to shhh. "To do some laundry," he whispered. It was a response seemingly prepared for anyone he might encounter. He stepped out of the front door as I slowly followed, instinctively knowing something was amiss. He made his way down several steps before he turned to me standing at the doorway. He put his finger to his lips again as my questions followed him, a distant look of melancholy in his eyes. He said, "I'll be back." He walked down the stairs … he never came back.

FIVE

God Gets Hurt

T hings got much worse after Jaci left. Om became more impatient and physically abusive. As time passed, he began to dole out severe whippings for the smallest disobediences. He told me that we had to move again because Jaci was going to tell the FBI where we were. So, again, we moved, first to a six-story hotel somewhere in Mexico City.

I spent most of my time out on the streets with the various women. They had perfected the new scam now. Or maybe it wasn't new, but I was just old enough to participate. It went like this: A single, very beautiful, white woman, with what appeared to be her son or little brother, depending on the couple that day, would walk up to tourists on the streets, most times at tourist sites, and say: "Excuse me, sorry to bother you. Can you help me?"

The tourists' defenses were down because she spoke English, and besides, she was a well-dressed, pretty, white lady, and she presented no threat. In a poverty stricken country, the last thing a German couple would think is *this is a scam.*

"My son and I are from California, and someone stole all of our belongings last night. We have to wait for my parents to arrive in two days. We just need a few dollars to get by."

That worked like a charm with some people, European mostly. People asked questions like, "Why don't you go to the Embassy?" The reply was (depending on the person and the con), "The embassy has a three-day wait." This was true, but we didn't know that at the time. So, after executing this scam for 15 hours a day for months at a time and walking many miles a day, we were able to make thousands of dollars. Since there were five women, the money just rolled in.

During the con, the mark (the person/persons we were targeting) would ask me questions like: "Are you okay, young man?"

"Yes, just hungry, that's all."

The thrill of fooling people was exciting, and participating in the "assignment" was sure to put me in good graces with Om. When we arrived home, we always had to report everything that transpired during the course of our assignments. I was outgoing and precocious in nature and that turned out to be a commodity for Om.

We learned that people's defenses lower when a handsome, articulate child is part of the "story." I was happy to be out of the house and away from Om and from the hours of endless silence and the monotony of being confined indoors 24 hours a day. I was also happy to get away from Omson and Freedom.

In this routine, the days turned into weeks and the weeks became months. I was proving to be a major asset to Om and his cult. I wanted nothing more than to please him and get his approval. This was my way of getting into the Kingdom of Heaven and for getting the love and attention that every boy needs and wants. I found some self-worth in my ability to articulate and charm people; I saw that I was liked and that people were interested in me.

Inspiration became my surrogate mother because I spent most of my days out with her, but, as we broke the daily income records, the other women petitioned to bring me out with them to boost their sales and make their quota, too. In the morning meetings before we went out on assignment, Om would assign me to the woman who had the lowest score from the day before.

I observed that each woman had a different approach to "alms collecting," the name given to our con. Lovelight used her sex appeal. We were not a good match. Perfection was far too introverted to overcome the hundreds of rejections we faced every day. And she was envious of my ability and willingness to talk to every single person who looked like a potential mark – coupled with the fact that I shined over her sons, Omson and Freedom.

Devi was always the lowest income earner. I hated being assigned to her because her work ethic was worse than Perfection's. She spent the majority of her day wandering the streets with her head in the clouds, occasionally finding some guy who thought she was cute and who was willing to part with a little cash. It was no wonder to me that she never made much money.

Although I did like being out just for the sake of being outside, I knew coming back empty-handed was not going to be good for either of us. Harmony was the workhorse. She pounded the pavement as hard, if not harder, than Inspiration and me. But her haven was the Chinese Mexican community, and I was a dead giveaway for her story, so we weren't a good match either.

Om decided that Inspiration and I would maintain our partnership. We made tens of thousands of dollars together. Under Om's and her tutelage, we perfected our pitch, worked extremely hard every day, constantly walking at a pace that was a slight jog for my small legs. Our daily assignments took us across the entire city of Mexico, D.F. We traveled on the subways and buses, hitchhiked, and took cabs. Cabs were my favorite because they allowed me to rest.

We were attacked, accosted, spit on, yelled at, and chased by people of every walk of life in a city of 15 million. There was a one-armed lunatic who wielded his own feces. There were Federales who demanded to see our papers. There were mobs, women, gang members, and even children who attacked us.

One kid threw a brick, hitting Inspiration on her head. All I could make out of his Spanish was that he wanted us to leave his neighborhood. Her head was split and bleeding, and we were lucky a bus arrived just as she got her senses back. We formed a special bond, like mother and son, like brother and sister, like a teacher and student.

I even tried to have sex with her while on an assignment in Guadalajara. We lay naked in bed together, but she denied my advances, telling me I had to get the Lord's permission first. I was eight or nine years old, and I was feeling like I might actually have a place among God's chosen people. But, as soon as I felt somewhat comfortable and safe, she would betray me.

I was always reminded of my place as a slave in a sick, messianic, doomsday sex cult. While we were out, I would inevitably make a mistake or do something that got me in trouble. If she told me to meet her at a certain place at a certain time while on assignment, and, when she got there, I was making small talk with a stranger, or I wasn't in the exact spot she told me to be at, she would report it to Om at the end of the day. Or, if I confided a secret feeling, she would report that, too. I was always under strict orders not to talk to any "worldly" people.

Depending on his mood, my disobedience would either mean a hard slap across the face or severe chastisement followed by being sent to stand in the corner. Once after having made one of those mistakes, we returned and Om wasn't there to punish me, so Inspiration told me to go sit in the closet until Om got back. I was hurt and shocked by the punishment. The closet was covered with the wall-to-wall carpeting that covered the entire apartment. The darkness and isolation were terrifying. I cracked the door to get a little light. I sat thinking about how much I hated everyone and everything, my existence, and my mother.

Later that night, after waiting to be let out and no one coming to tell me it was okay to leave, I took it upon myself to come out of the closet. I thought I would tell Om that she made me sit in the closet. I expected the "Lord" to see the injustice of her punishment and criticize her for her stupidity. To my surprise, he said, "The closet? That's a great idea. Return to it."

He left me in there overnight. Omson brought food to me at mealtime.

The next day, I was sent out on assignment again with Inspiration. Om knew I was mad at her and made me go out with her anyway to show me I had no say, no rights. He stripped me of having any feeling of self-worth. He wanted me to know that how I felt did not matter.

Inspiration and I worked so much for so long, we started seeing the same people twice in a city of 15 million people. The whippings became worse and worse, and I was now constantly experiencing full-fledged physical and mental abuse. There always seemed to be some justification for every beating, no matter how small the offense. Whether it was a lack of enthusiasm when chanting, or if I looked at one of the women with discontent, I got beaten. If I didn't clean up thoroughly enough, I got beaten. If I made the slightest sound while the leader was sleeping, I got beaten. Not only did I get beaten, but I was constantly ridiculed for poisoning the other children with "old world" influence.

Deep inside, I was thankful that I had the "old world" in me, and I longed to go back – back to the streets of Berkeley, back to the Med, back to my family, back to being allowed outside. I longed for home, but was too afraid of being destroyed by the all-powerful vengeance of the Lord. I was confused and aroused each morning when I was forced to sing and pray to him while he would have sex ("sacred fucking") with one, two, or three of his "illustrious Goddesses."

One afternoon, while the Lord was sleeping, most of the women were out collecting alms. That meant I was able to roam through the house without any "guards" on duty. I wanted to sneak downstairs and go to the corner store to steal some *paletas de cajeta* (caramel lollipops). On the way to get my shoes from the closet, I had to pass the sleeping monster. The room was blackened by the thick drapes that hung over the windows. I had to be very careful not to touch the bed because I knew it would wake the beast. So, I tiptoed over to the closet to get my shoes, keeping in mind the beating I would receive if I got caught.

"*Whatever you do, don't touch the bed,*" I thought. The bed was about two feet from the closet. "*Stay away from the rickety closet doors,*" I thought again. Exactly at that moment, the closet door slid violently back and forth on its tracks. The monster jumped out of bed and headed right for me. Simultaneously, I thought, "*I know I didn't touch that door or the bed!*"

"*He was waiting for me the way a crocodile waits patiently for a thirsty zebra to drink from its pool,*" I thought. But instead, he ran past me like a scared chicken. The closet doors were still shaking violently. In fact, the whole room was shaking. I stumbled after him into the living room and saw the chandelier smacking the ceiling on both sides of itself.

An earthquake!!!!! Why would the Lord of the Universe be scared of an earthquake? I didn't have time to ponder that. I instinctively followed him out the front door and down the six flights of stairs to the lobby. He took huge leaps down four or five steps at a time, leaving me far behind. On the way down, a Mexican couple came out of their apartment to let all the people who were running from their rooms know that it was just the elevator. No one listened. The building was still moving, and there was now a crowd of grownups running past me.

When I got down to the lobby, I immediately began scanning the room for Om, but he was nowhere in sight. The lobby was noisy and people looked confused. Women held their kids and huddled together in the arms of their husbands. Some ran outside. Giant slabs of marble fell from the support beams in the middle of the lobby. A huge crystal chandelier dropped on top of one of the janitors, and he lay there howling in pain as some men tried to pull it off of him. Broken glass and dust filled the air, and crying, screaming, and panic filled the lobby.

I ran past it all looking for God, somehow knowing by the speed of his jumps that I would find him outside. There he was, standing amidst a crowd of people in the middle of the parking lot, all of whom were looking up at the building to make sure it wasn't about to come down on them.

The streets were filled with people who had fled their homes, stores, and businesses. A telephone pole fell on top of a car, smashing its shape into the hood and roof as the electrical wire snapped and sparkled wildly in the street. The huge PHARMACIA sign that lit the small street at night had crashed as well, and its debris covered the sidewalk and street below it. Smoke billowed from a distant building.

It was an amazing experience, and I thought of the day I would be able to tell Jaci about what happened. As I looked at Om amidst the crowd, I saw not God the Almighty Creator of the Universe, but a man – a mortal man – who had fear in his eyes. I made my way over to him, bewildered and shocked – not by the destruction that surrounded me, but by him. He saw me and just smiled. As we made our way through the crowd, I noticed he was limping. I looked up at him, his hair was disheveled and confusion was reflected in his face. I wondered about his mortality. It was the first time I saw him as just a man, and I was confused.

Inspiration and I continued to traverse all across the city. Sometimes we would ride the subway for hours, fighting the thousands and thousands of people who packed the metro each day. It was so tight in the subway, I could barely breathe. The air was hot and muggy, and the people's body odor was repulsive. The filth and grime that filled every crevice of the subway disgusted me. Chaos and confusion kept me clutching to Inspiration at all times. At any given moment, if I lost her hand, I could have been swept away by the crowd.

SLAVE

Starving, homeless children constantly begged us for money, food, or any kind of help. Sometimes we would be bombarded by a group who would beg us over and over again very aggressively for pesos. Other times, in the corridors where several tunnels met and split into different directions, there would be a small child, lost and terrified, sobbing for its parent.

People by the thousands passed them, not even looking twice. I thought to myself, *"There is no way they will ever find their parent again."* Maybe they were abandoned. Left to fend for themselves. It was very sad to me, and, though their predicament was similar to mine, it made me grateful for what I had – grateful that, although I lived as a slave and was mistreated and unloved and had been abandoned by my family, my situation was not as bad as these kids.

I was happy to be the kind of slave I was. The kind who had a warm closet to sleep in and food to eat.

After a journey of several hours, we'd exit the subway in an entirely new section of the same city and scope out the area briefly and cautiously. If we discovered it lacked the demographic we needed – tourists or middle class Mexicans – we'd jump back on the subway again. Sometimes a neighborhood was just too dangerous, and we'd turn around right after exiting and be back in the overcrowded, unventilated ocean of filth and stench of 100,000 people.

Not one day went by without some strange man groping Inspiration. Often, while packed into the train like sardines and unable to move in any direction, she would suddenly jerk and start yelling at someone. A man would be standing behind her with a hard-on pressed into her ass. She would try to move, but there wasn't an inch to give, so she had to bear it until the next stop. The man's face would be without expression or he would sport a look of bold expectancy. Other times, he would be a real pervert, blatantly getting off on her. But it wasn't just her; thousands of women were being violated every day on the Metro. Violence, crime, mayhem, and even death took place every day on that subway.

The streets of Mexico City were my home away from home. I was learning the language faster than all the women and Om. I thought again of the questions that had plagued me at different times ... *Why doesn't God speak Spanish? Why are God's knees, feet, and elbows always being rubbed after his tennis matches? Why did God say "Ow!" after knocking his knee on the table? How could God make the mistake of knocking his knee in the first place? How does God lose a tennis game? Why doesn't God know I'm pocketing money when I go out into the city? Why do I speak better Spanish than God?* I asked myself all these questions constantly after the earthquake.

The earthquake forced me to experience a quantum leap in my growth and maturity. I never looked at him or the cult family in the same way, but I still functioned in a semi-brainwashed state.

Then the con had to change because the Mexican police were now investigating some of the women. Apparently, some of them had mistakenly tried to con an undercover police officer and got in trouble. I could only glean bits and pieces of what happened from eavesdropping on conversations between the women.

Om had decided to use their physical beauty to make money, so he'd sent them out to meet unsuspecting lonely, rich men. The women would lure them with the promise of sexual favors. But, once back at a predetermined hotel, they were to drug the men and steal whatever money they had.

Lovelight was pregnant, so she didn't participate in this con. Inspiration came back with stories as to why it wasn't safe. Perfection was too introverted, and Devi was too dumb to pull it off. Harmony never stopped using her connection to Chinatown. Overall, it proved to be a bad idea and was eventually abandoned.

During the time they were perfecting the con, however, I was kept inside. I was not allowed to leave the house for any reason unless directed by Om himself. My job was to take care of the littler children: Triumph, Prosperity, and, the newest, Marvel. It was my job to change diapers, feed the young ones, clean, and supervise the house while the women were out working and Om played tennis. I shared these responsibilities with Omson and Freedom.

Being kept indoors for such long periods of time with no adult supervision, we grew to hate each other. The only thing that kept us from doing the stupid things kids our age might do when left alone was the fear of the beatings that would await us once Om got back. We were in a constant game of tattletale trying to get each other in trouble.

Sometimes, if we tattled too much, or if we failed to have the house in order by the time he returned, we were all punished. One of the punishments for bickering and fighting was that we were made to face each other in a triangle and slap the person to the right. I slapped Omson, Omson slapped Freedom, and Freedom slapped me. Omson and I had a special hatred for each other. I reveled in slapping him, and he reveled equally in slapping me when Om told us to change directions in order of slaps. Now he slapped me, I slapped Freedom, and Freedom slapped him. I could tell when they were teaming up on me because the slaps they gave each other were soft and the ones to me were especially hard.

On the days Om stayed in, it was relatively quiet. We were each told to stand on a particular spot on the floor. If we left that spot other than to use the bathroom, we were beaten. Om often took long naps during the day, and, if he was awoken from his sleep for any reason other than the earth shaking violently, he arose in a rage and we all got a severe beating.

If I was able to please him, I received small privileges and freedoms around the house. One such freedom brought me to a box of cassette tapes. I was trying to find some recordings of Inspiration talking about the miracles that Om supposedly performed on some of his old disciples. I had heard these tapes once before in passing, and I was very intrigued. She talked about how Om had healed a severed hand, cured deathly ill people, and had levitated. I got permission from Om to search through them. Because it glorified Him, it was allowed.

In my search through countless tapes, most of which were devotional songs and talks he'd given, I came upon a red cassette tape with the word "Beatles" written in small block letters in faded black ink. Actually, I couldn't read the letters – B – E – A – T – I gave up trying to read it. Not knowing how to read bothered me tremendously. My life was so sheltered and isolated. I was in a foreign country and there were no barometers for me to gauge my illiteracy.

Not knowing how to read the signs on the streets or papers or billboards was not too troubling; I was, after all, in Mexico. I was seldom reminded of my deficiency, except in situations like this. Or sometimes, after Om read from his book, I would pick it up and look at the letters, wondering which words were the ones he had just spoken.

I put the tape in the small, handheld tape recorder and plugged in a pair of headphones, so I didn't disturb the quiet or draw any unwanted attention to myself. After a couple of crackles of dead air passed, I heard the most amazing sounds, the kind of sounds I hadn't heard in years. "Old World Music" …

Yesterday.

I immediately related to the words coming through the headphones … I looked up in a mild panic, hoping I wasn't being watched. I knew immediately I had to hide the tape from everyone, especially from Omson and Freedom. The tape player and headphones were far less valuable in comparison.

However, they, too, were important. Having no belongings to call my own, if I ever dared claim anything, it was taken and made very clear to me that all things belonged to Om. Even the clothes I wore. If I said "my pants" I was corrected … "the Lord's pants." I was a slave. I had no rights. So, I had to be sneaky and clever about how and where I hid the tape. Also requiring as much cleverness was how, where, and when I would listen to it.

The Beatles brought back so many memories of Mom, Jackie's house, my grandmother's sugar-coated strawberries, Dawn, Telegraph Avenue, The Med. I wanted to be back there so badly. All of the songs brought me comfort and a sense of normalcy, while simultaneously breaking my heart and depressing me. I now doubted Om's claim of being the Creator. *Why did he not know about the things I did behind his back? Why was he getting hurt?* I escaped to my red tape whenever I had the opportunity.

During all the time I'd been a slave in the cult, my identity had been systematically dismantled. Now, it seemed to me like the Beatles were describing my life on the tape. The next song was ... *Nowhere Man.*

I felt like a nowhere man, because I didn't know where I was or where I was going. I escaped to those songs anytime I could, which made my existence in that hellhole a tiny bit more tolerable.

It was as though someone had made this tape especially for me. Someone knew my pain and sorrow. When I finally heard *In My Life*, I felt so broken, so lonely, so destitute, I considered jumping off the balcony of the building we lived in.

I fantasized that Dawn was my love. Suddenly, the door of the closet swung open rapidly. It scared me and I jumped. I had unknowingly been crying, and my whimpering was so loud that Om heard me. I immediately pulled the headphones from my ears, looking up scared, startled, and busted.

He asked, "What do we have here?" He always intentionally asked questions in a manner that caused confusion and fear in me.

"A tape I found," I responded.

"Did you get permission to listen to that tape?" Another tricky question.

He knew I asked permission to listen to some tapes, but he also knew I didn't have permission to listen to that particular tape. So if I said, "Yes, you gave me permission," he would ask to hear what I was listening to. My only choice was to say no. When I did, he calmly reached down and took the cassette player and headphones away and closed the closet door.

I sat terrified in the closet, wondering how he was going to punish me. Hours later, he called for me to come to the bedroom. It was Harmony who opened the closet door.

"The Lord wants you."

I got up slowly. My bladder had not been emptied all day. I asked her if I could use the bathroom first. "No," she coldly replied.

When I got to the bedroom, he told me to take off my clothes. He then got up from the bed and grabbed his thick brown leather belt. He whipped my naked body so hard it forced me to pee all over the room. Grabbing my penis to prevent it from spraying all over his bed and the floor, I peed into my hands before he realized what was happening and screamed at me: "Go to the bathroom!!"

I was humiliated, hurt, and shamed. The abuse was getting more and more violent, and the women began to give really bad beatings as well on Om's instruction. In the beginning, the women were not allowed to discipline the children, but, after Isabella and Jaci left, that rule was abandoned. Jaci had been the scapegoat. He had taken the brunt of everyone's unhappiness. Now the animosity was aimed at me.

I was slowly becoming more disobedient. I would sneak out of the house when I was ordered not to go out. I talked back to the women disrespectfully. I fought with Omson and Freedom. All of these things earned me whippings and varying degrees of other punishments. Talking back to Lovelight earned a whipping with the belt. Talking back to Devi meant three hours of standing in a corner at about three inches away from the wall without touching it. That punishment was very common. I often spent 10, 12, and sometimes over 16 hours, just standing in the corner, only allowed away to use the bathroom.

If I requested to use the bathroom too often, I was denied. I was forced to hold my pee for such long periods of time so often that it has had a post, traumatic effect in my adult life. I was not allowed to drink water or eat any food. If I was caught drinking from the sink, I was beaten. Sometimes it was so hot and I was so thirsty, I would take a beating just to have some water. Or, if I thought I could make it to the kitchen while on a bathroom run, and had the opportunity to snatch a crumb from somewhere, I would do it – and I would be beaten again.

I often heard Perfection complaining that I was a bad influence on Omson and Freedom. My disdain for everyone grew stronger and stronger each day. My disbelief in Om's claims also heightened. More and more, my actions displayed my discontent, which lead to even more beatings, each punishment more severe than the last.

However contradictory, I still longed for his acceptance. I needed to feel love, and I longed for his approval. I did my best to do the things that pleased him. I cleaned windows or the bathroom and picked up lint and dust balls off the floor without having to be told. I would make tea or ask if he wanted his feet rubbed. "Holy Father, would you like a foot massage?" If he noticed my efforts, he would reward me by sending me out on alms collecting assignments with Inspiration or one of the others.

I so wanted to be in good graces with him that I began to secretly memorize his morning dissertations, thinking it would please him. Eventually, I could recite large portions of his book. One morning, after chanting and worshiping his "holy fucking," as we did each day before breakfast (if breakfast was even served, since he would often force everyone to fast), and after we were done with the silent meditation that preceded his morning readings, I raised my hand. I had my eyes fixed on him, so that the moment his eyes opened he would see my hand in the air. I knew if Lovelight and Inspiration did their "job", he would be in a good mood and would be more inclined to call on me. His eyes opened and he smiled big at me. He called me by my new name, the one I longed to know and hear. I was filled with a warm tingling feeling. Everyone in the room noticed, Inspiration was especially happy for me.

"Yes, Sovereignty?" he gestured as a king would from his throne.

"Holy Father," I said in an inquisitive tone, "yesterday I learned …. In the beginning just before the creation, the Lord of All said, 'Let this creation be a creation of light and joy in the self, by selfless labor and diligent repetitions of *I am*. Let this self come into being …'" The smile on his face grew. His eyes fixed on me, his body leaned in towards me as he listened intently to my words. I continued to recite his own teachings back to him. When I was done, he clapped very enthusiastically and everyone followed suit. It felt really good to get such an acknowledgement. Everyone smiled and talked about how good it was.

But Perfection was outwardly bitter and jealous that I was able to recite Om's words and had caused such a positive response to come from Om. She envied that her children, Omson and Freedom, were not capable of the same. She blurted out at Omson and Freedom, "Why don't you recite something?"

"I don't know how," Freedom said.

It felt good to me that she was so upset and to know that it was because of an ability I had that her kids did not.

I witnessed much ugly envy and jealousy from all the women. They were constantly bickering and fighting, backstabbing, and positioning for Om's attention. I often rooted for Inspiration and sometimes for Lovelight because I wanted to have a sexual encounter with her. Eventually, Om decided it was time to move out of D.F. He decided on Cuernavaca, the largest city in the state of Morelos, Mexico.

As usual, we split into different groups, and, this time, Om sent me off with Inspiration. Very shocked and equally happy, I reveled in Omson and Freedom's jealousy as much as I did in the excitement of being away from Om. There were far more freedoms with Inspiration, like an occasional ice cream or even some juice. Besides the ice cream, my favorite was that corn on the cob with the mayonnaise and cheese.

I was more relaxed, since, for the time being, I didn't have to worry about being hit or kicked or slapped. Om had no reservations about beating me in public or humiliating me in front of whomever he wanted. Anytime away from him was time well spent, all things considered. I gained enough trust after proving myself out on assignments to now travel with Inspiration. I felt proud of myself, like I had some value.

I had fun with Inspiration. I liked her, and she liked me. As always, I desperately needed to feel love, kindness, and acceptance. When we were alone, she was kind and funny like a mother, a sister, or a friend. I was happy, confused, and heartbroken all at the same time.

SIX

Anger Arises

As was typical of all of the transportation systems in Mexico, the bus station was chaotic. Hundreds and hundreds of people scurried around as the PA system blasted an unintelligible Spanish voice that directed people to the buses that would take them to their faraway destinations. Also, as was typical, there were flower carts, cotton candy sellers, Popsicle carts, newsstands, and young children selling Chicklets.

I had become accustomed to the culture, but the filth was something I could not get used to. At the beginning of the trip, while at a small café on the way to the station, a sweet little old lady who worked the cash register gave me a handful of candy similar to Brach's hard candy. When she handed it to me, her big smile revealed the absence of her front teeth. She gestured to me to keep quiet because when she'd asked Inspiration if it was okay for me to have some, Inspiration had emphatically replied, "No!" Candy was NEVER allowed.

The elderly lady put her index finger up to her lips and said, "Sshh!", then softly, with a grandma's touch, tapped me on my head and said, "Adios." She made me so very happy. She reminded me of Grandma back home in Berkeley. I remembered her well. I kept the candy in my pocket, waiting for a chance to eat some without being caught.

The bus station was too busy to go use the bathroom. So, I waited for the right time to get away. While we stood in line to get the tickets, I suddenly realized the candy was in the same pocket that I was holding some money in from earlier in the day. I had to be very careful not to let Inspiration hear the crackling of the wrapper as I tried to retrieve it before we reached the counter. But there was no avoiding it. I fumbled through my pockets when she asked for the money. It was pretty obvious I was trying to hide something.

Inspiration forced me to place all the contents of my pockets on the counter, then looked down at me with disdain.

"I can't believe you. Why would you throw away all of the freedom and trust the Lord bestowed on you? I'd hate to be in your shoes when we get home."

I was speechless and terrified. A horrible sinking feeling in my stomach intensified when she said, "The Lord is going to be very displeased with you."

All of the good feelings, all the bonding Inspiration and I had shared up until then, evaporated. She scowled at me, and, after buying the tickets, she walked off without saying anything to me. I followed behind in terror. I considered losing her in the crowd and going to the U.S. embassy. I learned that's where Americans go when they need help while on assignment. But I was too scared.

Inspiration didn't speak to me for the rest of the trip. Everything was ruined, the rest of the trip was hell. Every time I relaxed, she would look at me with an evil eye, reminding me I was in trouble.

The buses were old, outdated school buses. Green and red lights lined the interior windows, though it wasn't Christmas. Gory-looking crosses featuring a bloody, torched Jesus hung from the rearview mirror. A statue of Mary Magdalene staring helplessly up into the heavens was glued to the rusty dashboard. The morbidity of Mexican Catholicism was unnerving to me, but that, too, had become familiar.

A dark black, charcoal smoke blew into the air from buses that pulled in and out of the station. There was no air quality control. The seats on the bus were ripped. Some of them didn't even have cushions. Some people held chickens in small cages, while others seemed to have no luggage at all. The stench of the overcrowded bus filled with people who hadn't bathed for days was so bad that Inspiration and I had to cover our noses with our shirts. Inspiration made sure to get us a window seat, but it didn't help much because the hot, thick, polluted air outside had an equally repugnant scent. But none of that really mattered because, whenever I thought about the trouble I was in, the smell and the noise disappeared.

It was a 12-hour bus ride through the mountains that surrounded Mexico City. Eventually, we made it beyond the city limits, and the air outside offered some relief from the stench. We stopped once or twice in little pueblos for passengers to use the bathrooms and eat.

At one stop along the way, I marveled at the site of the huge fountain in the central square. I thought, *Wow, I'm going to love this place – once I survive my beating.* The bus slowly departed, and I saw children playing. Unlike other places we'd lived, the streets here were pretty clean. I also saw a movie theatre. *Batman* appeared on the marquee, and I knew I would come back here when no one was looking.

It reminded me of the premiere of *Superman* in Mexico City. The theatre there was gigantic, with blinking lights and huge searchlights, just as if it was Hollywood. Inspiration had once taken me to see *Superman* as a reward for all the money we'd made. The bus pulled over to unload many of the passengers, but then continued driving past all this cool stuff.

"What's going on?" I thought. I asked Inspiration where we were going, if not to this town. She responded with the same old vague answer. The bus stopped at random corners, dropped people off and picked up new ones. It stopped so frequently, it felt like an inner-city bus. We traveled for several more miles through winding roads filled with tropical life and vegetation. It was like being deep in the Amazon.

We arrived at sunset. The red dirt road gleamed brightly against the jungle-like green hillside to the right and the shallow valley to the left. The bus stopped at the top of a road that led down into the small community of partially developed houses. In the distance, I could see all the surrounding farmland and tropical vegetation and the little shack-like houses that were sprinkled throughout the valley and rolling hills. Pastures and long fields of grass for the grazing cows were further off in the distance. There were only a few houses completed in the development, and I hoped our house was one of them. The rest seemed abandoned, except for the smell of tar that permeated the valley. None of the roads were paved. There weren't any stores that I could see in any direction. By the time we arrived, the entire cult was already there.

The first thing that came out of Inspiration's mouth was, "Om, Sovereignty disobeyed your will!"

"How?" he asked.

She showed him the candy she had saved in her purse. He looked and said, "Oh. We have a place for you. Go down that hall to the room directly at the end and stay there until I call for you."

As I started to turn around, more directions stopped me.

"Take off your clothes." I did. Jacket first, then shirt, then shoes, and then pants all the way until I was completely nude. "Now go to the room."

Everyone in the house was told not to speak to me. Anyone that did would be punished more severely than me. They were also instructed not to give me anything to eat or drink without His permission. Being totally nude was still very uncomfortable to me. Nudity was normal, but rarely as a punishment. So that made me very uncomfortable.

I was confined to that room for a long time. For a period of time, I was only fed water. Then slowly, they began to feed me small amounts of food. As soon as I began to expect the food, they stopped delivering it.

Sometimes, when I was allowed to use the restroom, I would sneak water from the faucet. But I got busted for that, which tacked on more time for me in the room. Whenever I went to the bathroom, I would hear a voice from outside yell, "I better not hear that faucet running!"

So I began licking the shower wall and floor for the moisture it provided. I was tempted to drink the toilet water from the bowl but came up with the clever idea of drinking the water from the tank behind the toilet. Day after day, night after night, and week after week, I spent alone in that room with no one to talk to, no food to eat, no clothing. The only light in the room was a small, red lightbulb.

I tried to engage the other boys in conversation, but they screamed out, "Stop talking to me! Om, Sovereignty is talking to me!" And that led to yet another beating. Om showed up in the room shortly after that incident and asked me if I had been talking to them. Knowing that I had, he kicked me with a front kick to my stomach that sent me crashing into the wall several feet behind me. He knocked the wind out of me, causing me to gasp for air as I rolled in pain. Then, calmly, he ordered me to get up. As I did so, he slapped me with the palm of his hand against my ear and head so hard my feet came out from under me, and I dropped to the ground again.

The cool ceramic tile floor felt good against my inflamed cheek, ear, and head. I tried to impress him with my ability to recover and stand up, but I was too dizzy and had to bend down onto one knee. For some reason, even with all of these beatings, I still wanted to please him, to make him proud of me, and to show him I was his best soldier.

The next morning, the entire household left, some to play tennis, others to go on assignments. I was left behind. Part of me wanted to be left alone so I could sneak some food; the other part of me was even more saddened with the realization that I plain and simply was not loved. I waited for the door to close, then peered out the small window in my room to see if I could see the van driving away, but I couldn't. I was too small to see over the cinder block brick wall that separated our backyard from the neighbor's. I waited as long as I could before sneaking out into the rest of the house.

I had never had the chance to see all of the rooms or the layout of this place because I'd been sent to the room as soon as I'd arrived. I peeked through everyone's stuff (except Om's) to find money or anything that would satisfy my curiosity. I found a bunch of coins – 1, 5, 10, and 20 pesos. I got lucky. I even found some peanut butter and bread and scarfed it down, along with a couple of heaping spoonfuls of yogurt. I was extra-careful not to leave a mess or anything out of place.

Then I went back to my room to ensure my safety. With a little food in my stomach, I was able to fall asleep. Eventually, they left so often I began going outside. But first, I'd borrow one of the boys' pants. Slowly, I got to know some of the neighbors. I had learned to speak the language and was able to communicate with them. They all wondered why I was always the one left behind.

Even though I wanted to tell them the truth, I was so brainwashed I would make up lies to protect the group. I also knew that these very poor, humble people in the middle of nowhere Mexico would not be able to help me. I told them I was sick or that I had to watch the house, or sometimes I told them I was on punishment. One time when everyone was gone, I went about doing the usual inspection of the house and then went off to visit the people outside. I was very lonely and starved for love and attention.

Eventually, I got caught. I was outside talking to the construction workers and neighbors when, from around the corner, came the van. I calmly stopped talking, turned around, and went back inside to prepare for what was going to be the worst beating ever. I walked quietly to my room and waited. The door swung open; it was Inspiration.

"Why was she here?" I thought, making the anticipation even worse. She asked me why I kept disobeying the Lord.

"What is wrong with me? I must be the dumbest boy in the world."

Inside, another voice emerged: "Fuck you, bitch! You're the one who got me here in the first place"

SLAP! Oops. I realized I wasn't thinking but speaking.

"How dare you say that to me after all I've done for you!"

This time I only said it in my head: "Fuck you bitch! I didn't ask to be here!"

She looked at me, saw the contempt in my eyes and said, "I feel sorry for you. I'm not going to tell Om what you said, but you better straighten up your act. You better not ever talk to me that way again, or I'll give you a whipping worse than you've ever gotten."

She rambled on and on, but I faded out her voice, thinking to myself, "Why did Mom do this to me? What did I ever do that was so bad?" I thought of the times when Mom was mad at me. "Why did Jaci and Isabella leave me?"

"Do you hear me?" was the next thing I heard from Inspiration.

"Yes." I wanted her to leave so I could hurry up and get the beating over with. She walked out, leaving the door open. A few minutes later, Om came in. I sat in the corner nude with my back against the wall in the meditation position. I jumped to my feet and stood at attention at the sight of Om. As soon as I got to my feet, I was slapped back down to the ground with a blow so hard it spun my body completely around. I ended up on my hands and knees. Semi-unconscious, when I was able to get up, Om was gone.

I thought, "Wow. I got off easy." Then, I realized he wasn't sending any food my way. I was given only water.

I wondered what time or what day it was, what month or even what year. Eventually, I stopped wondering. My only concern involved knowing when I was going to be released from the confines of that room and when I would be given some clothes to put on my body. I would climb onto the windowsill that looked out back behind the house and position myself so I could see over the backyard wall. All I could see was part of the street and the house across the street.

I looked out that window so often I learned the pattern of the family that lived there. It was a small family consisting of one boy, who I'd met while outside, and a girl, whom I'd never actually met in person but who I knew because I always waved to her while I was crouched in the window and she always waved back. Their parents left every morning and returned every evening.

Life went on second by second, minute by minute, hour by hour, day by day, and week by week. After the fear wore off from that last punishment, I got the nerve to go about the house again. But when I tried to open the door to the outside, knowing everyone was gone, it was locked. This saddened me very much. Discouraged, I cried and went to sleep. When I awoke, I heard people on the other side. I knocked. In the back of my mind I thought if they ask me why I was knocking I'd just say that I needed to use the bathroom. So, when I knocked again, I was surprised, embarrassed, and confused when two cleaning ladies opened the door.

First, I was confused because normally no stranger was trusted in the house. They looked alarmed to see that I was naked and locked in the room. I asked them where everybody was. They didn't know. I asked if anyone else was there. They said no.

I was embarrassed and yet my ego was no match for my hunger. I decided to ask the cleaning lady for some food. Because I was speaking in Spanish and the communication factor worried me, I asked every question twice. I didn't know how to say banana in Spanish so I asked for "the food monkey eat" in Spanish. After a couple of tries, I conveyed my message, and the lady brought back one. She also taught me how to say banana, "Este es un plátano. Plátano." (This is a banana.) I never forgot that word or that lady.

My nudity was making both them and me feel uncomfortable, so I grabbed a towel from the bathroom to cover myself.

Once I was convinced there was no immediate danger, I ventured out of my room. I still had those pesos that I had stolen from the last time I snuck out, and now I had the perfect opportunity to spend them.

I went outside to feel the fresh air and see what I could see. Kids, neighbors, workers. Any kind of interaction. The maids were very nice. I knew they could tell something was wrong, but only kept on asking if I wanted some more food.

"Quieres mas comeda?" (You want more food?) They brought their own lunch and fed me. Tamales con arroz y frijoles. (Tamales with rice and beans.) I scarfed it down as fast as I could, and I could tell by the look in their eyes that they were shocked and confused.

I pleaded in clean, unaccented Spanish, "Please don't tell my father." They agreed and continued on with their work. I went outside and saw the paleta man, the neighborhood ice cream man, pushing his cart across the field. A group of kids and adults surrounded him. I calculated how long it would take me to run across the dirt field of the half-developed subdivision. But my train of thought was interrupted by the two cleaning ladies. They told me they were leaving, and since the door to my room only locked from the outside once the door was closed, I was forced to go back inside.

I figured out how to open the window and stood naked in front of it many times. My desire for a paleta was so strong that I didn't care about the consequences. Well, I did, but I thought, *"Fuck it!"* So out the window I went, a small drop onto the weeds that grew wildly. I walked along the wall that ran behind all the houses on that block. Once I crossed the border of my house, I was able to see the contents of the neighbor's yard. It was completely empty.

As I continued, I relished the fresh air. I wondered what Hippo, Aki, my other friend, Lion and the rest of my old friends were doing at that moment. As I got closer and closer to the paleta man, I could just about taste the delicious, icy cold Popsicle in my mouth. It was extremely hot that day, and I was sweating already. The group of neighbors that crowded around the paleta cart seemed to have gotten bigger. Damn! A longer line, a longer wait.

They were all very happy to see me. They bombarded me with questions in Spanish I couldn't understand, but just to have people treating me like I was special was a very cherished feeling. While we chatted, someone noticed the van coming way up at the top of the road where the bus had once dropped me off. I turned in panic to see the van I hated, and all of my new friends could see the panic in my eyes. They were sympathetic to whatever the reason was that I was so scared.

I took one gigantic bite of my paleta, dropped the Popsicle where I stood, and ran like the wind. Behind me, I could hear them all laughing. There was no time to respond. I headed back across the dusty field to the gray brick wall that separated the houses. The van was parallel with me, but now, on the wall, I couldn't afford to look and lose my footing or take my eyes off the top of the wall. If the driver only looked to the left, I would be caught. But, as luck would have it, their eyes were on the road.

Jumping off the wall into the yard was a good feeling, but I wasn't in the clear yet. Up through the window I pounced without making a sound, then I leapt down to the floor. I took off the pants I had hidden in the closet and jumped onto the sheet and blanket; I was safe. Voices chattered and I heard the scurrying around of many feet. Everyone was home, and I wondered how they could have missed me on the wall. Maybe they had seen me, and this was just another mind-torturing game before the beating. Five minutes, 10 minutes, 30 minutes … and nothing.

After several hours, I was finally able to doze off to sleep, only to find a nightmare waiting for me as I slumbered. I awoke from the nightmare to a red room and heard the sounds of two women, Inspiration and Devi, who were talking. The sun had long since fallen, and the pitch-black darkness of the countryside blackened the window. The red glow of the little red light bulb made the room look especially sad.

Unsure if I had been seen earlier, I was afraid to show I had awakened when Inspiration peaked into the room. She noticed my eyes were open and told me to go get some dinner. Still afraid because I didn't get direct permission from Om, I didn't move and Inspiration repeated herself, "Go get some dinner." This time she pointed with an angry gesture.

"Did they see me?" I wondered. *"Is a beating waiting for me out there?"* Fear and hunger drove me to the kitchen. On the way, I passed some of the other family members who ignored me. That hurt a little but was the least of my concerns. Food and whether or not I was going to receive an ass-whipping, were the only things on my mind. If a beating was to occur, how long would it take? If not, what would I have to endure before I could eat?

As I walked through the house, I noticed the children were playing. That could only mean one thing – Om wasn't there.

A huge sigh of relief blew from my mouth. There was no danger, and, since Inspiration gave the go-ahead, no one could stop me from eating. I headed straight to the kitchen for a nice big bowl of soup, bread, and veggies. While preparing it for myself, Perfection walked in with a shocked look on her face. She asked me who had given me permission.

I told her and she replied, "You've taken too much food. Put some back. The other children haven't eaten yet."

I wished I could have replied, *"Bitch I haven't eaten a meal for days!"* (Except for those delicious tamales earlier, supplied courtesy of the cleaning ladies.) *"If your fucking kids weren't busy playing games, they would have eaten already!"* I knew the "other" children she referred to were hers; she wasn't talking about all the children in the house. I knew this because she had a reputation for neglecting the children who weren't her own.

I returned to my room with a small bowl of soup, a small slice of bread and a little bit of veggies, but I was very happy to have received anything at all. When I got back to my room, Inspiration was waiting. Devi had gone. It was just the two of us. She was being kind again, the way she had been before the horrible candy incident. She told me if I just behaved for a short while longer, I would get out.

Obviously, no one knew what I had done earlier that day, so what could she mean? Just behave? As far as she knew, I had been contained to my room, and, therefore, how could I have misbehaved? But, I listened as much as I could while stuffing my face.

"Slow down," she said.

"You try not eating for days and then take your time when you finally get some food," I thought. I paused momentarily, then continued to devour my food.

"You know why you're in here, don't you?"

"Yes, because you betrayed me," I thought. "Yes," I said.

"Why?"

"Because I had that candy," I said.

"Not just that," her voice began to fade. "It's also because …"

I began thinking to myself, *"How long does she want to talk to me? And why? She's not on my side, so why does she keep pretending?"*

"Do you hear me?" SLAP. The slap shocked me more than it hurt, but it made me cry. Reacting to my tears, she stood up and left. I was glad she disappeared. All I wanted was to be left alone in my room. I felt very sad. That slap reminded me of where I was, who I was, and what had happened.

Where was my real family? Why did they all abandon me? Where were all my friends? What were they all doing? Once more, I cried myself to sleep remembering all the fun things we used to do, the places we used to go, like the campus to watch Pio play drums and sing, or to the Lawrence Hall of Science to check out all the cool stuff that was there. Just to have the freedom to go outside whenever I wanted to or to be able to eat. Although there were often times when there was no food in the house at Mom's, at least I was with family. At least everyone was as hungry as me. Back then, my siblings and I could always go hustle some money for food on Telegraph, and there was always Grandma and Jackie. I just wanted to go home. Where was Hippo, my best friend? And Aki and Hilary?

I stayed in that room for another week despite Inspiration's speech. I hated that little red light. I hated that room and these people. I hated myself for whatever it was I had done to be left with them.

Most of my time was filled with thoughts of vengeance against my family and the cult. I fantasized about what I would do to Om, how I would torture him by putting needles in his dick, and how I would starve Mom until she apologized and told me why she left me. I fantasized cutting off Jaci's hand, the one he waved goodbye with. Hatred and anger consumed me as much as sadness and despair. My contempt grew stronger and stronger. I didn't care if I didn't eat because hatred was my food. When someone opened the door, I closed it. I hated myself. I wanted to poison them like the Jim Jones people. I had learned about that in one of Om's many lectures, how all the rest of the world's religions, cults, and organizations were all apostates.

I ate only that which would keep me alive. Om noticed this behavior and would visit at strange hours during the night. I had become an extremely light sleeper because I never knew what kind of punishment or torture I might receive. So I always noticed when Om or anyone else came into the room.

Sometimes I would be sitting in the meditation position, meditating, when Om would visit. Om would sit directly across from me in the same position until I opened my eyes. As soon as I did, Om would smile his big smile, get up, and leave, or sometimes start conversations. I fell back under the spell of Om when he did that. It made me feel good that someone cared enough to visit, especially Him.

I was more brainwashed than I knew. Although I had doubts in my mind, I wanted to believe he was the Lord because that provided a reason as to why my mother had given me up. And it explained why these women were so devoted to him, why they gave all their money, time, love, and energy to this God, who seemed to me to be a man. I wanted and needed a father who loved and cared for me; I was torn and confused.

One day, Freedom came down to the room with a message from Om. He was instructed to invite me to the morning meditation and chanting. I wasn't sure what to expect, so I did what I was instructed to do and left the room. Moments later, I was face to face with Om. He sat on a huge piece of furniture, a solid piece of wood about 10 feet in length by 5 feet in width. In the center was a huge bed that sat about a foot above the floor, and, at either end of the bed were three drawers, each about three feet high. Carved into each drawer were His sacred animals: a horse, a tiger, an eagle, and a dolphin.

Detached from the main structure was a second piece, a large half-circle of orange and yellow leather upholstery that sat behind the main structure in the shape of the setting sun, similar to the Japanese flag. It was like a bed-throne-dresser. He sat on this monstrosity of a piece of furniture, declaring his dominion over all of us who sat below him. He was proud of it. Everyone was there. Inspiration, Perfection, Lovelight, Devi, Harmony, and also the kids, Omson, Freedom, Marvel, Triumph, Prosperity, Justice, and a new baby, Dominion.

As usual, everyone had his or her role. One woman cooked, one looked after the kids, one massaged his feet, one combed his hair, and his favorite sex goddess, Lovelight, performed fellatio. She had had another child since I saw her last. Dominion was now about four months old and was being watched by Harmony. Shortly after the Lord's climax, breakfast was served.

Happy to be a part of their society again, I was eager to please in any way I could. Since there was nothing I could do outright, I decided to show off by sitting in perfect meditation position, eyes closed, back straight, legs crossed left over right, hands placed on knees, index fingers closed against the thumb – something I had mastered in confinement.

Breakfast was served to everyone, but I was last. Although I was out of the room, I was treated like I still hadn't made it back into the family. It was similar to a National Geographic Special where a beta monkey is ostracized for a time, but is eventually let back into the clan.

It was some time in 1979. Om decided to give Omson, Freedom, and me permission to go out into the neighborhood and play. I was the ringleader as usual, so I took them to the house of the little girl that I had waved to from my window. I was curious to know if she was as cute as she looked from so far away. *"Was she nice? Did she speak English? Maybe she, or her brother, would like to come outside and play."*

The other boys were too scared to walk up to the door with me, so, after a brief argument about it, I went by myself.

KNOCK, KNOCK, KNOCK. The door slowly opened. On the other side stood the cutest girl I had ever seen, and I thought I'd seen a lot, traveling all over Mexico. But they all paled in comparison. She had long, silky, black hair that fell just past her shoulders and glowing caramel-colored skin. Her eyes were amber brown, and, when she gave me a welcoming smile, I noticed her teeth were shining white and all perfectly straight, except for one adorably cute eye tooth that was ever-so-slightly crooked, which made her all the more attractive .

I heard a couple of voices in the back speaking to her in Spanish. I concluded they were asking who was at the door. She turned her head and screamed something back. I hoped it wasn't, "It's the little naked boy that stands in the window."

Suddenly, pushing from behind her was her brother, chewing on some food. He pressed past her and closed the door, so he stood outside while she remained on the inside. There went all of my hopes. He spoke to me in broken English. Between the two of us, we could communicate fairly well.

"Hey, where have you been? Locked in that room?"

"I was on punishment. Does your sister want to come out and play?"

He shrugged his shoulders and waved his hands suggesting, *"She's a girl. Who wants to play with a girl?"*

I let it go. However, in the back of my mind I wanted to spend the rest of my life with her. This was one of my many crushes since Dawn. The little boy's name was Hector. His sister's was Gabriella. Hector showed me all the cool places in the community, like the private swimming hole and a ranch with a wild bull. He took me to meet a farmer, who grew marijuana, and another farmer, who had fathered five beautiful daughters. I met all of them, but none compared to Gabriella. He was molesting them, according to Hector.

I had such a good time meeting all these people and doing all these things. I felt great, like a child should. The next day, I went by myself to Hector and

Gabriella's, excited to see her again. I was a little scared and nervous. *"What will I say?"* I thought. KNOCK, KNOCK, KNOCK.

This time, the door swung open violently. On the other side, it wasn't the cute little girl from before; it was a mean, old-looking man in dirty work clothes. He had messy hair and a scruffy beard. Behind him stood Gabriella and her mother. They were both crying. Hector was nowhere in sight. Everything seemed to be moving in slow motion at that moment. The old man's lips moved, but I couldn't hear the words coming out of his mouth.

My heart went out to Gabriella and her mother. *Were they victims of a tyrannical leader? Was she suffering the same injustices as me? Was there some shameful family secret hidden behind these walls?*

"Puede jugar Héctor?" I asked. (Can Hector play?)

"No." Some more Spanish words came out of his mouth that I didn't understand.

Then Hector showed up at the door and told me he would meet me in one hour at the old man's ranch. I walked to the ranch, worried about Gabriella, but was soon distracted by the beauty of the countryside. As I approached the farmhouse, I wondered what life must be like for these people. I thought it must be easy to just feed the animals and go to school. They had a life I could imagine myself living, although, I was no fool; these people were dirt poor. They did have a certain kind of freedom, but they lacked the luxuries of the life I had known, despite all the injustices I had suffered.

As I walked up the road to the house, there was a huge grass field on my left of perhaps a few acres. It was surrounded by a brown fence. Inside were about 60 cows and a few horses. On the far side of the fence stood a huge group of trees, all different kinds. Beyond the fence lay some train tracks where a boy had met his death during the time of my stay in the room.

On my right was a large plot of land where the earth was a brownish red. It was much more faded than the deep red of the road up on the hill. It was surrounded by a fence that bordered a farm house and held a variety of small animals – dogs, goats, chickens, cats, and a pen of pigs. A screen door that barely hung on at its hinges protruded from a tiny, rickety, white house. On the side of the house, a long rope held a line of freshly washed clothes. As I approached, the dogs gave curious barks, and one of the sisters I had met on my last trip outside opened the screen door. She had a big grin on her face and yelled to everyone else about my arrival. They all came from around the house and stopped their chores to talk to me.

"Bali! Bali! Como estas?" (Jabali, Jabali, how are you?)

"Muy bien, y tú?" (Very good, and you?) They loved the fact I spoke the little Spanish that I did. They called me, "flacito" (skinny).

"Ven! Ven!" the mother told me, (Come! Eat!) We all went to the kitchen.

I wasn't going to ever turn down food. Even though I was allowed some freedom, there were still restrictions concerning food. So, I gladly followed them into the kitchen where about 10 thousand flies buzzed around. The horde of insects didn't seem to bother any of them; they rarely even bothered to shoo them away when they landed on their eyelids, lips, or any other part of their faces.

It was very gross to me. But flies on my face were a small price to pay for the wonderful welcoming and loving treatment I received from this family. The mother made me some delicious tacos from scratch. After a while, Hector showed up. I really didn't want to see him because I was getting along so well without him, but there was nothing I could do. After eating and practicing my Spanish, we left to go home. I had stayed away quite a while and wondered if I was in trouble. As the two of us walked back, I thought about how nice it would be if I never had to return to Om and the cult.

A short time after, we moved ... again. I was sad but had become accustomed to letting go of people and of expectations. I never got a chance to say goodbye to my friends, except for Gabriella. She was standing in front of her door. As we drove passed, I pressed my hands against the window, waved goodbye, and she wiped her eyes and waved back.

SEVEN

Inner Strength

In my darkest hour I found my greatest strength.

O ur move was sudden and unexpected, as it always was. This time, it was further from anything I could have ever imagined. The neighborhood was very rich. There were no signs of the immense poverty that was a reality for so many people just a few miles away. There were two main streets that ran through downtown, as I remember it. One was the road in and out of town that ran east and west, then there was the other main road that ran north and south. They intersected at the giant fountain.

About a mile south, down the road that ran north and south, was the huge mansion where we were to live. It was surrounded by a giant white wall about 10 feet high. At the top of the wall grew lots of green foliage and beautiful purple morning glories that hung down its sides. The entrance to the house was on a side street that led into a neighborhood of equally stunning homes.

The entrance was through a 12-foot black wrought iron gate, split down the middle so one side could open while the other stayed shut. Immediately to the right was a three-bedroom cottage where the groundskeeper and his family lived. Between the cottage and the house, a driveway led up a small incline. At the top was an old dirt tennis court. It looked like it had been abandoned for years.

The house faced the main street, so entry through the gate led to the side of the house. Directly behind the house was a swimming pool that sat atop a small grass hill. Down that hill were a variety of fruit trees: banana, avocado, plum, apple, and oranges. Along the far side of the house and all around the grounds were rose bushes, very nicely kept by the groundskeeper.

The entire property, besides the tennis court, was manicured and kept very clean. The house itself was huge, the likes of which I had never seen anywhere. I was amazed at all of its beauty, that this was going to be our new home, especially after where we had just left. I thought, *"Wow! This house has a lot of places to hide or stay out of sight."*

On the far side of the house from the gate entrance was the old groundskeeper's quarters; they were set beneath the house. Upstairs at the top of a circular staircase was a small, round room. I thought this could be my room, away from everything with a full vantage point of the entire grounds. The whole house had beautiful dark hardwood floors.

There were four bedrooms that were on the east side of the house facing the tennis court, and a huge dining room that ran the entire length of the house and faced the backyard, towards the pool and fruit trees. I couldn't wait to explore every corner, to eat from the banana trees and the orange trees ... there was so much to see.

The pool was by far the biggest attraction. But I knew better than to show my excitement, and I knew before I could explore I'd be forced to clean, scrub, and disinfect every inch of the house. I knew to immediately go to Om and offer myself as his servant before he could call on me. "Holy Father, how may I be of service to you?"

I was far cleverer than the other two boys and he knew it. He smiled and told the three of us to get the brooms from the truck and to meet him in the house. He methodically showed each of us which room we were responsible for and what needed to be done to each room.

First, a thorough sweeping, followed by scrubbing the floors with a bucket of soapy water and rags. This would require me to be on my hands and knees. Mopping was not allowed. After the floors, all the windows were to be cleaned inside and out. I tried to work harder and faster than Omson and Freedom while also doing a really good job. I didn't want him to check my work and have me go back and do it again, something he did often.

So, I worked hard all day without asking him to check my work like they did. I prided myself on my ability to clean and do a thorough job. I did each chore twice with the exception of the windows that required a third cleaning. Sometime after dark, I was done. I proudly went to get Om to have him inspect. He came in and looked around, nodding and smiling. He ran his fingers along the window sill, a place I knew to clean because I overheard him telling Freedom to clean that spot earlier when Freedom asked him to inspect his room at the fourth attempt.

He smiled at me, put his hand on my head, and rubbed it affectionately, and, with a playful push, he told me to go eat. I felt so good inside, so proud. I felt loved. This wasn't the only time he showed affection towards me, but because they were so few and far between, I relished every single time I got it.

The next day after the morning rituals, Om told the three of us he had a special assignment for us. He told us to take the wheelbarrow down the side street that led into the neighborhood and retrieve as many bricks as we could from a construction site about a mile down. We spent the next three days filling that old, beat-up wheelbarrow with bricks over and over again. From sun-up until sundown. We fought about whose turn it was to push the wheelbarrow and whose turn it was to pick up the bricks. If we snitched on one who helped the least (which was always Omson), Om would punish all of us. We collected hundreds and hundreds of pounds of bricks.

The next part of this assignment was to clean the old tennis court of the weeds and patches of grass that had overgrown it, along with any pebbles that were larger than a Tic Tac. First by hand, then we were to rake the entire court and smooth out any potholes. The next part of the assignment was to crush the bricks into a fine powder. Om made me get up first thing in the morning, before any food and before I could use the bathroom, to begin crushing the bricks. I couldn't even attend the morning rituals, which I began to actually miss. Omson and Freedom always joined a little later.

I had to sit on the patio that faced the court and crush all day long. At first, he had me use large rocks to crush, but he realized rocks weren't effective, so he bought us hammers. After a few days, he figured out the best way to crush these bricks down was to do so in three stages. The first stage involved the initial breaking of the bricks from whole down to medium-sized pieces. It required a lot of force and hard work and became my job. The second stage was to crush down the medium-sized bricks into even smaller pieces. That was Omson's job. And, finally, the last stage was to create a fine powder, which was the easiest job. That belonged to Freedom, his favorite.

At the end of each day we were to load a large sifter with the brick powder and sift it evenly onto the tennis court. Hour after hour, day after day, week after week, I sat out there in the blistering sun crushing bricks. I began to enjoy my time alone. No one bothered me; no one talked to me, except the groundskeeper's son, Alfonso. He was a nice little boy whose innocence was only matched by his curiosity and appetite.

I could tell that he and his family felt sorry for me. Sometimes he would show up with a cool glass of lemonade. Depending on if I thought I could get away with it, I would guzzle it down as fast as possible. Other times I said no because the risk was too great. I was kept naked, which was offensive to the groundskeeper's very Catholic family.

None of the women were allowed to have me do any of their chores. I wanted to impress Om with the good job I was doing, so I worked hard, and, eventually, I was allowed to go swimming during breaks. I loved that! It took months to complete my gargantuan task, and, towards the end of the assignment, I was doing all three stages. Alfonso's father, Alfonso Sr., brought me a sledgehammer. That allowed me to work three times as fast. I took pride in the discipline and hard work I showed every day.

After Omson and Freedom's inability to stay focused got them out of having to do any of the work, he put them to work in other places around the house. Om lined the court with white chalk, using string tightened by ground stakes to keep the lines straight.

Harmony made a net with her sewing skills, and, once again, the squares were sewn too big for a tennis net. Om was mad at her for not doing it right and berated her. Eventually, he got a regular net and the court was complete. Om rewarded me with "open freedom." That meant I could go anywhere on the grounds without having to get permission.

This was the happiest time of my life as a child slave. I made a pact with myself to not get in trouble with anyone while we lived here. There was too much freedom within the walls of this beautiful prison. Days went by without me getting into trouble. I did my duties. I learned to recite more pages from His book. I slept. I played tennis, swam, and had a lot of free time to explore and be away from everyone. But I was still at the beck and call of anyone who needed something done.

But it was only a matter of time before my curiosity got me in trouble again. All the women were gone on assignment, and I was left to take care of all the children with Om. That meant I was responsible for the well-being of the kids, their food, the changing of the diapers, the discipline, and everything else, while Om stayed in his room writing his book. So, I was sent to the store for food, which gave me a chance to meet some neighborhood kids. We were able to communicate through my broken Spanish. As we talked, I told lies about who we were, what we were doing, and how we got there.

My need for normalcy, for regular interactions with the outside world, caused me to stay out way past the time it should have taken me to complete my assignment. I hated to return to the reality that, on the other side of that wall, I was living the life of an abandoned, abused, afraid, lonely, and sad child, and that, once I returned, I would no longer be the charming, good looking, rich American boy from Berkeley that I had invented for my new friends.

The late afternoon turned into early evening before I began to hear in my mind, the sound of his calm, intimidating, militant voice asking me where I'd been. It was like waking up from a trance.

I abruptly told the kids I would catch up to them the next day, but I had to leave right then. I knew I was in big trouble, and I knew I was facing another beating. It was now dark and the sound of the iron gate squeaked as I entered; the only light that illuminated the dark country night was the small lightbulb that hung above the entryway. The sound of the gate opening brought Alfonso

Sr. to the window above the gate.

I waved nervously, receiving only an annoyed glare. Up the path, the darkness was blinding as the light behind me lost its potency. Onto the patio, where I spent the summer crushing bricks, I received a blow from out of the dark. I didn't know what hit me, only that I was on the ground fighting to find a sip of air. Then there were two more violent slaps to each side of my face. Om was squatting over my small frame, one leg on each side of me. His face looked larger than normal. I tried to focus, but bright lights whizzed past my eyes like shooting stars. I was dragged across the floor by my foot the entire length of the house. I tried to turn and roll to avoid the burning sensation on my back. My hands and elbows bounced across the ground as I attempted to adjust. His pace was too fast; I had to stop trying to catch myself and just let him drag me. All the time, I wondered when this was going to be over.

Eventually, we ended up at a closet on the far end of the house. When we entered the room, I thought there was going to be more beating, but, instead, he lifted me up with one hand and threw me into the closet upside down, slammed the door, and locked it. I was trembling, and urine saturated my pants.

I awoke several times in the night, conscious of my surroundings but in fear of what still lay in store for me. I half-wished one of the ladies were there because I knew their maternal instincts might motivate them to speak on my behalf. I curled up in the fetal position and cried myself to sleep. The next morning he returned, ordering me to take off all my clothes. Then he shut the door again and locked it. Locking the closet door was not customary. That told me I was going to be in there for a long time. I had held having to go to the bathroom for as long as I could. I didn't want to bring him back, but eventually I had to cry out, "Holy Father, please may I use the Throne (toilet)?" I cried out over and over again until Triumph heard me and told me he would ask the Lord if I could come out.

"I said no!" was the reply.

"I just need to use the bathroom very bad," I pleaded.

I didn't want him to misunderstand my bathroom request for a request to be let out of the closet. Finally, Triumph returned, unlocked the door, and I ran past him. Over the next few days, a thunderstorm rattled the house. The cold air blew under the door onto my naked body, and I caught a terrible flu. Om came to the closet and told me he was going to leave the door open so that I could use the bathroom but not to leave the closet for any other reason. The powerful storm was still pounding the house and rattling all the windows. I was so weak, I could barely move, but I felt if I didn't get some kind of food or liquid in my body I was going to die. I gathered all the strength I could and limped slowly and cautiously to the kitchen despite his orders.

The house was dark, only momentarily illuminated by the lightning strikes followed by violent thunder. The house rattled and shook as I made my way to the kitchen. I was so weak, I could barely lift the bottle of apple juice to my lips. I could feel the juice go down and land in my stomach. I tried to be as quiet as possible as I slowly made my way back to the closet. Just as I got to the entrance, I was kicked from behind. Too weak to put my hands up to protect my head, my body smashed against the closet wall. I heard his voice, but could not make sense of the words. I fell to the floor, and recoiled into the fetal position. After one or two kicks to my ribs and stomach area, I suddenly could not feel the tough, dry skin of his foot, nor the splinters from the floor in my back, and I could not hear his heavy breathing.

There was a silence and a calm, a stillness that was greater than the circumstance. I floated out of my body. I found myself hovering not far over his shoulder. I was looking down at him as he kicked my body, yet I felt no pain. As I watched him, from a painless peace, time was still and serenity overwhelmed me. I was connected to an infinite, extraordinary power, yet also acutely aware of who I was and of the person who was kicking a helpless, sick child. In that moment I realized that, no matter what this man or any of his women did to my body, they could not reach this place. They could never reach the thing they wanted the most.

I saw that I had a power greater than my body and my mind. I had found the power of the human spirit, my spirit. I was untouchable, unbreakable, infallible, and invincible against all external forces.

I was now connected to, and had access to, an immeasurable power that would guide and protect me for the rest of my life. *"I am Jabali! Not Sovereignty. They can't break me! They can't harm me! They cannot access the real me. No matter what they do, I am invincible! I am!"*

The next morning, the closet door was opened. The light was blinding. He stood over me, grimacing at the smell. "Go take a shower." As he followed behind me, I didn't know what was going to happen, and when he said, "You should have told me," my heart sank into my belly. I heard remorse in his voice for the first time ever. And, when he put his hand on my head, I cried. Never at any time did I cry during a beating. That was cause for a worse beating, and I prided myself a lot about that. No one was ever to cry, but they all did, even the women. I left to go wash up. He directed me to the bedroom to lie on a bed. I did so and fell asleep for a very long time.

I thought about everything that had happened, of all the things that had led to that moment, and then I knew without any doubt that I was going to survive. I had come upon the indomitable essence of the human spirit, a place that was unreachable by anyone else, by any of man's evils. I had accessed a deep place inside myself that was so profound, so safe, that encompassed so much peace, light, and love, that I was forever changed. I knew that, no matter what they did to my body, no matter what they said, nor how bad they made me feel about myself, not he nor any human being for the rest of my existence on this planet could ever break or blemish my spirit. I was connected to God, the great Spirit, Jehovah, Allah, Krishna.

I questioned the existence of Jesus, Buddha, Krishna, Allah, and began to ask myself questions, wondering and doubting all that had happened. I remember wondering how old I was. What year was it? What was my last name? When I asked, I got the runaround. *"There is no such thing as age; time does not exist, therefore there is no such thing as years; your last name is Om."* I knew that keeping this information from me was intended to keep me in the dark so I wouldn't be able to run away, but these questions burned inside of me. I knew I could find the answers out in the world.

One day, Om hit a ball over the wall while playing a tennis match and told me to go get it. I was elated to see what was on the other side of the wall. I ran fast, as he always instructed me upon receiving orders. But this speed was for selfish reasons. When I got beyond the wall, I found a man and his two sons.

"Que año es?" I asked immediately (What year is it?) He looked at me like I was out of my mind, like *"Any child your age should know what the year is."* Then he replied, "Mil novecientos ochenta." (1980.) I didn't understand him, and he could tell. So he signed the numbers to me using his hands. I couldn't believe it.

Where were all my friends? What were they doing? I truly wanted to go home.

I possessed a knowing that I was going to make it, that I was going to survive this horrible experience. The physical pain of that night eventually subsided, but not the memories of the cruel punishment I learned to endure.

Life behind the walls of that mansion, secluded and sequestered away from the rest of the world, mirrored how I felt in my heart. I decided I was going home. I didn't know when, I didn't know how, but I knew the walls of the prison in my mind were coming down. The seed of this knowing was planted, and it was now just a matter of time. I learned how to hide my feelings and thoughts so deeply that no one could read my inner convictions, not even the Lord, this highly intelligent fraud.

I read him before he read me. I developed an acute awareness of the energy and intention of the adult world around me – a defense mechanism that was wired against psychological intrusion and physical abuse. Through this awareness, I created a mental minefield of trapdoors that kept him, his treacherous women, and everybody else out of my secret, sacred place that was Jabali. I was not Sovereignty, not a boy, not a human being, but the spirit that dwelled within a child's body.

Unexpectedly, after the morning rituals, the announcement was made that we were moving; we were to pack up the house that morning. Where? I knew better than to ask. I wished it was back to the U.S. But my wishes rarely came true.

EIGHT

Special Assignment

t was Oct 31ˢᵗ, 1980, Dia de los Muertos (Day of the Dead). We were living in a storefront in Tijuana, Mexico. It was very cold and unwelcoming. Three giant, white sheets were used to divide the front from the back, and cardboard was taped to the giant front window to prevent anyone from seeing in.

It was damp and dark on the inside, and the scent of incense wafted over the smell of mildew on the cold cement floor. A long work table made from old wood ran along the wall to the back, left by the previous occupants. We used the front half for storage, and the back half behind the white sheets was used for kitchen items like dried food and pots and pans, although there wasn't a stove or even a refrigerator. Underneath the kitchen table was a small space where I was made to sleep. I was given some leftover material from the sheets for my bedding.

Of course the cult leader had a giant, king-sized bed with plenty of blankets, pillows, and comforters. The other children were given small futons with pillows and all the works.

That it was Halloween meant nothing to me, but, for some reason, Om instructed us to go out and collect candy. Not to go have fun trick or treating – it was an assignment, a job. I didn't care. It gave me a reason to get out of there, and I got to sneak candy. The three of us wore colored paper masks with the eyes and noses cut out and string to hold them on our faces.

We went out into the city, me leading the pack. It was very fun. There were fireworks and streamers, and kids ran all through the streets. The night sky would periodically light up and I could see everyone's costumes, as smoke and the smell of gunpowder filled the air. By now, my Spanish was good enough to engage in conversation with other kids. I made friends with a group of them while Omson and Freedom stuck together and tried to keep up.

The last time I could remember being out on Halloween was back in Berkeley when Jaci and Isabella took me out. I remembered being dressed as Batman and being scared by a Dracula rising out of a coffin. Jaci got a big laugh out of my fear, while Isabella reassured me there was nothing to be afraid of. As always, I thought back on the time with my family and yearned to be back with them again.

I felt like the time for me to leave these people was upon me. I could feel and understand that I had a choice. An inner light was brightening in my mind daily about how easy it would be to get back home. It was a light that told me it was all a lie. This light shined upon my independence, my autonomy. I was unbreakable; they could never take or break my inner being.

As the three of us worked our way through the neighborhood and collected as much candy as possible, we ran into some bullies. At first I thought I could make friends with them. They were a couple of years older than us and, like all bullies do, they found the weak link: Freedom.

They began talking about his Afro and pulled at it and laughed when I tried to come to his assistance. They got very serious and started cussing. They asked me what I was going to do. I was so scared I forgot all my Spanish and I began stuttering as I tried to translate my English thoughts into Spanish words.

Before I knew it, one of the boys had lit a firecracker and thrown it at me. It exploded at my torso. Luckily, I flinched and turned as it let out a BANG. The flash from the explosion caught my polyester shirt on fire. As it burned, I ran down the street screaming, flailing my arms up and down, trying to put out the flames. From out of nowhere, a man grabbed me and began beating me to put the fire out.

I was so shocked and in so much pain I couldn't understand him when he asked me questions. In the back of my mind, further removed from the situation, I thought, *"I'm going to tell Om I want to go back home."* That was something I could never do before. I was afraid of disappointing Him (God?).

For those few moments in that man's arms, I felt no pain. I was limp in his arms – head, legs and arms dead. It all seemed to be happening in slow motion again. The next thing I remember was being able to make out what he was saying: *Donde vives? Donde vives?* (Where do you live?)

The fear of what might happen next raced through my mind. What if the Federales came? Taking them back to the storefront was not an option. My fear turned to strength and determination. I told the man and the small crowd that had gathered that we lived very close and not to worry, I'd be all right. I hurriedly pointed in the direction of our place and walked as fast as I could. Omson and Freedom tried to console me. They had picked up my bag of candy and gave it back to me in a gesture of sentiment and camaraderie.

If we were in any state in America, I don't think the adults in that situation would have let a nine-year-old boy walk away with second-degree burns all over his torso without at least walking him home or calling an ambulance. Although I was very grateful that the man put the fire out, the fear of home and what was waiting there prevented me from thanking him. I knew because of the language barrier that I could escape.

When we got home, Omson and Freedom blurted out all of the night's activities. I was hit with a barrage of questions I couldn't answer; the pain was so great. I don't remember how I actually got home that night. Om examined my wounds and gave a series of commands to the ladies.

Inspiration spent the whole night picking the melted polyester out of my skin. It was the most painful night of my life. I screamed every time the sharp metal end of the tweezers was pushed into my open flesh wound. It felt as though the tweezers had been heated up in a blacksmith's oven and were being used to torture me. In fact, they cared for me better that night than any other time in all my experience of being with them. I felt loved and was finally treated like I belonged. Om was helpful too, offering his bed to share. Although I did not sleep one wink, I was very appreciative of all the kindness I received.

It took several agonizing weeks for my wounds to heal. As I approached complete recovery, the treatment I received began to return to that of a slave. At one point, Om told me the good life was over, that the care and attentiveness I had been given was done. I didn't care. I had found my own inner strength, which I knew would now and forever guide me through any difficulties I would face.

I returned to my space under the kitchen counter. Life resumed to "normal"; there was the chanting about His greatness in the morning while he had sex, listening to him lecture, meditating, and then cleaning. A little free time could be stolen from time to time during the course of a day.

One day, when everyone had an assignment out in the world selling incense, conning for money, and so on, I was left at home with the instruction to not leave my designated spot. Well, of course, as soon as I determined the coast was clear, I moved off of it and decided to snoop around outside, and it paid off. I found the mother lode, my dream find, the kind of find that was worth all the beatings … it was my bag of candy from that fateful night. It must have been forgotten in the panic and chaos. I discovered it in between some boxes that were stacked on top of each other. The thrill of this find made the risk of having left my spot all worth it. I felt like Julie Andrews in "The Sound of Music."

I knew it had been forgotten by the condition of the bag, which was faded and wrinkled. It had been a month or two since Halloween, and it had been that long since I had stepped outside. My disobedience, curiosity, or foolishness may have led me outside that day, but finding this treasure kept me occupied. My mind raced. How was I going to keep it? Surely I couldn't eat it all now. I couldn't hide it with me in my spot; Omson would find it. He was always going through my things, however miniscule they were. A light went off inside of me; I'd keep it right where I found it. Not even Omson had found this spot. So now, whenever I got a free moment and the coast was clear, I could devour as much candy as I possibly could. My hiding spot worked well, with the exception of getting rid of the wrappers.

Eventually, I got down to my last piece, a strawberry hard candy with a chewy soft filling. I had purposefully saved this one for last. It was my favorite; the wrapper was the color and print of a strawberry. I decided to wait until everyone was asleep before I ate it. I knew I had to be extra quiet when I unwrapped the cellophane wrapper. The lights were out, and the whimper of dreaming babies broke the night's silence. The faint smell of hours-old incense lingered in the night air. It was time.

I began slowly, methodically, millimeter by millimeter to unravel the last of my delicious sin. I had successfully consumed all of it without notice. That fact made this piece even sweeter. As it opened completely, I could smell its sweet flavor, and my mouth started watering. Just as I closed my lips on its heavenly goodness, I heard, "What is that?"

My hand clenched around the wrapper and the sound of it cracking was deafening against the silence. Time slowed to a standstill. The candy lost its entire flavor and I could not answer. The candy was in the middle of my mouth, switching it to either side would have made a clattering against my teeth.

"Come here," was the next command. As I slowly walked across the dark, cold room, my mind raced. The faster I thought of an answer, the slower time moved. I could not see him, but I knew he was there waiting to do something that would hurt me. When I got to the edge of the bed, I knew he was even more livid that I had not yet answered his direct question.

The only thing I could do was try to swallow it, but it was too big. As the tension mounted and the empty feeling in my stomach grew to a tremble, I knew it was going to be bad. He struck a blow to the side of my head that lifted me off my feet. I knew this pain well. To this day, if I incur a head strike or injury, it creates a profound feeling of déjà vu. This time, it was especially memorable because the piece of candy that I had had a moment ago and loved so dearly was now lodged in my windpipe by the powerful blow, and it was now my worst enemy; it was taking my life. I began gasping for air. He seemed to be done with me, but the hard candy with the chewy center was not. I vaguely heard him say something, but this was now a life-or-death situation. All I cared about was removing this object from my throat.

I stumbled away with my hands holding my neck. I wasn't breathing, and I was afraid to wave at someone for help. I even tried standing on my head for a moment. I felt alone and completely helpless. *"These could be my last breaths."* This quick thought raised through my consciousness, then I felt a sense of calm. *"Stay calm, take your time."* My ordeal probably was over within two minutes, but it seemed like an eternity.

Finally, the gooey wad slipped down my throat, saliva having shrunk it. I didn't care how it happened, I was just glad it was done. That was my first time facing the real possibility of death. I was nine years old. Little did I know I would face death a dozen more times in my life.

I went back to bed scared, afraid of death. I cried myself to sleep that night, wishing I were home. What was so wrong with me that my family would all leave me behind to die, to be tortured, to be starved and beaten? My heart was broken, I had thought my mom loved me. She used to tell me she did. But now it was obvious that she didn't.

The cold, hard floor, the thin sheet that I lay on, and Om's beating were all harsh reminders that I was alone and unloved.

When I awoke the next day, it was as though the night's events had never taken place. Everyone went about his or her morning chores. The idea that I almost died plagued me to the point that I decided it was the right time for Om to know that I wanted to go back home. He always told me whenever I wanted to go home to tell him, and now, after about five years, I was ready. But I was too scared to tell him myself, so I got Omson to tell Him for me. We were in the front of the store, in front of the partition.

I whispered to him, "I want to go back to my family," and, sure enough, without hesitation, he screamed out, "Holy Father! Jabali said he wants to go back to his family!"

I had never uttered anything remotely close to that sentiment before, so his words cut through the morning air like church bells on a cold winter morning. Everyone in the house froze where they were, and a soapy-eyed figure peered from where he had been standing behind the shower curtain.

"Jabali, come here," came the voice from the other side of the curtain.

It was done, my pent-up feeling had finally been spoken aloud. There was no turning back. I was scared and relieved at the same time. What in the world was going to happen next?

The room began to move again with whispers and quiet talk of conversations long overdue. The figure from behind the shower curtain began to sing, "I am God, I am the Lord, I am God, I am the Lord ..." A morning classic.

Although the offer of going home was often reiterated to me, the underlying message was that I would be a fool to leave God's presence, to go back to the Old World, and this was a very powerful brainwashing and programming agenda. I was in the company of the Lord, the Creator of the Universe, the

Father that Jesus spoke of, and to stray from His Will was a fool's choice. This had confused me immensely.

But, as I had gotten older and had become more disobedient when I realized I could get away with it, the evidence of Om's human frailty became more evident. He didn't read my thoughts. He didn't know what I did behind his back. He didn't know about the candy I had hidden. But still, 12 hours a day of lecture, chanting, and worshipping the "sacred fucking" were all very powerful brainwashing tools.

Ironically, when I found my inner strength in the depths of my most severe beating, and accessed the place where God really lives, that sacred place within me that no human could ever reach, I realized I was all powerful: I was king. And, from there, I mentally began the journey home.

***

I have drawn from this inner source of power ever since. It has been my source of peace, resolve, compassion, love, and forgiveness. I came to believe, though not overnight, that these qualities are in all people, no matter their experience. It's this clarity that I hope to convey through writing my story, that there is indeed always a light at the end of even the darkest tunnel.

***

When he emerged from the shower, Om asked me if I wanted to go home, and, with all the inner strength I could muster, with all the hatred for him and all his women and kids I could gather, I said ... "No!"

From the other side of the partition, Omson's voice rang out, "Yes, he did. He said he wanted to go back to his family!"

Om told me to go stand in the corner until I had something to tell him. As I turned and walked away, he quickly kicked me in the back and said, "That will give you something to think about."

I slowly got up and said with barely any breath in my body, in almost a whisper, "I want to go home."

He pointed me to my living space under the counter with a gesture similar to how you tell a dog to go outside. I was glad to be leaving his presence, back to the only place where I could secretly cry and feel sorry for myself.

Now I just hoped he would oblige me. In no way did he let on whether he would comply. I lay bruised and hurt, wondering what would happen next.

The next day, I realized we were heading back to the U.S. when I saw the metering lights at the border in Tijuana. I was happy to be off of the cold concrete floor and didn't care where we were going. I hadn't grasped that all the packing that had occurred earlier at the storefront was for our move back to the U.S. Inside, I lit up like the Fourth of July; it would be a lot easier for me to get home now. I didn't know where we were going, but, as long as it was in America, it was closer to home.

I had spent three-and-a-half long years in a foreign country, and I was ecstatic to be going home to the United States of America with its clean streets, grocery stores, clean air, the English language, and Americans.

All the brainwashing about the evil Establishment had no effect; I still longed for the USA and to be one step closer to my friends, my family, and home.

We settled into a small apartment in San Diego, a couple of blocks away from the Balboa Tennis Club. Being back in San Diego brought up feelings of sadness and anxiety, but I ignored those and waited for my opportunity to disappear from the cult.

Omson, Freedom, and I were allowed to walk to the club as long as we were playing tennis. I enjoyed playing the game, but mostly I wanted any reason to get out of the house. When we finally got there after fooling around in the streets, we'd play each other sets. Omson and I were better than Freedom, and there was a fierce competition between Omson and myself as to who was Number One. Sometimes it was Omson and sometimes it was me.

I was now a pretty good player after having had our own court. Om read all the major tennis magazines and often lectured on tennis. He claimed he would win Wimbledon one day. We spent a lot of time at the local tennis club, and I began to develop relationships with the club pro and other faculty members. Omson and Freedom hated me for that. I don't know if it was jealousy or because we were forbidden from talking to strangers, or to anyone from the Old World.

I could sometimes talk the pro into serving me a couple of balls. After they blew past me, he would let up and let me return a couple or just volley with me – never for as long as I wanted, but I was happy with the attention. I was also secretly going into the men's locker room and stealing wallets while the guests showered. It was my personal hustle to keep a few dollars in my pocket to spend whenever I had the chance to get away. I knew better than to tell Omson and Freedom, or anyone.

I was feeling good overall at this time and there were very few beatings. Om was a lot more relaxed for some reason, and that spread throughout the group. He had bought a locksmith license and kit using a false ID, and was teaching us how to make keys. He explained how there were master keys to every Ford car. He owned all these keys, about 300 in all. One day, he sat me down and explained an assignment he had chosen for me and only me. He said the other boys couldn't handle it.

I was to steal, or "liberate," a Ford Econoline 250 van, similar to the one he drove. Lovelight, Harmony, and I were to keep an eye out for such a van.

One day, while at the court, I saw a young white guy with long hair getting out of a brown van. I went to see if it was the kind that had been to me. It was. I ran to the tennis court to tell Om. He said, "Okay," and the wheels were in motion. We waited to see if the van would be there the next day, and, to my surprise, it was.

Harmony was the lookout. We parked parallel to it and opened our passenger side door to block the view from the rear, and the front passenger door to block the front. It was very nerve-racking to sit in our van, reach over, and test key after key while wondering if the next would be the lucky key to open the driver's side door of the Ford. I checked every key until I found the correct one. It took me twenty minutes – twenty minutes of exhilaration, fear, and excitement. Finally, on the second to the last key, I felt the door unlock.

All the tension lifted, and, in a single second, fear turned into joy, and then back to fear. I looked at Lovelight and we slid out of our van into the Ford. Within seconds we were on our way back to Mexico. Meanwhile, Harmony closed up our van and drove off in the other direction. As we drove, I went to the back of the Ford to search for valuables on Lovelight's direction. I found about $75 in some old pants and I took $25 for myself and gave the rest to her.

Once in Tijuana, we took the van to a person Om had befriended who owned a paint shop, where the color was changed from brown to black. Harmony showed up not long after, picked us up from a restaurant at a predetermined location, and drove us back to the apartment in San Diego. Upon our return, I was the star of the day. Om was very happy with me and that made me feel very proud, once again, like I had value. I was important.

Meanwhile Perfection was sketching a prototype for the fake license plate that would be used. The process took a couple of weeks. After failing many times and being ridiculed for incompetence, she finally got it right. It was made of clay that was hardened and painted blue with gold letters that read: "AUM 76."

Shortly, we received word that the van was done. He sent Harmony to drive it back across the border. We were on the move again. On our drive from San Diego, we made many stops for food and rest. At one of the food stops, the two boys and I were sent into Safeway to "liberate" some "food spirits." My item was strawberry Yoplait yogurt.

As we spread throughout the store I studied all the people I saw – shoppers and employees – they were like strange foreign caricatures from my memory. I wanted to talk to them all; I thought that any of them could be capable of rescuing me. There was no longer a language barrier, no longer a cultural divide.

All I had to do was speak up, say something, say anything. But then I convinced myself that this wasn't the time or place, and carried out my assignment.

"There will be a better opportunity," I thought, *"to get away."*

I saw Omson at the other end of the store looking for his quota. I found myself on the toy aisle momentarily captivated by the Star Wars action figures and audio cassette stories, even though I didn't know anything about the Star Wars movie. I decided to get myself a treat. No one would know. I'd just tell him or her that some employees were on to me, but I knew I had to get rid of the wrappers before we got back to the car. After I put the Luke Skywalker figure and audiotape under my jacket, I asked an employee to direct me to the bathroom.

"Oh sure, I'll walk you."

Omson saw us walking together from down one of the aisles. He probably thought I was busted and immediately left the store. How perfect. It was even better than I'd planned. Now all I had to do was get rid of the packaging in the bathroom without making too much noise. I assumed Freedom caught wind of my apparent apprehension from Omson and had also left.

After a few seconds in the bathroom, I turned on the faucet to drown out the crackling sound of the wrapping. Coughing and flushing the toilet also helped. I took the lid off the trash can, dumped all the wrappings in it, covered them with paper towels, and put the lid back.

With the tape pressed against my navel and the action figure stuffed into my sock, I made my way to the exit, slowly passing an old man who was stocking the shelves.

He smiled and asked, "How are you today?"

I said, "Fine." I asked out of nervousness where the yogurt was. He smiled again and pointed in the direction I had just come from.

"You just passed it."

"Oh, thank you." I turned around in the direction of the yogurt, stopped, pretended to read the labels (which I could not), acted as though I was disappointed by swinging my shoulders down in case someone was watching, and walked away from the yogurt.

Now heading back to the car, I had about two minutes to think of a lie, as to why I had been walking with the employee, and what had taken me so long to come out of the store, and why I had no yogurt.

But when I stepped outside, the van was gone. I was stunned. I knew better than to panic, so I walked the length of the small shopping center, past the small businesses that lined the walkway, wondering if this was it. Was this the moment when I would be free? But, like so many times before, my fantasy was cut short with the emergence of the van as it slowly pulled around the corner of the building. They were surveying the area, looking for me and possibly also for the police.

This extra bit of time was enough for me to formulate my lie. I told him that the employees had their eyes on me and that there was no opportunity for me to retrieve the yogurt. That is why I had to make it appear as though I was just there to use the bathroom.

Knowing that Omson told him about my walk with the store clerk, Om trusted my decision-making when it came to "liberating food spirits" because I had become very good at it, having impressed him with my skills on many occasions. I returned to my designated spot in the back of the van.

Inside, I was thrilled at my new acquisition. No one knew; I showed no outer sign of my accomplishment, but I reveled in the fact that I carried my new companion in my sock.

We arrived in Las Vegas, where the temperature was extremely hot. On this occasion, the group consisted of Him, Lovelight, Omson, Freedom, Triumph, Prosperity, Marvel, and me. Because secrecy and invisibility remained paramount, the kids were instructed to stay out of sight in the van while he checked in, but he had Freedom and me accompany him inside. He wanted the motel management to know he had some kids, in case they saw the other kids. This way they wouldn't know exactly how many kids there actually were.

My lips had broken out with severe fever blisters that were worse than I ever had before. My entire mouth was swollen shut. I was embarrassed and felt ugly. But I was happy to see a pool in the center of the courtyard, although there was no guarantee I'd be able to go swimming.

For the next several days, all of us kids were dropped off at a small park. The reason was never explained; I was just happy to be outside. Each day, I noticed a group of children with two adult women at the park. They were daycare teachers out on their routine walk. On the third day, while we were playing, the police showed up and asked us why we weren't in school. I imagined it was the daycare teachers who reported us.

I had been instructed to tell anyone who asked that we were traveling with our parents and had just gotten into town, and that we were not yet registered for school. It was an easy enough story for me to repeat if needed, but Omson and Freedom were not capable of communicating it to the police. This was partly because they were afraid of the officers, since the police were the evil "dragonflies" who were looking for us at every turn. The other reason may have been because their general mental aptitude was below average.

The officers realized I was the only one who was able to articulate in a coherent manner, so all their questions were directed at me. Soon after trying to explain the phony situation as best I could, the police took us to the local foster care facility. I was scared that I'd said the wrong thing and failed to prevent us from being taken. I kept going over the story in my mind, knowing I'd repeated it exactly the way I had been instructed. I was terrified. What was going to happen? The officers could tell something was wrong by the presence of fear on all of our faces.

We arrived at a small brown building that looked like a school, on a small tree-lined street. Inside, the building sparkled; the floors looked like they had just received a wax polish and the posters of smiling children that decorated the walls told me this was a place for kids.

The receptionist stared at me with confused interest. I was separated from the other kids, but was reassured by the officer that I would be reunited with them just as soon as my father came to pick us up.

"This is Scott," said the officer.

"Hi, Scott," the woman said as she led us through a small swinging door. "Have a seat right here, and I'll be right back."

She and the officer walked across the office to speak privately. A second woman then appeared from behind a closed door that led to another office. She nodded and shook hands with the officer, looked at me, then continued talking to the two of them. Eventually, the trio turned and started walking towards me. I could feel the sweat collecting in the palms of my hands and the vibration of my heart pounding against my chest. In the back of my mind I thought, *"All I have to do is tell them who I am,"* but fear and shame disabled me.

The woman who had entered from behind the office door was an older woman. Years of experience shone on her face. She wore a brown skirt that stopped just below her knees with matching brown boots and a white blouse. Her feathered hair made me think of Charlie's Angels. Her pretty smile and motherly tone made me feel a little better.

The officer said goodbye. The receptionist went back to her seat, and my Angel escorted me down a long corridor. The sound of her boots clacking against the shiny waxed floor echoed down the hall. We turned left at the end of the hall and continued walking. To fill the awkward silence and hide my fear of what was going to happen next, I asked her where my brothers and sister were. She told me I would see them soon enough, but first she wanted me to meet someone.

We pushed through a pair of doors that led out into a courtyard where there were lots of kids playing games and talking. Many of them stared at me as we walked across the courtyard to another office. Instinctively, I surveyed the area, looking for the troublemakers, the girls, and the overall sentiment from the children. Were they happy or unhappy? I liked the feeling I got from the kids, and I felt like I recognized them from my old life.

The next thing I knew, I was sitting in front of a much younger, cuter angel who began asking me questions and had me repeat my story. She said she was confused because my story didn't match that of my brothers.

"They are your brothers, right?" She said in a fair but suspicious tone.

"Yes," I responded, "they're just a little, ya know ..." I tried to insinuate their deficiency, then quickly asked, "Really? What did they say?"

"Why don't you tell me exactly how you ended up at the park again?" she said with a smile.

I'd told the story so many times, fear and confusion made me doubt I was telling it right. From the window that looked out onto the courtyard, I could see the kids eating outside.

"Are you hungry?" she asked.

"A little," I replied.

"Oh …," she said, mildly embarrassed that she hadn't offered me anything.

I was really very hungry. She got up and went outside to get me some of the lunches that were being served. I hadn't had a peanut butter and jelly sandwich for years. The chocolate milk and cherry-flavored Jell-O made me want to go home. This was my opportunity! All I had to do was tell her. But I was brainwashed. I wanted to say something but couldn't.

She continued probing and my story was falling apart. "We came from Mexico …"

"You came from Mexico?" she repeated.

"This is my chance! Speak up. Tell her!" I thought. But the Jabali who was from Berkeley was locked in a prison of silence and could not speak. She asked more questions, but I couldn't hear her.

"Scott, is there something you're not telling me?" she asked.

My silence and behavior was speaking loudly to her behavioral studies degree. I coached myself to speak up. *"Say something,"* I said to myself. *"Tell her."* The words were making their way up to my tongue from the deepest reaches of my soul, from under almost six years of pain, shame, and silence. The phone on her desk rang once, then twice. She picked it up on the third ring after studying the caller ID button that was flashing red.

"Yes?" Her tone implied it was an unwelcomed interruption. "Oh?" Her back straightened. "Okay!" She listened for a few more seconds then said, while hanging up, "Your father is here." I tried to pretend I was excited and happy, but the little boy who lived as a prisoner in my heart was pulled back down to the darkness of that prison, the prison of silence.

We settled into the another motel, also with a pool. Om let us kids go swimming. There were of couple of old guys in the pool. Meaning no harm, they began to ask us questions about our names and ages. I knew these two fat guys weren't FBI, CIA, or police, so I responded with lies, of course. Nevertheless, we began conversing. Freedom, like the snitch he was, went and told Om. And, again, like clockwork, I was beaten and put in the closet. I stayed in there for the duration of our stay at that motel.

About a week and a half later, we moved to a middle-class community in Las Vegas. The homes all looked the same: Two stories, brown, shingle roofs, small lawns in front. There were five or six different designs, all clearly laid out by the same architect. There was a community pool, a playground, grass fields, and, best of all, tennis courts. They were all connected by small pathways that ran in all directions from the homes, each one with a perfectly manicured lawn. Sycamore trees shaded the paths that got extremely hot in the Las Vegas sun.

I couldn't wait to go explore this new wonderland. Since we were back in the States, I knew I was that much closer to getting home. Everything was so clean compared to Mexico. I was really excited, but I knew not to show it. We moved into this new place, and I was directed to my living space – a closet in a downstairs bedroom. But I didn't care; I was so happy to be in a warm, carpeted space. I gladly took my place there and patiently waited to be released.

At least I could lie down flat in this one. I stayed in the closet for a month or two. It was hard to keep track of time because there were never any clocks or calendars kept in the house, although, by this time, I knew that time did exist. Still, we were never taught the days of the week or months of the year.

Searching for the truth through the labyrinth of lies was a constant chore. I had to decide for myself what would be my truth. That truth became a double-edged sword because I believed that I was stupid, unlovable, unworthy, ugly, unwanted, and not good enough to deserve basic kindness and decency.

I spent half my life in that unbreakable prison of silence. There were countless hours standing in corners, and endless days and months in dark closets, deprived of food and being beaten. I hated everyone. Every time I thought I could trust one of them, they were quick to betray me. I hated my mother, brother, and sister. They betrayed me first. Did anyone care about me? I must not be worth anything. I hated the world. I hated myself.

Once, while everyone was out, I snuck out of the closet, really desperate to get out and see where I lived. As I looked through the house, I remembered Om kept his guns under the bed. I was so miserable, I thought I would just end all of the pain right then. Then they would all know how much pain I felt. And I thought how sorry my family would be for giving me away. I found the .45 pistol and put it to my head. As I did so, all the memories of my younger days raced through my mind. I remembered the bad times and good, my hatred for my mother and family, the hatred for this "family," for my father, who I barely knew, and for my grandmother and uncle, none of whom reached out to save me. I wished I could use the gun on them.

I also recalled the good times, playing with Hippo and Dawn, and riding my Bigwheel on Telegraph. I began sobbing uncontrollably, something I hadn't done in years. As I cried, something sparked in me. At the very bottom of my heart, I remembered my inner strength, my power, my connection to something greater than myself. I remembered my promise to myself, to never let these people break me. Even if my real family didn't want me, I'd make it without them. I didn't need any of those motherfuckers. Sorrow turned to anger, anger turned to pride. I remembered that, no matter what they did to me, they could never get inside me. I became a warrior, but also a prisoner of my hate. He could beat me, put me in a closet, and starve me. But he would never, ever break me. That was my chant.

I put the gun down and returned it to its original spot. I dried my eyes with angry wipes and went back to my closet. I had successfully kept my new Luke Skywalker friend from the watchful eyes of the group. I didn't care about being punished, as I had been secretly playing with my action figure hero.

As soon as I felt it was safe, I went rummaging through boxes looking for a tape player to play the cassette I had stolen. Adrenaline coursing through my veins, with heightened alertness and a keen sense of my new surroundings, I searched like a stealthy cat hunting its prey. This new house was like nothing I had ever seen, except maybe on *The Brady Bunch* back in Berkeley. It looked brand new. The wall-to-wall carpet was light brown, clean, and thick. The walls were bone white with light brown trim that matched the carpet. As had happened at other times before, I was walked straight to the closet when we first arrived, so I didn't get a chance to examine the layout. So, on this trip out, I was able to see for myself a real Brady Bunch house. I was surprised to find the same tape player I first heard those Beatles songs on. It was in a five-gallon paint container. Before I returned to the closet, I continued my exploration of the house. The kitchen was huge, with a white linoleum floor and a futuristic looking stove. It had a black glass front with silver trim, and what I later learned was a microwave oven. The refrigerator was something out of *The Jetsons*, which my starving stomach forced me to open. I found milk, honey, and some leftover rice and beans. I stuck my fingers aggressively into the mixture and scarfed it down, then took a couple of big swallows of milk. I knew this was grounds for an extreme beating, but my hunger forced me.

On the counter next to the refrigerator was something that did not belong that stood out even more than the new appliances, the house, the pool, and the neighborhood. It was a box of Hostess white-powdered doughnuts. I was thrilled and now twice as scared, because sitting in front of me was my great weakness. It was about half empty, and I hesitated only for two seconds, convincing myself I could get away with it. I eagerly stuffed my face with one, two, then three giant bites. Some white powder dropped onto the floor and counter. The thrill and excitement and delicious taste gave me great joy.

In addition to sugar, which was always forbidden, all processed, canned, and boxed food were strictly off limits as well. A very strict diet of "health food" was enforced. To see those doughnuts was a shocking and surprising thing, more evidence that it was all a lie. Again, I reflected and knew my time there was coming to an end.

When I heard the key slide into the lock, panic and fear shot through my body. I closed the doughnut box and put it back exactly how I'd found it, lengthwise against the back of the counter. I grabbed the tape player and ran as fast as I could down the hall, closed the bedroom door behind me, went back to the closet and slid the closet door closed. I put the tape player under my blanket and lay stomach-down on top of it. I closed my eyes and pretended to be asleep in case anyone came in. My heart was pounding in my chest, my breathing heavy and frantic. If someone had come in, it would have been obvious I had been out.

My tape, tape player, and action figure were with me. I looked forward to my solitude and now hoped to be left alone. I knew someone would pay me a visit before the day was over. I just hoped it wasn't Him but, preferably, Devi or one of the boys. I still had only eaten those bites of beans, the swallow of milk, and that oh-so-delicious doughnut. They had been feeding me one small meal a day fairly regularly, so I was expecting that last visit before I dared turn the tape player on.

I had scored some headphones already but knew better than to disconnect myself from a possible command uttered from the door of the bedroom. I slept with one eye open and never knew what would awaken me. It might be a cold glass of water poured on my head, a kick to the stomach, a lashing from a leather belt, or the soft naked skin of a woman.

Finally, I heard the bedroom door open, then a voice telling me to open the door. Freedom entered the bedroom, turned the light on, and set the food down just outside the closet door. It was the same beans and rice from earlier. I tried to chitchat with him to see what had been going on outside the closet, but I could tell by his silence that he was under orders not to talk to me. I eagerly scarfed down all the food, partially out of hunger and of fear that, if the doughnut was discovered missing and that I was the culprit, I would be denied food or given other punishment.

Being confined to a dark closet for days and weeks was now a familiar feeling for me. However, I welcomed the simple pleasures of an overhead light being turned on or the closet door being left open for an extended period of time. My tape and toy took a backseat to light and something for my eyes to fix upon – even if it was only a blank wall with plain, white blinds and a window to appreciate. Sometimes, I would build up the courage, after rehearsing it in my head over and over, to call out, "Holy Father, may I open the closet door for a while?"

If, after several attempts at being heard, I was not answered, I knew to quit. Sometimes I heard an abrupt, "No!" Other times I heard, "You may, for a spell." If I felt bold enough, I would let him determine how long "a spell" was, or I would try to win his affection by closing the door before he came to do it, hoping my willingness to suffer impressed him and he would be inclined to let me out.

The room went black. A voice instructed me to close the closet door. It was Him. I was scared, but happy at the command for it meant the doughnut was not yet discovered to be missing. A bit more patience and I would be clear to turn on my tape.

The tape turned out to be *The Empire Strikes Back*. The sounds of light sabers thrashing through the air, Chewbacca roaring, and the wisdom of Obi Wan Kenobi took me far, far away from the pain in which I was living. It brought a welcomed disconnect to my sad reality. I was in awe of the story. What an amazing, wonderful world Luke Skywalker lived in.

I liked Han Solo, too. I played that tape over and over again until I memorized all the characters' lines, word for word. I could tell that story as though it were my own.

I spent a long time in that closet, maybe a month or two. That was the easiest "time" I ever did, thanks to George Lucas.

During the days, I could hear the kids playing in the pool outside the bedroom window and I sometimes snuck out to watch them. When I was finally let out, there was a different vibe and feeling in the house. It was much happier and more relaxed. He seemed less godly and more manly. The kids were allowed to play outside much more frequently. The women slept most days and were gone at night. He had bought a brand new stereo system that he played old blues records on, like Muddy Waters, Lightning Hopkins, BB King, Albert King, and even Perry Como.

This was so different, so strange. I didn't know what to make of it. It was almost like it was in the beginning. Now it was like a more normal feeling than I had ever experienced since being with the "Om Lovers."

But everything could change in a minute. I was always adapting and changing to match the environment, to try and read his mood. The trick was to adapt and conform before he noticed me. He often sat on his "throne" in the meditation position with his eyes closed. If I could quietly enter the room, sit down in front of him, and assume a meditation prayer position before he opened his eyes, I was sometimes given extra free time.

Or, if he was really in a good mood and I stayed in one of those positions for a great length of time, he would call me up on the throne to sit with him, which I longed for and relished. I wanted so much to be loved and cared for. I wanted to be considered his son. I wanted him to be the father I never had. The loneliness and helplessness I felt everyday would be washed away when he was kind to me; just an affectionate stroke of my head lit me up inside.

On a few occasions he let me brush his hair. Those little signs of affection made me feel loved, and, looking back, they helped me understand the importance of showing and giving love through affection and kind words.

My bed was now outside the closet on the floor. I positioned it under the window. Across the hall was His room. He often shut the door during his morning sex rituals. He had a John Holmes pornography book that he worked from. The images were so sexually graphic that I couldn't help but look through it whenever I got the chance.

While the door was closed, I was free to roam around the house. I relished any time I had out of the closet without being supervised. The new stereo was very intriguing. I wanted so much to poke and push all the buttons. I wondered which one turned it on. I still couldn't read. I knew only small words, so I had to guess, but I knew better than to jeopardize my newfound freedom so soon. I restrained myself.

I decided to clean the bathroom to win his favor and increase the possibility of being let outside later. As I was cleaning, I heard his door open. I was happy to be in there cleaning at that moment because he could actually see me in the act. As he walked by, he said, "Take a shower." It was not the response I was hoping for, but at least he saw me working. That would give me the courage to ask to go outside later. As I undressed, Lovelight came in, walked passed me to the faucet, and turned the shower on. She was already nude, having just had her "Holy fuck."

Looking at her naked body, I became aroused and tried to fight it off by telling her he had ordered me to take a shower. "Get in then," she said as she pulled the shower curtain behind her.

"Get my shampoo from under the counter." I'd fantasized about having sex with her in the shower, wondering now if it was really going to happen. I didn't want to get in with an erection, but I couldn't help it. I had always fantasized about her throughout all the morning rituals. She had long blonde hair, green eyes, and a Playboy-sculpted face. Her body was firm and fit. She had very small breasts with abnormally large nipples. The curvature of her legs and ass resembled a 1940's pin-up poster you would find in a mechanic's shop. She was always distant and seemed to be emotionally unavailable. She had a very nasty temper when she was mad, but her beauty always won me over.

One of the objectives of the women's work every day was to go out and find followers to give up all their worldly possessions and join the cult. On many occasions, Lovelight would recruit men who were willing to follow her home to meet The Creator, in hopes of sleeping with her … which they did, after getting permission. This caused problems with the other women. They were always jealous of each other, cat fighting and arguing over who had to do what, especially when Lovelight brought someone home.

I took her shampoo into the shower, embarrassed by my condition, but I had grown accustomed to ignoring what little morality and dignity I had left.

Her back was turned, her hands swiped over her face and hair as the water glided down her back like a river rushing over her buttocks; her butt cheeks were like two giant boulders unable to hold the water back. I wanted to put my arms around her and press myself against her body. She turned around and stepped out from under the water and reached for the shampoo. I coyly held it in front of my body, hoping she wouldn't notice.

When she took it, I was exposed, more than just my naked body but my whole being. I stopped there for a moment, motionless. It felt like an eternity. As she reached out to pull me underneath the water and slide past me, I felt her soft skin and pubic hairs glide against my chest. She smiled and told me that I would have to get permission before we could do that.

She lathered the shampoo, and, as I watched, I became more and more aroused and tempted to do something, anything. She told me to turn the water nozzle to bath mode and to soap up. She took some of the shampoo and began to wash my hair and body. As she scrubbed and washed my back, the powerful smell of coconut filled my nose. She turned me around to face away from her and lifted my arms to wash under them. Her hands slid down my torso to my waist. Full of suds, her hands washed me. She told me to rinse off and get out so she could finish up. I did and didn't dare show my disappointment, not out of fear, but pride.

After watching and participating in the daily sex rituals and orgies for years now, I felt like I was ready to start having sex. I was 10. The visits to me at night had stopped, and, even though they were unwelcomed, I wondered if there was something wrong with me.

As I settled into this new, more casual, less sickened life, violence kept me alert and on my toes. We had been given permission to go outside and play, but we were to stay within the tennis courts, which were about 100 yards south of our house. Our boundaries included the main walking path that curved through the sycamore trees and divided the housing community and the main street. It led through a large, open grass field with benches and barbecue pits. I could see all the neighborhood kids playing football when we drove in and out of the community and they saw me. Now I could join them.

Since I was a very friendly child before my abduction, making friends on the playground was easy for me. "You want to be my friend?" was my go-to line. I don't recall ever being turned down. My extroverted personality earned many charmed admirers, especially adults. This trait was never lost, and, although it earned me many beatings, solitary confinement, and ostracism from the cult members, it was something I relied on for my survival. It was a God-given gift, interwoven into my core since birth.

On a hot day in the Nevada sun, after all the morning rituals, I got permission to go play outside. As soon as the door closed behind me, I was forming my story about myself and this crazy group of people that I knew had been observed by the kids and neighbors. I ran straight to the football field. As I got closer, I slowed my run to a casual walk. I didn't want to seem too eager to all the kids. When I approached the field, I heard their voices, and joy-filled butterflies danced and fluttered in my stomach. They were in the middle of a game. The quarterback saw me first. He was really big, towering over the rest of the kids by a foot. He stopped in the middle of calling his play and yelled out, "Hey, we need you! You want to play?" His voice was deep and he had a dark peach-fuzz mustache. He was a teenager.

"Yeah," I said confidently.

"What's your name?" he asked. My mind went blank. *"Who am I?"* I forgot about that question. I was so busy thinking of explaining "them" that I had forgotten about me. I had long since lost the new name He gave me, Sovereignty. I didn't like the name Jabali, that was the name of the worthless, lying, good-for-nothing son of a woman and family who didn't care about whether he lived or died on the streets of Mexico or in a basement closet. So, I became "Scott" once more.

"Scott!" I called out.

"Alright, Scott. You're on my team! You're gonna be my running back."

"I thought I was your running back!" another kid said.

"No, you're going to play wide right," the older boy said to him.

I didn't know what wide right meant and was happy he didn't give me the position. I knew what running back was, though, because I remembered OJ Simpson. He was everyone's favorite, and all I had to do was run with the ball, not get tackled, and get to the other end of the field. In the huddle, he introduced me to all the other kids on my team, including his brother, the now wide receiver. The play was called an "I" formation call. I didn't know what that was, but the quarterback told me where to line up.

"On three, break. HUT 1 HUT 2 HUT 3 … HIKE!"

As everyone began to move, the entire world slowed to a snail's pace, the quarterback dropped back to hand me the ball, and they all looked like they were standing still. I moved straight up the middle and one defender moved straight at me. I cut right, dodging him, then cut back left to avoid a second. The third kid dove at my waist, but I sprinted out of his grasp. I could hear the quarterback cheering me on. Now, it was a foot race to the end zone with all of them chasing me, the defensive back their last hope to cut me off.

"He can't catch me," I thought. And I ran harder, leaving them all behind. When I got into the end zone, I looked back to see the quarterback and my teammates cheering with their hands in the air, running toward me. It felt so good to be acknowledged and admired. They all gave me high fives and congratulatory pats on the back.

I was an instant star. I then noticed a group of kids watching the game on the sidelines. Girls and boys were all pointing and talking about me. Some girls were whispering in each other's ears, as girls do. Then the questions came, "How old are you? Where are you from? What school do you go to?" I answered them all with my pre-rehearsed lies.

I was Scott. Ten years old. From Berkeley, California. My mom was a teacher so she home schooled us. The quarterback, Jason, was an all-time quarterback, which meant he was now quarterback for the opposing team. He threw the ball off for us, as we all charged down the field. The kid who caught the ball kneeled down on one knee. Some of his teammates yelled at him for his decision, which stopped the play and automatically started their downs from their twenty-yard line. The field wasn't marked, so it was up to the quarterback to estimate. They gained a few yards on a couple of plays and finally scored a passing touchdown. They now threw off to us, everyone wanted to run it back, but fate would have it that it rolled to me after Jason's brother Dylan dropped it. So I picked it up, and scanned the field for holes in the charging army of kids. Again, they all slowed down. I saw the weak links and headed for them. My speed and agility shocked everyone, even me. I had no idea I had these skills, and, as I realized them, they seemed to increase with every step. I ran the length of the field, evading capture.

"Oh my God!" screamed Dylan. "How do you do that?"

I was just as amazed as he was but didn't show it. I shrugged my shoulders and accepted the praise. They told me I should play on a team. The kids on the sidelines were just as excited as we were. It was the best first impression a kid could ever wish for. I was an instant hit. We won that game, 35 to 7. I scored four of the five touchdowns. After the game, we all hung out at the field talking. I was navigating through a barrage of questions. Some were harder than others.

"What grade are you in?" stopped me in my tracks. I had no idea. I had no idea what the appropriate grade for my age was. So, I repeated the question back to Dylan.

"What grade are you in?"

"Fifth," he answered.

"Me, too," I said.

The sun was setting and most of the kids were going home for dinner. There seemed to be an agreed-upon curfew by all the parents. Jason had left much earlier and Dylan and I were the last to leave. Even though in the back of my mind I was worried about the time and whether I was going to be punished for staying out so long, I stayed until the very end. There was no guarantee that I would ever see any of them again, so I was going to enjoy that feeling as long as it was available.

On the way home, half-terrified of going back, I reflected on the day. It felt so good, being good at something, being liked and admired. I fantasized about going to school and living there forever. My mind went back and forth between the possible impending doom and my newfound talents and friends. I was happy Omson and Freedom didn't show up. I knew at some point I would have to explain them and their inability to socialize.

Playing football that day, I learned that I had talent and skill, that I was good at something. It gave me self-confidence, and a sense of self-love that was profoundly important to my development. I cherish it to this day; it was the single best day of the entire six-year ordeal.

When I got back, I could hear music playing from outside the front door. I slowly opened it to see Omson and Freedom playing and dancing in front of the stereo. *Man Child* by Muddy Waters was playing, and I was shocked at the freedom they were expressing. It was fun without fear. Triumph and Prosperity came running in, having been dancing and playing, too. I joined in, hoping to blend in so that when He came back to the room it would appear as though I had been there for some time. This was a tactic I didn't have much faith in, but it was the only one available to me at that moment.

The kids were having so much fun that the jealousy and adversarial feeling that would normally have driven them to immediately report me were lost in the music. I thanked Muddy Waters.

Orders came out of His room to turn off the music and go to bed. I couldn't believe it; I didn't have to face Him, and the best day of my life would end without any physical or mental or verbal abuse. It truly was the happiest day of my life to date.

The next morning, I was woken up and told to come to the Lord's room. Now I was terrified. As I approached the door to his bedroom, I tried to prepare myself for a beating. There was no particular formula that I knew of, just a spontaneous mental preparation for extreme pain. The room smelled of incense and sex. He was fucking Perfection, which was about as rare as me going outside and playing all day. She didn't seem to care for my presence. With her back to him, facing the door and me, she closed her eyes. He was sitting upright with his back against the headboard in his usual position with his book held close to his face. I walked to the side of the bed so he could see I was there and kneeled down. Perfection let out a moan of satisfaction, and he rested the book on the small of her back and told me he had an assignment for me. With his hand still on the book, he spanked her lightly with it, forcing her off, then gestured for Lovelight to come get on, which she did eagerly.

I secretly enjoyed this and became aroused as she backed herself onto him, her body shiny from the oils she had slathered on herself. I became transfixed by her. Our eyes met for a brief moment and she smiled as if to say she knew what I was thinking, and then we lost eye contact.

My assignment was to go to Montgomery Ward's with Inspiration and liberate/steal an electric hand drill. I was proud that he picked and trusted me enough to give me the assignment, and it also meant I could go out into the world and see life. I was dismissed and went to get ready for the day.

When I found Inspiration preparing the morning meal, she was in high spirits, moving quickly around the kitchen, humming. When she saw me, she gave me a huge smile and said, "Good morning, handsome." This kind of behavior could only mean one thing, that she was picked first for the morning rituals. Her happy, perky, upbeat behavior repulsed me. She was so transparent, even to a 10-year-old boy. But I didn't care; everyone seemed happier. It actually felt kind of good in the house. I smiled back at her and offered to help.

After all the morning rituals were over and breakfast was done, Inspiration and I went out on our assignment. She was dressed down from her usual attire, which resembled a mass up of Rajneesh, Hare Krishna, and Muktananda clothing (other cults found across the world).

I wore tennis clothes for the most part, sometimes a pair of blue khakis and a polo shirt with tennis shoes. This day, I wore Adidas sweatpants with a matching jacket that was a bit oversized in order to conceal anything underneath. She and I were always a pretty good team. We always beat the other women and kid combos that went out. There were competitions to see who could bring back the most money and goods at the end of a given day, and she and I were hands down the best. Harmony was second, Lovelight was third, Perfection was fourth, and Devi was always last.

I had proven myself an asset, and the reward was going back into the field. The fieldwork had changed since we got to Vegas. The women were working the casinos at night, and, during the days, we went out "liberating" whatever was on his list of things he wanted. This time it was that hand drill.

We found the store, parked, and went over our plan of action. We were to go in together and find the tool and toy sections, in that order. I was to survey the area and choose the drill I was going to take. Then she would continue to appear to be shopping while I went to the toy section (with strict orders not to take any toys), hang out there for a few minutes, then go back to the tools and quickly put the drill in my pants.

On my first attempt, I realized I would have to tighten the drawstring on my pants because of the weight of the drill, which meant I had to circle around the aisle one more time. On my second attempt, looking quickly up and down the aisle, I stuffed the drill into my pants and under my jacket. I knew by the weight I wouldn't have long before I would have to be adjusting it, so I made a beeline to the exit. The whole event took 10 minutes, tops. As I got to the front exit, I made a curious and lost head gesture as if to say, "Where did my mommy go?"

It also let me know if anyone was following me out, in which case, if they stopped me, I would cry and say, "I just wanted to surprise my daddy for his birthday!" I saw Inspiration as I glanced over my shoulder. No one else seemed to be near or notice me, so I walked to the exit.

We met back at the car and celebrated.

"The Lord is going to be so pleased with you!"

I was happy at the thought of making him happy and imagined another day of playing with my new friends. As we entered the housing community, I saw the kids out there playing again, and they all waved, beckoning me to come play. I reluctantly waved back. I didn't want Inspiration to know that I had made new friends because it might be considered a security breach, in which case I would not be allowed out anymore, and violent disciplinary actions would be taken.

Inspiration was notorious for betraying my trust and was instrumental in shaping my hatred and mistrust of women. I knew it was going to get back to him, but hoped, in the light of the success of our recent assignment, she wouldn't make a big deal about it.

We got back, and he was sitting on his throne playing his guitar along with BB King's *The Thrill is Gone*. I wanted to be the one to give him the drill and so did she, but, somehow, it worked out in my favor.

He was pleased with me, and, even though I hated him, I still continued to long for his approval.

"Your son has made some little friends," Inspiration said with a bit of poison on her tongue.

My stomach dropped out from under me, terror pumped throughout every vein.

"Great," he said, seeming to recognize her witchery. "You're free to go outside."

I didn't respond. I just turned to the front door and walked out, excited to go back and play. I ran the whole way back to the football field, this time, not bothering to hide my enthusiasm. They were all gathered around the cinder block wall that separated the homes that ran the length of the field.

As I approached, they were picking the teams, but my presence forced them to start over. There was a group of girls that had gathered nearby, and it was obvious through their pointing that they were talking about me again. The two team captains were arguing over who had first pick, which was settled with a coin toss.

"I got Scott!"

"See! I knew you were going to pick him!"

I was proud to be first pick but was distracted by the girls and their giggling.

Then out from the middle of the crowd came the prettiest girl. She had short, curly, brown hair, little red stud earrings that matched her red shirt, and shiny lip gloss. She walked over to Dylan and asked him a question, putting her hands on her hips. He was obviously annoyed and responded with, "I don't know. Get out of here." She stormed back to her friends and the team picking resumed.

It was another good day for me on the field. I scored three touchdowns and won the hearts of even more kids, especially the girl in red. After the game, we all hung out on the wall. The awkwardness of our obvious juvenile attraction to each other wore off between us. She turned out to be the baby sister of Dylan and Jason, and her name was Sarah. Dylan did all he could to embarrass her, but she was a little spitfire with enough wit and sass to handle any kid our age, especially her big brother. Had I not been exposed to the experiences I'd been forced to live through, she would have intimidated me; I don't think there was a shy bone in her body. She was full of questions that made it hard to keep up.

The lies that worked with the rest of the kids didn't work on her. She knew I was lying and wanted to know what about. Eventually, she cleverly let me out of my lies. Her good looks, charm, wit, and sass won my heart. The streetlights were coming on and I knew if I ever wanted to see her again I would have to get home early.

When I said goodbye for the day, she put her hands on her hips and said, "Aren't you going to walk me home?" We all said goodbye and Dylan walked away from us towards their house. I tried to follow, but she put her hand on my arm to stop me, making some small talk to get some distance between him and us. I loved all the attention, but a deep fear was growing in the pit of my stomach. I wanted so much to enjoy this moment but was torn between taking advantage of my current freedom or hurrying home in hopes of being allowed out again. She seemed to sense my nervousness and asked, "What's the matter? Do you have to go home?"

I reluctantly said, "Yes," so she picked up the pace to her house.

Suddenly, she took off running and yelled, "Let's race!" So, we raced down the rest of the block until we got to her house, laughing. When she beat me there, I told her she cheated. We walked halfway up her walkway when she stopped me. Now, she was looking nervously back and forth to the front door. I'll never forget that moment.

She said, "I don't know how to say this, but I have a crush on you."

Time slowed to a standstill as she leaned in to kiss me. I could feel her warm breath on my cheek and the smell of her cherry lip gloss as it slid against my skin. It happened in the blink of an eye but lasted for an eternity. Then she ran to her front door as if for safety and closed it without looking back.

I stood there for a moment in disbelief, then came to my senses, turned around, and ran all the way home. My heart was pounding with excitement and joy. I had a girlfriend. When I got back and knocked on the front door, no one answered. After several attempts I went around to the side door of the garage, which led to a door into the house. The house was empty.

The day couldn't have ended better. I had no one to answer to, the whole house to myself, and time to reflect on the now new best day of my life. For the first time since this whole nightmare began, I felt happy, like I had something to look forward to.

Eventually, the day came when I had to explain Omson and Freedom to my new friends. Up until that point, I had hidden the fact that I had any siblings, but I knew if I kept playing with the neighborhood kids the day would come when I would have to introduce my "brothers."

Omson called himself Josh, and Freedom called himself Michael. I made up these names for them to help them blend in. We had been thoroughly brainwashed into believing that everyone in the outside world was most probably working for the police or the FBI.

It was a fact that He had had run-ins with both federal and local law enforcement agencies, but I knew none of these kids were "plants." Omson and Freedom had no reference to the outside world, so they believed all the lies, and why not? They were the sons of God Almighty. They had plans on inheriting the Kingdom of Heaven, so the warnings of the dangers of talking to worldly people fit into their paradigm.

Since talking to the public was strictly forbidden (unless on an assignment), the new freedom I was experiencing confused me. Surely they knew I was talking to the kids. Omson and Freedom followed along with the story but were never really able to blend in. Dylan and the other kids always asked me, "What is wrong with your brothers?" I told them we had different moms, but it never really explained their oddities and social ineptitude.

One day while Omson, Freedom, and I were at the tennis courts, an older kid (bully type) was asking us questions about who we were. He asked Omson if he was retarded. Omson angrily replied, "No!"

Insultingly, the boy said back, "Yes, you are!" and grabbed the keys to the tennis courts out of Omson's hands and threw them over the dividing wall into a patch of undeveloped desert. We all knew that losing the keys meant punishment for all of us, and we all gasped as the keys flew high into the air. My eyes followed exactly where they would land, and we all ran and jumped over the wall like our lives depended on it. The kid started laughing and taunted us. We searched and searched but to no avail; the keys were gone, and we were undoubtedly going to be punished.

We climbed back over the wall, unsure as to what to do. The boy hadn't stopped taunting us, and I felt everything slow down again. I felt a burning, hot hatred for him. It triggered the humiliation boiling inside me from all of the heartbreak, sadness, and injustice I had endured. I felt the cumulative pain of my mother giving me away, my sister and brother leaving me, and my father not protecting me. No one loved me.

It all turned to rage. I started running toward him. He, being much bigger and stronger, smiled and welcomed a fight. His mouth was moving as he got off his bike. I couldn't hear any of his words. As I got closer, I realized I still had my tennis racquet in my hands, a metal Wilson T-2000. I waited until I was just close enough not to miss, but far enough that he couldn't reach me before I hurled it with all my strength right at his face. When I released it, I knew it was not going to miss. It flew end over end, hitting him directly in the mouth.

The metal head of the T-2000 exploded against his braces. His lips disintegrated into red mush. He made a muffled whining sound as his head flew back from the force of the blow. He grabbed his mouth as the blood and meat filled his hands. "My braces!" he cried as he knelt over a newly forming pool of blood.

I reveled in my victory as I watched him change from a mean, insensitive bully who would pick on a retarded kid to a whimpering child paralyzed with fear at the sight of his own blood. There were some other kids watching from a nearby sandlot on the other side of the tennis courts. I could hear them groan at the moment of impact.

I got up close to him and asked, "Are you retarded?"

Omson and Freedom insisted we go home. I picked up the racket and we ran home. After explaining what happened, I was rewarded for defending my brothers with "the freedom to go outside until further notice." I didn't know why I was being extended so many freedoms. I felt like something was going on, but I didn't know what. Looking back now, I think that, perhaps, they were preparing to let me go, and they were trying to make up for all the damage they had done.

He told us to stay in for a couple of days in order to let the incident blow over, just in case the kid's parents got involved.

Back at the house, Perfection and Lovelight were painting portraits and scenes for God's book, which he called *The Song of Om*. Perfection and Lovelight were artists. Om would sometimes spend weeks, and even months, in front of his typewriter. The endless tapping of the keys as they slapped the papers of his books became a rhythmic conversation. Tack, tack, tack, ding, tack, tack, tack. I listened from behind the closet doors.

Perfection was by far the better painter, Lovelight, the better lover. This was part of what fueled their rivalry and competition to be his top Goddess. Perfection was creating a replica of a California driver's license so they could make fake IDs and assume different identities for the scams they were planning.

I was never made aware of exactly what they were going to do. I got the impression that Inspiration and Lovelight were prostituting themselves, but I was never sure. This new fake ID project was a very big deal, and He constantly berated Perfection for making mistakes and threatened to give the assignment to Lovelight.

For the next couple of days, I watched Perfection create what He was calling her "greatest work." I couldn't wait to see Sarah again and tried to be the best "son" I could so I would be allowed out again.

I did everything in my power to stay in His good graces. I cleaned his bathroom, toilet, and polished his sink. I handpicked the carpet of all its dirt, cleaned the kitchen, cleaned the windows, dusted his throne, wiped and dusted the new wall unit and stereo, cleaned the stove, and swept and mopped the garage. I cleaned his new waterbed, changed the bedding, and stayed away from Omson and Freedom.

Perfection noticed my attempts to be in good graces and told Omson and Freedom to do the same. As always, she was very jealous of me and my abilities to take action, and angry about the inability of her kids to do as I did.

After about the second or third day, I worked up enough nerve to ask for permission to go outside again. He told me what a good job I had been doing and exclaimed, "Of course you can go outside."

All I could do was guess at his intentions. It was a packed day at the field, and it seemed as though all the kids were out that day. I think it must have been a Saturday. The game had already started, but I didn't care because I wanted to hang out with Sarah. And there she was in the middle of her circle of girlfriends, wearing a little white sleeveless dress and sandals. She was playing with something. Some parents were there barbecuing and celebrating a kid's birthday, which added to the day's excitement. Colorful balloons decorated the BBQ pit and tables, the smell of meat grilling filled the air, and a beautiful cake sat majestically on a white tablecloth that covered the brown park bench.

When I got over to Sarah, she put the thing she had in her hand behind her back abruptly and said, "Guess which hand?" I picked the right hand. She showed me there was nothing in it. Then she produced a Rubik's cube in her left. I had seen the toy before but had never played with one. It was a gift for me! I had not been given a gift since my sixth birthday, when James had given me seven silver dollars. I had forgotten what it was like to be cared for, and here I was receiving a gesture so fundamental in human interaction, from a 10-year-old girl, no less. But I was paralyzed with fear and doubt, unable to accept it.

"Here, it's for you. It's a Rubik's cube."

I gathered myself together and forced out a "Thank you."

"Don't you like it?" she asked.

"Yes! Yes, I like it, but I like you more," I said.

She blushed and smiled big. It was another spectacular day in the middle of a miserable life. I was invited to dinner by Sarah's parents. She told me they wanted to meet me. The idea of having a meal with her and her family was very enticing but also dangerous.

I had permission to play with the kids, but interacting or speaking with adults was an absolute violation of the "law" and was punishable by lashings, food, and clothing deprivation, isolation and/or all of the above.

I didn't want to risk all my newfound freedoms, so I told her I had to ask my father. Her invitation was very innocent and she had no way of knowing the pressure and stress it put upon me. She accepted my response as if it was expected. I thought I was being clever.

The smell of burgers and hot dogs called to my empty stomach. I had been accustomed to not eating for lengthy periods of time and this day was no different. In my eagerness to get outside and away from all of them, I didn't ask for permission to eat. When I saw Sarah, I was too embarrassed to ask her directly for some food, so I asked a lot of questions about the food. She understood me somehow and ran over to the grill and brought back a hotdog and soda. Eating that kind of food meant punishment. I had not had a hot dog in years. Just the smell made my mouth salivate, and defying the "law" made it taste even better.

The first game came to an end and all the kids were lining up for the second. We all lined up against the wall, which was customary. I really didn't want to play football anymore. I just wanted to spend time with the angel known as Sarah. I did enjoy all of the attention, but it paled in comparison to how she made me feel.

I played a painfully embarrassing game. I was trying so hard to show off and impress Sarah. I fumbled several times and struggled to get out of the back field, where days earlier I was the master. I was so frustrated, I told Dylan to put me in as wide receiver to see if anything would change. He agreed and sent me on a slant pattern, which ended in my only touchdown of the day.

I took the opportunity to fall and get hurt as I scored, got up limping, and had one of the sideliners take my place. Dylan and some other kids on my team expressed their disappointment, but I didn't care. I got to be with the sweetest, kindest person I had ever known.

We spent the afternoon playing with the Rubik's cube. She asked me if I wanted to see her room. I agreed and we headed across the field toward her house. Up until she asked me that, I felt very comfortable and at ease, but the thought of being alone with her in her room made me very nervous. She, on the other hand, was still very poised and confident. She kept up the conversation, and that made me feel more relaxed. She explained that her parents had taken their eldest son Jason to shop for a new motocross bike. He was one of many neighborhood kids who rode dirt bikes at the local motocross track a couple of blocks away.

She lived in a very modern, middle-class home. The architecture was similar to our house with a living room, dining area, and kitchen all closely connected. She walked me straight to the stairs, which led to the second floor where all the kid's rooms were. It was a very "girly" room. Teddy bears covered the shelves that lined all four walls about a foot from the ceiling. The walls were peach with white trim. A white desk sat under the window that was covered with papers and pencils, and a portrait of her sat in a small glass frame. She had posters on the walls of people I mostly didn't recognize, except for Farrah Fawcett. I knew of her. Sarah's bedcovers and pillows matched the room, including the metal bed frame, which was also painted white. The closet door was half open, revealing a full wardrobe. There was a record player in the corner with a stack of 45 records placed neatly under it. Some clothes were strewn over the bed as if she couldn't decide what to wear that morning. She closed the door behind us and on it were more posters and pictures angled askew, attached with tape and tacks.

She went over to the record player and asked me what I liked. I didn't know any artists or songs, so she picked the one that was sitting on top of the player. It was Rick Springfield's *Jessie's Girl*. We must have played it 50 times that afternoon. She danced around the room playing with different things, showing me pictures and artifacts from trips to Disneyland and vacation places she and her family had been.

I longed so badly to be part of her family. I wished they could adopt me. I wanted to have sex with her and thought that was the reason why she brought me. But she was just an innocent little girl who had a schoolgirl crush. It was refreshing and appealing at the same time. Being around her made me remember and long for a normal life even more. We played that afternoon like kids.

That evening, I was given a "Standing Post" assignment, which meant I was to stand guard at the front door with a loaded .45 caliber pistol on my waist until further notice. The assignment started as soon as I walked through the front door. He was sitting on his throne reading his own book aloud. Without saying a word, he gestured for me to come over to him. I stood there just to the right of his throne in the customary attention position for a very long time, about 2 hours, as he read his book aloud.

When he was done reading, he instructed me to go get a belt that would fit me. I walked away wondering about my fate. When I returned, he ordered me closer to him. He reached out for the belt, and I flinched with fear as he turned me around by my shoulder. I didn't know what to expect. I hoped it wasn't going to be lashings.

Then he fixed the belt tightly around my waist. I heard the sound of a gun being loaded or unloaded, I couldn't tell. The next thing I knew, he had stuffed it into the belt, which kept it snug against my small waist.

There was something very exhilarating about having a gun on my person.

He instructed me to stand guard at the front door until further notice. I didn't know if this was a reward or a punishment for coming home late. He got up, turned out all the lights, and left the room.

I was so happy not to have gotten a beating that it did not occur to me that it might be a setup. Anything having to do with Om was always a game of psychological cat and mouse; I was constantly trying to figure him out and he was forever speaking in parables and deliberately confusing me.

As I stood there in the dark, I smelled a faint hint of incense from the back room.

Adrenaline was still pumping through my veins. My heart had been pounding since the moment I walked through the door but only now was I aware of it and my fear.

I slowly settled into my post. As my fear subsided, I began to reflect on the day I spent with Sarah, and the sweet smell of her cherry lip gloss that seemed to have made its way into my shirt.

I took another deep breath, but the smell had vanished. Minutes became hours and my eyelids grew heavy. To stay awake I thought of taking out the pistol and examining it, but he left me with strict instructions not to play with it. I thought it might be loaded, and I fantasized about walking into his room, standing over him, and pulling the trigger. But what if it wasn't loaded and he woke up? He would surely kill me, I thought.

I was awoken by his voice coming from the direction of the throne. He was sitting on it in meditation position. My body jerked up into attention.

"What did I tell you?"

"To man the post."

"Do you call that manning the post?"

"No."

"Come here." When I got over to him, he beckoned me closer – two more steps and I would be within striking distance. He reached under the belt and retrieved the pistol, took the safety off, withdrew the clip, and ejected the .45-caliber bullet that sat in the chamber. He sat everything neatly and methodically off to the side, fixed himself a little closer to the edge of his seat, and slapped the side of my head with so much force my feet came out from under me.

I felt a loud, hot popping in my ear and stars shot across my eyes like pixie dust. I knew the routine. I had been here many times before. I was supposed to jump back to attention and wait for more without crying. I did that several more times, each time getting up slower and slower, until the tears busted out of my eyes, and I couldn't stand another blow.

My body hurt and heartbroken, my spirit bruised, I called out, "Please … I'm sorry." I could taste the blood in my mouth, salty and bitter. But he was not done. He demanded that I get up. As I slowly got to my hands and knees, I prayed for the strength to endure another strike. Again I went down, the flesh in my mouth mangled against my teeth. Now, there was no strength in me to get up again, and I lay there in the dark, bleeding and helpless.

There is something particularly dreadful about being beaten in the dark. It left me feeling the emptiness of space and the hopelessness of death in the pit of my stomach.

"Take off all your clothes and go sit in the kitchen closet." He chose the kitchen closet because of the hard, cold linoleum floor and because it had no blankets. I paid special attention to the word "sit" which could have meant he was going to come check on me at any given time. I slowly rose to my feet and stumbled to the closet. I closed the door behind me and sat down in the meditation position, hoping to impress him if and when he came to check on me. But he never came.

I stayed in that closet for days, only leaving to use the bathroom. I could hear all the happenings of daily life from behind the door. Unlike all the other times, I did not want to join them. I did not want to be in his good graces or be the recipient of a kind word or blessing smile from one of the women. I hated them all and made up my mind to not be lured or convinced that somehow I belonged there.

I was going to make it back to Berkeley someway, somehow. I never got to play football again, and I only saw Sarah once more through the peephole of the front door when she came by to see if I could play. I was given strict instructions not to open the door for anybody. I wanted so badly to open the door and be with her just one last time and have one last kiss. I wanted to tell her to wait for me, that I would come back once I got away from these people. But, I couldn't. Omson was standing next to me wanting to see who was at the door, and he would have reported me. I think she came by several times while I was in the closet, but that was the end of this happiest of times. I watched her walk away, then went to my closet and cried.

NINE

Going Home

e left Las Vegas very abruptly, and I believe we were on the run for the crimes the women had committed. Half of the group was now in some other location, and, again, we split into two groups to prevent all of us from being apprehended at the same time. Om, Omson, Freedom, Lovelight, and I were now one traveling team. We settled into our new location, and I was just as oblivious to the plan as I had ever been.

Although I was purposely kept in the dark about the day-to-day operations and overall plans, I was now old enough to glean bits and pieces of information that gave me a broader understanding of my predicament. We had not made any incense while in Las Vegas, so the plan was to start up the incense selling business again, this time in Los Angeles.

Om sent Inspiration to connect with her contact at the Krishna Temple. But buying the incense sticks and oils from the Hare Krishnas was taking longer to negotiate than he had anticipated. The person who had been their contact was no longer a Krishna temple member, so Inspiration was trying to renegotiate, and they were having problems.

Om blamed Inspiration for the breakdown, which led to one of their violent fights.

He decided that we would sell scented candles with pictures of Guadalupe and other Catholic saints on them. I was now about 11 years old, and I could go out on my own and sell.

My quota was 15 candles a day, which sometimes required two trips home during the day. I began to learn my way around the area within about a 3-mile radius of our house. All the liquor stores, laundromats, strip malls, and

149

restaurants were open for me to sell to. I made friends with a lot of merchants who recognized that I was not in school and that I was a hard worker. I met lots of kids at an arcade in our neighborhood and slowly assimilated into the culture of south central Los Angeles.

Om was happy with me during this time because I was doing very well selling. The rules were always changing. Very strict rules about talking, eating, sleeping, working, and meditating would change suddenly. Om still spoke in riddles that needed deciphering, and it was never easy navigating through the minefield of His psychological trickery.

He would leave the front door wide open, something that went against every one of His security measures. The police, FBI, and all other government agencies were our enemies. I had spent countless hours listening and learning how to prevent security breaches like this one, and yet, He, the "Lord" of all, was putting everyone at risk.

This must be a test, I thought. If I closed it in an attempt to secure the perimeter, I could be punished for assuming I had the authority to make that decision. If I left it open, that may also have led to some kind of punishment for it implied carelessness to a security breach.

"Your freedom awaits you!" he said.

Free to go out and play? Free to take a look at the parking lot? Free to go back home to Berkeley? Another cryptic message to confuse me. Another chess move in a game I was still too young and weak to win.

I took the opportunity to go down the hall to Room 18 where my friend Desiree lived. We had become friends during our stay at this new apartment complex. On the days that I went out to sell incense, we would see each other in the hallways, at the bus stop, and at the corner store, and we had developed a crush on one another. Desiree had beautiful, almond-shaped eyes, her hair was always braided with little pink barrettes at the end, her teeth were perfect and white, and her ebony skin always smelled of cocoa butter. Her voice was raspy and quiet like a little mouse.

Her mother answered the door with a smile and told me that Desiree was down the street at the arcade. I debated whether to go without getting permission and decided to go for it. But first, I went to get some money I had hidden; I had been secretly charging extra for the candles and saved the extra money for myself.

As I began to understand over the years that he wasn't God, but just a man, I realized that I was not chosen to be a warrior who would help bring in the New Kingdom of God, that my mother had betrayed me for unknown reasons, and that I was alone in the world and had to look out for myself. So I began stealing for myself, selling extra candles and keeping the money, reporting back that I had broken the candles or that I had been robbed. These were little ways of securing my own comfort and safety regardless of the risk.

I found Desiree at the arcade playing Mrs. Pacman. She was really good at it and enjoyed showing off her skills. I met other kids in the neighborhood through her. I had to tell them the same lies again, but these were inner city kids so my lies were altered to fit my environment.

First, they would ask me questions about my ethnicity. "What color are you?"

One boy named, Anthony, or Ant, for short would always say, "You a white boy, huh? You ain't black."

I knew that he was trying to insult me, and I was insulted. Being mixed in an all black/white world was very challenging. In the black community, there is a secondary racism against lighter blacks that is traced back to slavery when white slave owners raped black slave women and they had babies. Those children were often treated much more kindly than their siblings and were given privileges, and, in some cases, even inherited freedom and land. So, to this day, there is a rivalry in black culture that maintains a subtle divide.

I had experienced it long before I'd landed in the clutches of the sex cult. I was four years old and the neighborhood kids in west Oakland called me a "Pissy Yellow Nigga," a name I never forgot. I thought the darker skinned a person was, the tougher that person was.

Ant was really dark skinned, and I knew he had it out for me because I was so light. So I was afraid to fight him, and used my wit instead.

It worked the first couple of times, but this day, seeing that Desiree and I liked each other, he was set on fighting me. Most of the other kids liked me, so I wasn't worried about getting jumped. At least it would be a one-on-one fight. Ant started telling everyone that he was going to beat me up when I left the arcade. Word spread like wildfire in the arcade; kids were whispering in each other's ears. I was in the middle of playing Centipede when Desiree came to warn me. I had noticed something going on but was distracted by my new high score.

"Ant is waiting outside for you. He wants to fight you. You should see if they'll let you go out the back."

I knew if I went out the back door, I would be running away and ashamed for as long as I lived there. Giant butterflies grew in my stomach. An empty hollow space filled my heart and sweat collected in my palms.

As I pondered my fate, I realized I had taken fierce beatings from a grown man who claimed to be the Creator of Us All. I knew that, if I lost, it wouldn't hurt nearly as much as that. I concluded that I could handle the pain, and doubt slowly turned to hope.

I remembered my brother Pio teaching the block-punch over and over again when I was younger. Pio was a fighter, and he would take me to see Bruce Lee movies and play-fight with me, a memory I cherished. Hope became courage, and, by the time I found myself outside, I was ready to fight.

The customary fighting routine for boys 9 to 13 was to first walk up close to each other, press our opposite shoulders against one another, walk in a circle, then abruptly push the other person away. I had seen it done before but had never experienced the ritual myself until that day. In the past when I had watched, the person who pushed first showed their dominance.

Unfortunately, he got off the first blow, which sent me stumbling back. His swing was what's known as a "haymaker", punching wildly with his right hand. Like so many times before in moments of heightened awareness, time slowed. All I could think was, *"Block! Punch!"* And, just as Pio and I had rehearsed so many times before, I put up my left forearm, blocking his punch. Then, I threw my counter punch with my right hand, which landed squarely between his eyes.

"Ooohhh!" the crowd erupted. He was a bit bigger, older, and stronger than me, so, when he charged me, he overpowered me and tackled me to the ground. Before he could begin pummeling me, the store owner grabbed him, saving me from a certain beating.

Some of the kids were on my side and some were on his. They all began debating who was the winner. When the store owner pulled him off me, his nose was bleeding. Most everyone concluded that Ant would have won if it hadn't been stopped, but I had earned everyone's respect for bloodying his nose and having shown heart. I definitely didn't want to fight anymore and the store owner held him there, giving me a head start home.

Desiree and some other kids walked me home, congratulating me and affirming that I won the fight. I was proud of giving Ant a bloody nose and thankful that I had a big brother somewhere who had loved me enough to teach me how to fight. I remembered Pio well and knew that somehow, one day, I would share the story of how our training had saved me in that moment.

I never told Omson and Freedom about my fight, as much as I wanted to brag about it, although they saw evidence of it a couple of days later in the alley behind the apartment complex. They had been sent to the corner store for some milk. A few minutes later, Freedom came running in the front door breathing heavily, scared, and pointing.

Om was asleep in the back room, and we were never to wake him. Freedom managed to convey that some boys in the alley were harassing the two of them. Having fought the toughest kid ever just a couple of days before, I was full of confidence as he and I arrived in the alley.

We saw Omson walking backwards toward us, away from a group of boys. I ran over to them and heard them questioning him. And, like so many times before, Omson's inability to articulate and communicate opened him up to being challenged and threatened. I recognized one of the boys from my fight with Ant and he recognized me.

"Who are you?" one of them asked.

"I'm his brother!"

"Where are y'all from?"

I pointed behind us to our building.

"What's wrong with him?"

"Nothing, he just don't talk much," I said.

I could tell these guys wanted to fight, but I had just enough confidence to stand my ground. The boy who remembered me told the others who I was under his breath and the leader said, "Who? Him?" and pointed at me. Then he asked me with a threatening growl, "Are you a Blood or a Crip?"

I didn't know what a Blood or a Crip was. For a moment, I thought he was referring to Anthony's blood, but somehow I knew that wasn't it. Having been scrutinized, cross-examined, and questioned by a master manipulator, it only took a fraction of a second for me to rebut with, "What are you?"

"I'm a Crip," he said proudly, and I answered, "Me, too." Immediately his growl turned to a smile, "Aww you alright den." Then he put his hand up to give me a high five. As our hands met he said, "I heard you socked that nigga Ant in the nose?"

"Yep."

"I don't like that nigga no way."

Omson and Freedom now had a new respect for me, even though Omson was now much stronger than me and could win an all-out fight. This incident made them revere me even more.

When we got home, Om was awake and ready to begin our beatings. Mine, for leaving without permission, and theirs for not being back when he got up. Freedom immediately began recalling the story to him, which he found amusing. To my surprise, he was pleased with me for being a good brother. It was a relief that no punishment was coming.

We were all watching the Lakers on the wall-mounted television one early evening after having Popeye's fried chicken for dinner. The one-bedroom apartment had the usual smell of incense and oils, but now with this new overlay of Popeye's fried chicken smell. Inspiration had not returned since her fight with Om, and we hadn't seen any of the others since we moved in. We all sat on the floor. Chairs or couches were never used. Om had his spot decorated with a colorful blanket that featured the Mexican eagle eating a serpent, a reminder of Mexico, and a time that seemed so long ago.

With no woman around to worship and suck his "Holy Cock," he was just another man eating fried chicken, watching the Lakers. He still commanded me around, as I was his slave, but, with these new freedoms, I didn't mind as much. I actually enjoyed not having the rest of the group around. He was a lot more relaxed and mellow when it was just the four of us – less like the Lord of the Universe All Powerful to be Worshipped and Adored. After the Lakers game, he went to sleep. I guess Popeye's made the Lord a little tired. He allowed us to stay up and watch *Charlie's Angels* reruns, which made me long for home even more, as that was one of Hippo's and my favorite shows.

The next day, Omson and I were sent to do laundry. This was a low level assignment that fit Omson's capability. I enjoyed getting away, no matter what the excuse. The laundromat was about a mile down Crenshaw. I had been there several times selling candles. Although carrying these very large bundles of laundry was difficult for us, we were accustomed to it. We had performed this task many times in Mexico.

Knowing the distance, I thought it would be smarter if we took a shopping cart from Thrifty's across the street. Once outside, I told Omson to wait for me at the bus stop while I ran and grabbed one. It made our job much easier, but I was embarrassed to be pushing our laundry down that busy street. I tried to convince him to push it down the alley, but he didn't want to because of the neighborhood kids who hung out there. So we agreed that Crenshaw was a safer choice and we could stop at the arcade.

When we finally got to the laundromat, it was business as usual. Except in child sequestered from social interactions for long periods of time, there grows a special curiosity about everything. On this day, that curiosity led me to rip a piece of newspaper into the size of a dollar bill to see if it would turn into quarters if I put it into the change machine. When it did, my stomach dropped. I had found the mother lode of all finds. I did it again and sure enough it worked again. I wanted to tell Omson, but greed and self-preservation prevented me from doing so.

I thought about how I could save enough money to buy a bus ticket back to Berkeley. I decided to keep the treasure to myself. I thought, *"If this machine takes paper maybe the washing machines would too,"* so I folded three pieces of paper, slid them into the slot and watched the wash cycle start. I was amazed.

All I had to do was convince Omson to let me do the washing and let him do the drying, and I could keep all the wash money, too. I had to trick him into it without raising suspicion, but I was unable to come up with a satisfactory story, so, reluctantly, I shared the information about the washers. He was just as happy as me, and, when I saw that, I appealed to his greed and explained how if we didn't tell anyone (meaning Om) that we could keep the money for ourselves and spend it at the arcade on the way back. He agreed, and my other moneymaking secret was safe.

The women often blamed me for corrupting Omson and Freedom. I guess it was true. On the way back, we stopped at the arcade to enjoy some video games and junk food. All the usual kids were out of school and said "Hi" to me. They asked me who Omson was and Omson was surprised I knew all of them. I explained that he was my brother and that we had another brother, too. I introduced him as Josh. But I couldn't really enjoy my time, mostly because I thought I might see Ant again and because we had a time restraint. I didn't want to be gone too long and raise suspicion about our whereabouts.

On our way out the door, Ant and another boy were just arriving on their bikes. Our shopping cart was parked just inside the store, which I was still embarrassed about. As we backed it up, I made eye contact with Ant. He gave me a smile and tilted his head up (a gesture that males use to acknowledge each other without actually greeting one another). I tilted mine and that was it. I didn't know why he didn't want to fight again, but was extremely relieved by his attitude. We hurried home and made it back before any suspicion arose.

The Lakers were playing again. After we put the laundry away, we joined Om and Freedom on the floor for a dinner of avocado, tomato, and cheese sandwiches on whole grain bread with organic tortilla chips and a cup of pomegranate juice to wash it down.

The next morning, I woke up excited. I couldn't wait to go back to the laundromat to my cash cow, my Rumpelstiltskin machine that turned newspaper into money. I knew I had to come up with a really good lie to convince him of why I needed to go out for the day.

So, I began the morning by picking up tiny dust, dirt, and lint balls from the carpet, that painstaking chore that could take hours to complete. Omson and Freedom were still sleeping when He walked past on His way to the bathroom. I was on my hands and knees below the television with my back to Him when he said, "You're free to go outside." I turned and he was smiling at me. I took the opportunity to try my lie.

"Holy Father, yesterday when we were doing laundry, one of my candle customers asked me to fill an order of five candles today. May I go deliver them?"

"Yes!" he said enthusiastically.

We went into His room to get them and I searched for a bag to carry them in . I needed to get out of there before Omson or Freedom woke up and asked if they could go with me. I was ready in a flash and out the door just as the two of them were waking up. The door closed behind me. I didn't want to carry the bag of candles all the way there, but I didn't want to risk the laundromat being closed, or worse, the machine not working, so I toted them all the way down Crenshaw as I had done so many times before.

The laundromat was open, and, to my surprise, empty. I put the bag of candles on top of a washing machine to look like I was doing laundry. There was Rumpelstiltskin, but I couldn't find my paper to turn into gold.

I decided to go next door to the liquor store and "liberate" the morning paper. I had become a very skilled thief, or kleptomaniac may be more ac-curate. I went back to the laundromat and sat down in the back corner to begin the manufacturing of the paper 'straw' that would become gold. I con-cluded that the most efficient way to work would be to first assemble one fake bill and see if it still worked, then begin the mass production. I went over to "Rumpelstiltskin" and fed him the one piece of straw. The machine accepted it and made a series of mechanical sounds. Then, like the sounds of the slot machines in the MGM Grand in Las Vegas, it produced shiny coins. Yes!

Back to my manufacturing plant in the corner, I made about 20 bills. As I completed the twenty, laundry patrons began to trickle in. I knew I had to be as inconspicuous as possible. If anyone asked, I would tell him or her I was doing a school project. Now, I could only do four or five at a time without drawing too much attention to myself.

I spent the whole day turning paper into gold. On my return home, I stopped to change the quarters back into paper at the arcade, but, instead of going inside and playing video games, I decided to steal Ant's bike. It was a 20" Red BMX. I made my mind up from seeing it lying on the sidewalk. I decided not to stop, I was going to walk right up, get on, and ride away. And that is exactly what I did.

When I got to our front door, I knocked the secret knock, "taptaptap, tap, tap tap." Om opened the door. He smiled, and I returned the smile. I had di-vided the money I owed him for the candles at one of the stores on the way home: $25 for him – and $85 for me.

Seeing the bike, He asked me, "Where did this come from?" I told him. Feeling very good about my pay and confident, I said, "It needed to be liber-ated." As I reached into my pocket and handed him his money, he laughed and gave me a small nod of appreciation.

Desiree and I had become close and she often invited me to her house. On occasion, her mom would invite me in, but, most times she told us to go play outside, which I preferred. Her mother was a very cantankerous woman who always seemed to be drunk. She drank the same whiskey that James drank. I could tell she liked me, but she tried to hide it.

One day, some of Desiree's cousins were visiting from another neighbor-hood and we all were hanging out in the alley behind our building. I was still in good graces and was enjoying socializing with the "worldly kids."

The "worldly kids" were trying to figure me out. Desiree's cousins were a few years older than me and wanted to know my story. They could tell I was lying, but their weak interrogation was far from cracking the wall of lies, secrets, and silence I'd spent almost six years cultivating.

Of course, as with all teenage kids, the topic of sex came up. Her older cousin, Tevon, asked me, "Are you a virgin?"

I scoffed and said, "Hell no. Are you?" He laughed and began berating me with questions about the female anatomy. All of which I answered, no problem. I remembered Dawn and Sierra and how we just took our clothes off and gyrated up and down, imitating what we thought were the sounds of sex. We were babies. On the other hand, I had been molested and wondered if that counted as de-virginization if it was against my will.

Desiree shyly admitted to being a virgin and didn't hold up as well under their interrogation. They teased and asked us about being "boyfriend and girlfriend", and, although we liked each other, we hadn't made it to that status. I didn't like them and it was making her uncomfortable, so I cut in and said, "Yes, she is my girl. So?"

Tevon said, "Let us see you kiss her then!"

Before I could reply with witty repartee, Desiree planted a giant, wet tongue kiss on me, which I returned out of shock. Everybody let out a loud, "Ooooh!" and started laughing. Then, one of the other kids dared us to "do it" in the janitor's closet. Before we knew it, the whole group was trying to get us to do it. Now, this was a lot of pressure, even for me.

Tevon said, "You like him, right?"

Desiree said, "Yes."

"And you like her, right?"

I said, "Yes."

"Then you guys should do it."

Desiree shrugged her shoulders and looked at me, asking with her eyes if I wanted to. I shrugged back, and so we both agreed under severe peer pressure. The crowd erupted with ooh's and aah's. As we sadly headed back to our building, the crowd followed, Desiree stopped and told them not to follow us, and I chimed in and said, "Yeah!"

She took my hand and led me to the janitor's room. I was really nervous and wondered to myself, *"Is this really going to happen?"* She closed the door behind us and asked with her squeaky voice, "Are you scared?" She must have seen the nervous look on my face on the way in. The closet was dark and smelled of cleaning supplies.

She now was far less shy, in fact, aggressive. She pushed me against the wall and kissed me hard. Suddenly, she pulled me down to lie on top of her. When we got to the floor I began humping on her, the only way I knew, up and down. She suggested we take our clothes off and that really made me nervous.

Even though I had been exposed to the most explicit sex acts a child could ever see, and had a grown woman molest me, this was making me extremely uneasy, nervous, and excited all at the same time. I could hear her cousins yelling out to us, and then laughing. I could feel her hairless body under me as we kissed and pressed our bodies against each other.

Her shorts were now all the way off, and she opened her legs wide. I was fully aroused and lost in her kiss.

The door swung open then, causing both of us to jump frantically. The silhouette of a tall dark figure stood over us as Desiree blindly grasped around for her shorts. I fell over trying to pull my pants up. The light outside the janitor's closet was out, making the closet hard to see into.

The voice said, "Desiree, is that you?"

She responded with a timid, "Yes."

And with that, the figure began violently grabbing down at us, striking us with slaps from his open hand. He cussed viciously, and, with one hand, snatched me up by my shirt and threw me into the hall. He speedily and clumsily ripped his belt from his pants and began swinging it wildly at Desiree. He screamed at me to go home and told me he would talk to my father later that night. Desiree didn't have her shorts on yet, so he stopped long enough for her to make several nervous attempts to get them on.

I stood there in shock and noticed none of the other kids were anywhere in sight. He grabbed her by her braids and turned back towards me. He feinted aggressively at me, pointed, and said, "Go home."

I slowly backed out of their way and watched him beat and whip her down the hall. She screamed and cried and begged him to stop. It caused such a commotion that some of the neighbors poked their heads out of their doorways to see what was happening. When they saw us, they quickly closed the doors, not wanting to get involved with our petty goings-on. His words were still ringing in my head: "I'ma tell your Daddy tonight."

I had broken one of the biggest rules of his manifesto: Don't draw attention to the group. Invisibility was paramount. Fear paralyzed me. Thoughts of the horrible consequences of my actions brought my hands to my head and forced me to squat down in disbelief.

I had had enough; I wasn't going to turn myself in like a good little soldier and pray and beg for mercy and forgiveness. There was only one thing I could do – run away!

I thought, *"I'm in the US now, in Los Angeles. That's close to home."* And, in that moment, I decided it was time.

I was so scared I was trembling. I felt sick to my stomach. I looked around nervously, sat down, and fantasized about how I might escape. I would have to do it quickly before Desiree's dad came back to tell Om what had happened. That meant, as casually as possible, going inside to get the money I'd stashed, grabbing it, and then taking off. I realized I didn't have a change of clothes. But I couldn't take the time to pack a bag.

There was a phone booth at the far end of the corridor. I had to pass Desiree's apartment door to get there. I thought about the courage it would take to walk past her door to get to it. There, I'd make two phone calls, one to a cab company and one to the Greyhound bus station.

The cab would drop me at the Greyhound station. I'd have to come up with a story for the ticket agent, like my father sent me in to get a ticket to visit my mom. Once in Oakland the next morning, with only the clothes on my back and about $45 in my pocket, I thought I would just ask the ticket agent how to get to Telegraph Avenue in Berkeley from the bus station.

It was two weeks before my 12th birthday, and, although I would be escaping from years of grotesque misery, I felt scared, like one of them might just pop up in Berkeley, grab me, and take me back. I figured I'd walk from the Greyhound station, then take a bus. I imagined I'd keep my head stuck to the window to see if I recognized any of the streets, buildings, or landmarks I once knew. And I'd ask the bus driver to tell me when we got to the campus, a landmark I remembered well.

My plan was to go to the Mediterraneum Café; that was forever etched into my memory as being my family's second home. I imagined as I approached Alta Bates hospital on Telegraph and Ashby that I would begin recognizing more and more of the buildings and streets.

I remembered the Co-op grocery store, where, when I was four or five, the police picked me up for being out at night with no parental supervision. I thought about the bank where my friend Mike Hughes used to get free candy. I knew that was somewhere on Telegraph. I thought about seeing my old school, Kilimanjaro/Odyssey.

I would look out the window at every fat white lady that passed by to see if she was my mom. I had forgotten what she looked like. When I got off the bus, I'd walk the block to the Med and notice the "Garden Spot" – my favorite store. I'd see the mural on the side of the building where Jaci, Mom, and I once took a picture and where James used to play his flute. Just a few more feet and I'd be home.

In my mind's eye, I walked into the Med ready to see Mom. I'd be back. But that was all a dream. A fantasy. In fact, I was too scared to leave, too crippled with self-doubt and a fading but still-strong Stockholm Syndrome as I recognized years later. I was resigned again to take my beating. I went back home and waited nervously for Desiree's father to come knocking on the door.

He never came. After a while, I was able to get some rest until I was awakened by Omson telling me we had been ordered to get up and begin packing all of our belongings. Half asleep and stricken with fear, I couldn't tell if I had been found out and was about to be surprised with some kind of punishment or if Omson was just messing with me. I soon gathered my senses and realized we were, in fact, packing up and moving. I couldn't believe how lucky I was. It was 2 a.m., and it appeared I was going to get away with it. It took us a couple of hours to pack everything into the old black van I had helped to steal back in San Diego.

As usual, I didn't know why we were moving or where we were going, but I was ecstatic to be leaving, though my heart twinged for a moment with longing for Desiree. The late hour and the hum of the van's motor made it easy to fall back asleep. We arrived at a dilapidated house in the ghetto of a city I didn't know. It was on the corner of 29th Street and Cutting Blvd. in Richmond, which at the time I didn't realize was very close to Berkeley.

I recognized we were in a ghetto because of the winos that were hanging out on the corner and the garbage that littered the street, not to mention the boarded-up house we entered. The three-bedroom house smelled of mildew and rot. I could tell by the stink and dust that rose from the central heating vents that the heater hadn't been turned on in a long time.

I hated it the second I saw it. I knew it was going to be hell cleaning every nook and cranny of this filthy, disgusting house. The bathroom was stained and revolting. That, of course, was my job. I spent a week cleaning and scrubbing and painting, along with Omson and Freedom. Eventually, it became livable.

Soon after we arrived, the rest of the group showed up. Even Harmony showed up, whom I had not seen in a long time. The entire cult was back under the same roof. Not long after, Om was sending me on assignments again. I was now a mature, capable con artist/thief who could be relied on to carry out assignments with relatively little supervision.

Harmony returned with her baby girl, who had been born around the time we were living in the storefront. Her baby was always sick and crying. Everyone was out on assignment during the days that followed. I was sent out with Inspiration, mostly on 'liberation' missions, and I sensed she had her own assignments on other days.

On an assignment that required taking the bus across town, I recognized the bus line. It was AC Transit, the bus line from Berkeley. I remembered putting quarters in the change receptacle as a kid and being mesmerized as I watched them fall through the glass case. "This is definitely the same AC Transit," I thought, even though I still didn't know how to read. I didn't want to ask Inspiration for confirmation either, so I just kept quiet and looked for landmarks I might recognize.

Riding the bus all day, stopping at different stores and businesses, not knowing what we were doing or why, I was happy to be out of the house and away from Om. Shockingly, all of a sudden, I realized we were on Telegraph Avenue!

I couldn't keep quiet any longer. "Hey, I know where we are!" We were on the corner of Dwight Way and Telegraph Avenue. "The Med is right up there," I said enthusiastically.

"How would you like to see your mom?"

"Yeah, I want to see her and Pio and Jaci and Isabella AND Hippo."

"Okay, let's go look for her."

We walked up and down Telegraph several times after checking the Med. Everything was the same – the smell of ground coffee and pastries, the loud swishing sound of the espresso machine, and the noisy, relentless chatter coming from every table. Even the paintings on the wall were the same. I looked up at the giant face of Poseidon, the Greek God of the Ocean. It had scared me when I was younger, but now it was just a harmless face. I walked around looking for my mom or any familiar face I might recognize. Eventually, we headed back home. I was disappointed, but I now knew I was back!

Inspiration asked me probing questions about how I felt, what I thought, and more pointed questions like, did I want to go back to my mom? I gave vague answers and felt confused inside. Partly, I didn't trust her not to "report" everything I might say. I didn't know if Mom wanted to see me. Maybe she didn't want me to come back. I just didn't know. When we got back home, Om was mad about something and Authority, one of Devi's babies, was crying.

Authority was standing in the doorway naked, screaming at the top of his two-year-old lungs, when Om walked in, snatched him up by his ankle, and tossed him into the bathroom. He was so shocked, he couldn't cry. He was gasping for air and silent as his lungs slowly filled. I went to the bathroom to help him, and, as I picked him up, he let out a blood-curdling scream. I carried him to the back room away from Om. His little body was trembling in my arms. I learned to take care of children very well, and I had a special bond with Devi's children because they were the least loved of all his kids.

Eventually, I was able to console him with a bottle of milk I'd received permission to give him. He fell asleep in my arms. The next morning, Om had the three of us boys unload the trash from the back of our moving truck into the garbage truck that was making its rounds.

We were trying to unload as fast as possible because the city garbage truck had a time schedule. I accidentally threw away the fake California driver's license board that Perfection had crafted back in Las Vegas. It was kept between two pieces of plywood. The second it left my hands I knew what it was, and I watched the metal arm of the truck snap it in two as it fell into the heap of garbage; the light blue color vanished in the depths of filth. Luckily, Omson and Freedom were so busy they didn't notice my hesitation and regret, which I instinctively hid.

This was the biggest blunder of all. I knew that, when Om found out, the outcome for me was going to be very, very bad. So, I decided I wasn't going to be around when he asked where it was. It was this blunder that made up my mind. I didn't care if Mom didn't want me. I was getting out of there at the very next opportunity.

The opportunity came while out on assignment with Inspiration. She told me to meet her on the corner of Cutting and San Pablo, after our assignment to liberate some "food spirits" from different health food stores in our local area. I decided this was my opportunity. I got on the 72 bus line that ran along San Pablo Ave. I asked the bus driver to let me know when we got to Berkeley. He asked me where in Berkeley, and I told him I wanted to go to Telegraph Avenue.

"University Avenue is your exit, then take the 51 line, and that will take you to Telegraph."

I sat near the driver so I could hear him when he called out my exit.

"University Avenue, this is your stop, young man."

I crossed the street as he directed me and waited for the 51. I was spooked that one of the cult members might see me, but I pressed on. I asked the new bus driver to tell me when we got to Telegraph.

When we arrived at the right stop, I was excited but extremely nervous. I walked down Telegraph looking for people I might know. I still thought every fat white lady might be my mom. I walked into the Med, this time thinking I would see a familiar face. I saw no one. So I went upstairs. There at the first table was a face I knew. I didn't remember his name or from where, but I knew him.

I walked up to him and said, "I know you!"

And he said, "I know you, too! What's your name, kid?"

"Jabali."

He jumped out of his seat. His face lit up with a huge smile and tears swelled in his eyes as his arms opened wide to embrace me. He said, "It's me ... Bill ... Bill Jackson." Bill Jackson was a friend of my mother's and father's, and he was the man who had introduced my father to the Jehovah's Witness religion/cult. Bill hugged me and asked if I was with my mom. I told him I wasn't but that I was looking for her. He immediately took my hand and said, "Let's go find her."

Bill asked me a thousand questions as he led me up the street towards campus. I answered some questions and lied about others but was happy to be with him. He asked me if I had seen my dad and assured me he would contact him if we were unable to find my mom. Then he walked me to a store called Dzinu House, which was Jackie's store. I was so happy to hear her name and knew that, if I found her, I would be safe. She wasn't there, but a cute employee by the name of Dari was, and, after an introduction, she made some phone calls and left messages. She assured me that Jackie would call back as soon as she got the messages. In the meantime, she recommended I stay close by and check back in 30 minutes or so.

Bill asked me if I was hungry and suggested we go back to the Med for some food and the possibility that we might run into my mom. Now that I had made contact with Jackie via her store, I really didn't want to hang with Bill anymore, so, on the way back to the Med, I asked if Silverball, the arcade, was still up the street. He wasn't sure and offered to take me.

I declined as nicely as I could and suggested we could meet back at the Med in a half hour, and, if he saw my mom, to tell her to meet me at either Dzinu House or the Med. He reluctantly agreed, and I headed to Silverball to play some videogames. After a couple dollars' worth of video games, I headed back to Dzinu House. Dari told me Jackie had not responded yet, so I left again. This time, I walked through People's Park and relished in the idea of being home. Then I walked down to The Berkeley Hat Shop, thinking I might steal a new hat.

While trying to look like a shopper, I was met with a surprise.

"It's me, your brother, Pio!" He welcomed me with open arms, and I gave him a huge hug and said, "I know who you are!" It turns out Pio and my mom had been sitting in the window of the restaurant where the old Garden Spot had been. They had watched me walk back and forth with Bill, not realizing who I was.. After Mom had gone home on the bus, Pio had coincidentally poked his head into Dzinu House, and it was Dari who had told him I was looking for my mom. He then realized it was me whom he had been watching, so he had taken off to look for me up and down Telegraph Avenue.

Pio and I walked down to Mom's house on 61st and Telegraph. We talked along the way and reminisced about the old days. I asked about Dawn, Hippo, Jaci, Isabella, Aki, Hilary, and my other good friends, Lion and Johnny. He assured me we would meet up with all of them soon.

I wanted to burst into tears and ask them why they'd left me. *What did I do to make Mom mad at me?* But I pushed those thoughts deep down in my heart and nervously awaited meeting my mom. Pio's excitement in seeing me made me feel so good, but I was unable to express back to him the mutual excitement I felt. I was afraid to show it.

On the way to my mother's house, my emotions went into full lockdown. I wasn't going to show any vulnerability whatsoever, a teaching I developed to ensure my survival under the constant psycho-emotional attacks from Om and his women.

Pio pushed the buzzer of a two-story duplex. It was across the street from a miniature golf course where I used to play. We walked up a long flight of stairs, and, at the top, the door had been left ajar. I walked in and saw James's acoustic bass leaning up against the wall. I was happy to see it there. It meant that he was still around.

My mom was sitting at a small round kitchen table, smoking a cigarette. A cup of coffee sat comfortably next to a half-smoked joint. Our eyes met, but she didn't recognize me. She looked at Pio then back at me, and said, "Who is this?"

"Jabali!" Pio said with a high-pitched screech that implied "You fool!"

Her face lit up. She stood up smiling, and we embraced. After fending off her questions with truth-colored lies, I explained how Om and the Om lovers tortured me, starved me, beat me, molested me, and took any and all dignity I had away from me. I told them how they humiliated me. She sat there listening in disbelief, not at the shock and horror of what her youngest son went through, but actually thinking I was lying.

I didn't know she didn't believe me or my siblings until 25 years later, when, in a conversation with my son's mother, she told her that none of those things ever happened. In fact, up until the finishing of this book, she has stayed loyal to Om – but not loyal enough to have committed herself to Him and the stringent lifestyle he and his followers led in 1977. But she had been willing to give up her sons instead of cigarettes. And she had offered up her daughter's virginity instead of her missing morning cup of coffee.

After talking for what seemed like an eternity and my several requests to visit Hippo, who apparently lived around the corner, Pio recognized my exhaustion and agreed to take me over, telling Mom we would be back later that night. We walked over to Hippo's, and, as we were walking down the street, I saw a figure in the middle of the street about half a block away. It was Hippo.

For some reason he started walking directly towards us. When he got up close, I could see that he was a full foot taller than me. I couldn't believe it. We hugged tightly and looked deeply into each other's eyes. I was so happy to see him. I loved him so much.

Hippo was my best friend. I immediately asked him if he remembered when we cut open our index fingers and pressed them together to become blood brothers. He said, "Of course," and then proceeded to tell me where it happened. Then he described another one of our many adventures, when I was five and he was six, and we'd gotten lost while walking to his parents' house on 63rd and Telegraph from Codornices Park in North Berkeley and had to knock on a stranger's door to ask for help.

After a while of reminiscing, we went back to my mom's and had a small reunion, absent of Jaci and Isabella. I would meet up with them later. The next morning, as my mom and I were leaving the duplex, I saw Inspiration across the street. She was peering into the window of a storefront. At first glance, a stranger would think nothing of a woman who was so curiously looking into a storefront, but I recognized by her body language that she was doing reconnaissance.

Om must have sent her after me once they realized I didn't come back the night before. My mom got really nervous and took me out the back, between the two buildings and off into the neighborhood. Walking briskly, we made our way to a friend's house, where I stayed all day until the nighttime. Mom assured me everything would be okay and that she would return later that night. I didn't know the woman whose house it was, but she was pleasant enough and let me watch TV. Eventually, she needed to leave the house, and she asked if I was okay being there alone. I told her I would be fine and she gave me the run of her house.

"You can have whatever you want. This is your house." I don't think that included the Swiss army knife I found in her son's room, but I took it anyway. ("Liberating" things had been so ingrained in me that I didn't give it a second thought at the time.)

This time, Mom really did come back, and she told me her plan. We were going to live in a place called Covelo up in the mountains. I told her I didn't want to leave Berkeley, but she thought the cult might try to capture me. So we moved to Covelo, despite my objections. Mom told me we would move back after things cooled down. She seemed happy to have me back, but I would not fully understand why she did what she did for another twenty years.

Covelo was a small logging town in the mountains of Northern California's Mendocino County that had a population of about one thousand people. I found out that Isabella, my sister whom I absolutely loved and adored, was living in Covelo with her two-year-old daughter, Liliah. I was really excited to be able to see her again and couldn't wait to be in her arms. I didn't blame her for leaving me; it hurt me, but I understood. Having to watch my sister be molested had given me a uniquely empathetic perspective.

The bus dropped my mom and me right in front of where we would be staying. It was a small, three-bedroom house with a cute little white-picket fence around it. It belonged to a friend of my mom's.

Isabella lived around the corner in a small studio apartment. She was waiting for us at the house. The door opened and there she was, just as happy to see me as I was to see her!

"Bali!" she exclaimed on my embrace. If I had been capable of crying, I would have shed a thousand tears in that moment. Her eyes were sparkling green, and I was now taller than her. More than her height was her now curly hair. It was almost like an Afro. That was so surprising because I knew it to be long and straight. She introduced me to my niece, Liliah, a beautiful little girl with amazing blue eyes and straight black hair like her mother's had once been.

"You're an uncle now, Bali," Isabella said.

I swelled with pride. Her pronouncement gave me my first taste of a long-forgotten feeling of family. Life in Covelo was a slow reintroduction to the regular world. I found the neighborhood kids and quickly made friends. Still full of lies, I made up stories of what grade I was in and why I wasn't in school, but at least I was back with my real family and I felt a degree of safety. I listened to Prince's "Little Red Corvette" and Pat Benatar's "Hell is for Children," which caused my sister to raise her eyebrows.

Although my life was getting better, and things looked okay from the outside, on the inside, I was still very brainwashed with the cult ideology, and I was plagued with nightmares in which giant waves were overcoming me and destroying me.

I had my twelfth birthday in Covelo. Some of the new neighborhood friends came, along with Isabella, Liliah, and Mom. They all sang Happy Birthday, not knowing that song hadn't been sung to me in six years. Mom got me a puppy, which I named Poppy. It was some kind of Japanese dog that was supposed to be super smart. I liked it, but I really just wanted to be back in Berkeley with Hippo and the crew. And I wanted to go to school to learn to read and write and do math.

But Mom wouldn't enroll me in school because she said it was the middle of the school year. She tried to convince me that I didn't need school at all. She said, "It's all bullshit, honey." But, finally, she agreed to do it the following year, and, in the meantime, we were going to move out of the town and further into the mountains.

I asked Mom if I could stay with Isabella, but Isabella was moving back to Berkeley, probably to get away from Mom. Mom and I moved into a small log cabin located about 10 miles up the mountain. There was no electricity and the bathroom was an outhouse about 20 yards behind the cabin. It was as if we'd moved back in time 100 years to 1883. In the middle of the log cabin was an old wood-burning stove, and a long, black exhaust pipe escaped straight up through the roof. Above it was a small window.

Someone had recently been living there. There was a bed pushed up against the far wall with the bedding disheveled. A pair of men's boots sat next to it, one knocked over on its side.

It turned out my mother had negotiated herself into a huge pot growing operation. She agreed to water and feed the plants for the harvest season in exchange for some of the proceeds. She didn't tell me any of this, but she especially didn't tell me that I would be her work mule.

When I figured it out after days of carrying water from a pump outside the house to the weed plot 75 yards into the brush, I protested, only to be slapped and beaten by her. I ran crying into the brush, sloshing the gallons of water, cursing her under my breath.

Why did I come back? Sometimes, she would leave me there overnight while she partied with the neighbors who lived about two miles up the road from us. All those years of solitary confinement allowed me to handle being left alone in a log cabin by myself at the tender age of 12.

The neighbors were a nice hillbilly family that consisted of Dale, the ex-biker-turned-logger dad, Janet, his wife, who had part of her arm lost due to a logging accident, and their son, Scott, who enjoyed fishing, hunting, and killing random animals for sport. They seemed very happy and content with their lives, and they all treated me very kindly, even though my kleptomania forced me to steal anything and everything that wasn't nailed down.

Dale and Janet thought it was amusing, but Scott didn't like it. He waited until we were alone and grabbed me by the front of my shirt with one hand, pulled me close into his face and warned me to give back the pen with the digital clock that I had stolen.

I did what he said, more because I liked him and his family, rather than just because I was afraid of getting beat up. Also, his name was Scott, my old alias.

Then someone came to the cabin while we were visiting Dale and his family and cut down and stole every plant I had watered. Mom decided it wasn't safe to live at that cabin anymore, so we stayed with Dale and his family.

Living with them was wonderful. I loved every day there and looked forward to every day to come. A wild bear broke into the chicken coop one night and ate three or four chickens right there on the spot. A couple of nights later, it was back, claiming more chickens. So, a plan went into action to rid ourselves of this very hungry bear. We decided that, since I was a very light sleeper (due to my post-traumatic stress which they knew nothing about), I would sleep out on the porch, and, if I heard anything, I would quietly come in and get Dale. So that night, as I slept, I was awakened to the sounds of chickens squawking and heavy rustling in the coop. I tiptoed into the house and whispered to Dale, "Dale!" He didn't wake up, I tried again. "Dale, the bear is outside!"

"What?" he shouted. "The bear?" He jumped up and tripped over his boots while trying to pull up his pants. He hit the floor with a loud thud, then screamed out, "Shit! Where's my rifle?"

It was a scene right out of the Three Stooges movies, as I watched him fumbling and tripping over himself in the dark. Meanwhile, Scott and his dad's hunting buddy shouted loud whispers to each other. "Get the rifle!" "Where are my boots?"

They were too slow that night. The bear had his dinner and disappeared into the dark. The next night, we decided that Dale's hunting buddy Tom and I would wait outside on the hill that overlooked the chicken coop. Tom was a better shot than Dale, and I was the light sleeper.

We settled on a perch with a direct shot at the front of the coop where the bear had been entering. We brought no food for fear of it being smelled by the bear. However, we had eaten a full meal of beef stew to get us through the night. Unfortunately, whatever was in that stew had Tom and me farting all through the night. When the bear didn't show up, I blamed it on our horrific gas. They all thought that was ridiculous and hilarious. They scoffed at me. *The little city boy thinks that farts kept the bear away.* The next night, we didn't eat the stew and perched ourselves once again at our spot and waited.

Tom and I had fallen asleep in firing position with the thirty-aught-six high-powered rifle aimed at the front of the coop. I leaned on his shoulder with a flashlight that rested directly on top of the barrel. Suddenly, I heard a rustling in the distance. I waited a few moments to be sure. I tried to make out a figure but could see nothing in the moonless night. Then I heard the branches snap under something's heavy feet. I struggled to wake Tom with a hard nudge. I whispered and pointed in the bear's general direction. He aimed the red laser scope onto the ground in front of the cage and told me to turn on the flashlight. We waited with nerve-shattering expectancy, and then, there stood a huge, magnificent bear. She was about 4.5 feet tall on her hind legs. Her head was enormous, her eyes sat about 12 inches apart as they reflected back a beautiful green hypnotizing emptiness from the flashlight. The red dot of death sat squarely between them.

Tom pulled the trigger. CLICK. The safety was on. The bear looked up at us as it surveyed the area, turned, and ran back into the night. Inside, I was thankful for the mishap. Tom cursed, removed the safety, and fixed a deafening shot blindly in the dark that echoed over the mountainside. Everyone came running out onto the deck, and Dale yelled out to us, "Did you get the sonofa-bitch?" Neither of us responded.

Tom stood up and in a disappointed sigh said, "No."

"What the hell happened?" Dale demanded.

"Well," I said, "we had the laser right between his eyes, but the safety was on."

"What?" Dale began ridiculing his buddy like an older brother does when his young sibling has ruined the game.

The next day, Dale organized a hunting party to track the bear and kill it once and for all. That afternoon, about 15 rednecks showed up in Jeeps with hunting dogs and an artillery of weaponry. The leader was Dale's cousin, a crazy looking white man with a cowboy hat and a patch over one eye. They converged in Dale's living room and held a meeting that was reminiscent of an old John Wayne cowboy movie.

I loved it and felt especially proud that I was part of this thrilling adventure. They asked me which direction the bear had come from the night before, and I proudly showed them. They began tracking her from an area by the trees just beyond the chicken coop. They allowed me to come along through the trees and underbrush. We came to a clearing a lengthy distance into the manzanita trees. There on the ground in the center of the clearing were the carcasses of all the chickens the bear had consumed and the wild turkey Dale had caught just days before the incidents began.

Dale was especially perturbed that the bear had made off with his

Thanksgiving turkey. It, along with several of the chickens, had been flayed open with what looked like one clean strike right down the middle of their sternums. Then their ribcages had been opened and cleaned out. The hunters were amazed at the cleanliness of each kill. They also determined it was a mother who was feeding her two young cubs. They decided to get in their trucks and scour the countryside since some of the dogs had picked up their scent. I wasn't allowed to continue on with the hunt after that.

Dale said I was too young, but his son Scott got to go, and that made me really mad. He was two years older than me and much stronger, but I still thought it was unfair that I wasn't allowed to go. Sadly, I stood at the top of the driveway and watched them all drive away, determined to kill a bear.

A short time later, while sitting in Janet's kitchen with one of her girlfriends, I told her my story ... the whole thing. She was blown away and flabbergasted to learn about what I had endured, and she immediately hated my mother, who was away in town on this particular day.

When Mom came back later that afternoon, Janet and her friend confronted my mom, which led to a violent screaming match that Dale had to referee. The next morning, we got on a bus back to Berkeley. Mom left everything we couldn't carry.

Mom screamed and yelled at me for hours, telling me that I was forbidden to talk about "it" anymore – ever! She used the same technique to keep me quiet as the cult did – fear, lies, manipulation, and bullying. She told me that the FBI might take me away and send me off to live with strangers. I didn't want to be sent away again, so I promised never to tell. I was kind of sad to be leaving the redneck mountain dwellers. They were nice people. And I was happy they never caught the bear.

Next, we moved into an apartment in West Oakland after staying at Jackie's house for a while. Finally, I was enrolled in Peralta, a year-round elementary school on Alcatraz and Telegraph in North Oakland.

I could not read or write or do arithmetic, but somehow, through the broken education system and my mother's 20 years' experience of manipulating social services, Welfare, and the entire system at large, I was able to be enrolled into the 5th grade, even though my academic level was at or below the first grade. However, through all the years of being preached to, I had developed quite a large vocabulary and an intellectual understanding that was far beyond my years. With street smarts and an acute ability to read people, along with an awareness of my environment, I assimilated into school life.

Still, I was always hiding an aspect of myself, forever keeping "the secret" safe; I wanted to be normal in order to not be found out. Sometimes I lost my sense of reality because I was living countless different lives and lies. Although this was not foreign to me, now that I was back, I wished and wondered when it could stop. I wished there was someone with whom I could confide all my secrets.

There was an innocence at Peralta that, on some level, was healing for me. All the kids were happy playing their schoolyard games, obviously unaware of the cruel world that existed just outside the gates. Their world of innocence was a "lie" I thoroughly enjoyed, but at three o'clock every day, it came to an end.

I spent most days on Telegraph Avenue with Hippo and Blaine. Blaine was a kid Hippo had befriended while I was gone. All of our parents knew each other before any of us were born. But Blaine and his older brother Pat were from Santa Cruz. They had moved to Oakland to live with their mother. Blaine was a little older than me but my same size. He had a competitive spirit that rivaled mine. He was a handsome, blonde-haired, blue-eyed kid who would take any dare, anytime.

Blaine became my new best friend for the next twenty years. Hippo, Blaine, and I were inseparable. They both had a huge weed habit, and everyday involved finding some weed to smoke. I was willing to smoke with them but didn't understand the need to smoke every day. Our adventures through and around Berkeley and Oakland, looking for weed, stealing, and finding and creating mischief wherever we could, was the beginning of my life of attempting to free myself of the horrible secrets that I still held in silence.

I barely passed the 5th grade that year. My teacher, Ms. Thomas, told me that I had a lot of work to do to catch up to my age group. I was thirteen when I was finishing the 5th grade. Mom threw a party for my 13th birthday and invited all her and James's friends, which consisted mostly of old ex-hippies, beatniks, and jazz musicians. A select few of my friends attended and had a pretty good time. Mom didn't get me anything. She said it cost money to throw a party. I guess when you supply all the food and booze, there's not a lot leftover for gifts.

When I showed my friends my room, they were startled to learn that I lived in a closet, and they asked me why. The truth was, like many war vets, ex-cons, POWs, and survivors of trauma and torture, there is posttraumatic stress (PTSD) to contend with. PTSD manifested itself in many different ways for me, one of which was that I felt safe in a closet after all the years where it had been my one safe place. I didn't realize how absurd this was, even after that embarrassing moment. I tried to move out and sleep in the living room, but didn't like it and moved back into the closet, where I stayed for the next year.

I attempted to go to the 6th grade, but felt so ashamed of my illiteracy that I dropped out of school for the next two years. But I still had a strong desire to learn, so I often sat down and wrote out the ABC's over and over again. I wanted to make sure my handwriting would be legible.

I spent most of my days sleeping in late. Mom had no understanding as to why I didn't want to get up early. I was depressed, but I didn't have the language to understand it or articulate my feelings. Maybe in a normal family after a traumatic experience, the parents and family would go and find a therapist to consult with, and maybe they'd hire a tutor to help with schooling. Maybe the child would even be allowed a voice to speak the pain that plagued him.

As much as I was glad to be home, I was heartbroken at what I came back to. Mom was sociopathic in her inability to empathize with what her children had been through. Pio was busy being a rock star in his band, "The Freaky Executives." Isabella was busy raising Liliah, and Jaci was growing into a bigger bully with the help of drugs and alcohol. It's fair to say they were all on their way to becoming alcoholics and drug addicts. James, one of the few I felt I could really trust, told me all the things that happened to me were good for me and would help make me a man. Although that hurt me, somewhere inside I thought he might be right.

TEN

Fun Fun Fun

I was now 14 and did not want any authority figure telling me what to do. Mom told me that if I didn't want to live by her rules I should move out. I spent the next year on the streets with Blaine and Hippo. The corner of Telegraph and Durant was the place where I would hang out with a slew of other street kids – Dave, Nate, Pat, Derrick, Mike, Ray, and Tony, among countless others.

We were a varied mix of kids from Berkeley. Some came from money but most didn't. Some were black, some were white, and some were Latino, Asian, and every mixture of race born out of the Berkeley 60s scene. We were half-cursed, half-blessed, and all lost.

All these guys were older than me, some over 21, and they all sold drugs to the "squids," the Navy boys from the Alameda Naval Base, as they were called. The squids created a steady supply of business when they came to town, along with the locals, Cal students, the drug addicts, and other regulars.

We played video games at Silverball, smoked weed on the Cal campus, and found trouble everywhere, especially on Thursday, Friday, and Saturday nights at the Cal Berkeley fraternity parties, or "the frats" as we called them. I was now well-acquainted with most all of Berkeley's young drug dealers, pimps, thieves, and con men.

All of my siblings had a reputation. Pio, the musician, public speaker, and activist would just as soon bite off the ear of a foe as come to the rescue of anyone he called friend. Isabella was the gifted consigliore of all who needed a loving and understanding friend. Jaci was the enforcer. If anyone needed unquestioned "back up," he was their guy. Then there was me, baby brother to all. I was given carte blanche in the city that I loved.

On early summer evenings, everyone would head up to "the wall" or "lookout" at the top of the Berkeley Hills above the Lawrence Hall of Science. It's a beautiful stretch of road that offers a spectacular view of San Francisco, Oakland, Berkeley, and the entire Bay Area.

Another hangout spot that attracted Berkeley's young hustlers was the Town and Country Pool Hall on University Ave at Sacramento. This was where I met some of the most ruthless, biggest pimps in Berkeley: Joker, Moon, and Yellow. Yellow was my favorite. He was a smooth-talking, light-skinned, black man with long, shoulder-length, curly hair. Short and muscular, he reminded me of my Uncle Stanley on my dad's side. He would give me money for video games and let me ride along in his 1979 Deville Cadillac as he checked up on his "hoes." He would tell me to collect the money from them through the passenger window.

When they saw my baby face, the harshness of the streets disappeared for a moment as each one looked into my eyes. Then, in the same fraction of a section, their look would transform back into the cold harshness of the pimp/hoe relationship as their eyes met his. I was shocked to see how much money they gave him, but he never seemed content with what they handed over.

He told me, "Bitches ain't shit! They got to pay to play!"

He would preach the pimp game to me as we drove around. Although it had an effect on me, it was weak in comparison to what I had been exposed to by Om – still, it was basically the same rhetoric: *"I am number one. Give everything you own to me or suffer a terrible fate!"*

What I came to understand is that Om took Jaci and me from our mother in exchange for the right to fuck her daughter. Mom knowingly, willingly, and enthusiastically acquiesced. She got "pimped." It wasn't until years later that a Muslim man told me, when I jokingly referred to him as "Big Pimp," that a pimp is a real man's worst enemy because a pimp will take your sister and pimp her, take your mother and pimp her, and, if you're so inclined, will pimp you, too!

But, back then, I thought I was going to grow up and become a pimp to make a living. The money, the respect, the clout, the women, and the life were very attractive to me. Yet, still I longed for something greater – to have fun! Fun was all I sought, no matter what.

I spent many nights at Hippo's house. His mom lived with a man who called himself the "Hateman." He was a local Telegraph Avenue crazy who, among other things, wore a dress, had a long, grey beard, and wore one Chuck Taylor High Top on his left foot and a lady's red patent-leather stiletto on his right. His head was covered in a balding Jew-fro and his angular facial features made him all the more puzzling.

If you greeted him with a "Hello," or a "Hi, how are you?" he would reply,

"Fuck you!" But, if you said, "Fuck you!" he would happily reply with, "I hear you!" The other peculiarity about him was, if you ever wanted anything from him, whether a question answered, a glass of water, or a hit of his weed, you had to "push." "Pushing" meant pressing the palm of your hand against his palm for a couple of minutes before he was willing to share anything. How attached he was to a given item or piece of information determined how long the "push" was required. So that became the way I "paid rent."

I tried sneaking in Hippo's window, but Hateman always heard me and would knock on Hippo's door and say, "Hey! You have to push if you want to stay the night!"

The rumor was that he had been a reporter for the New York Times and that he'd uncovered a government conspiracy so ugly he went crazy. It was also the perfect cover in case men in black ever thought that he was a threat. There were a lot of cliques in Berkeley, but I never related to any of them. Any kind of group repulsed me. I liked the individuals, but I stayed clear of the cliques and groups. I guess, on a sociological level, I did group up, but I thought I was maintaining my autonomy.

Some weeks, I would hang with Pio's musician friends, sometimes Jaci's hustling waterfront friends, or Isabella's beautiful girlfriends. Then there were my old friends and new sets of friends that I created on my own. One thing stayed the same – I was always lying to keep my secret safe. I was always silent, trying to protect Om, Mom, and the ugly shame of my past. I was still trapped, still imprisoned in the silence of a child's broken heart.

Before Mom moved back to Berkeley, she told me I was welcome to come live with her and that I would have my own room. I was tired of couch-surfing and decided to go back to school.

Mom reminded me I would have to live by her rules, which I apprehensively agreed to. The place was on Derby Street in Berkeley. I was happy to have a room of my own and looked forward to going to Willard Junior High. But, before I could enroll, I needed Mom to work her magic with the Berkeley School District. After an interview with a school counselor and some red tape, I was enrolled in the 8th grade.

Meanwhile, Mom was dealing weed, and she cut me in on the action. This allowed me to hone a much-needed arithmetic skill. I sold dime bags at school, then walked the four or five blocks to Telegraph and Durant to get rid of the rest. Blaine went to Montera Junior High in the Oakland Hills, and Hippo attended Berkeley High School.

We always met on Telegraph, but there were no cell phones, so it was often a hit-or-miss situation. While making a name for myself as the weed dealer to a smll group of kids, I met two precocious young girls: Sarah and Leila. Sarah was very pretty with long, brown hair and she dressed like she knew it. Leila was blonde, just as cute but not so sure of her beauty.

One Friday, after selling them a bag, we snuck over to the back of Willard Park, once known as Ho Chi Minh, to smoke a little before class. Sex was the topic, as it was with all kids our age. They were probing me about my sexual experiences, and I totally lied and bragged about my many conquests. Neither of them believed me and teased me about being a virgin. I have often wondered if the molestation I experienced was my de-virginization. Or was it when I was a willing participant, or when I actually ejaculated for the first time?

In any case, as the bell rang, I told the two of them to call me if they ever wanted to have a good time. They walked away giggling, and I walked toward English class, still wondering about my virginity. I was suddenly too high to go to class, so I decided to go up to Durant and sell the last couple of dime bags. It didn't occur to me that none of the dope users would be up this early in the morning. Luckily, I was only three steps into my journey when I had this epiphany about the smokers and decided to turn back and force myself through English with the hopes of seeing Sarah and Leila at the lockers.

That night, the phone rang while I was watching *Nightrider*. Mom screamed, "It's for you!" in her angry, burly voice from her smoky, alcohol infused room.

"Okay!" I screamed back, annoyed that I was being pulled away from Kit. The voice on the other end sounded raspy and cute. It was Sarah and Leila on a three-way call. They were inviting me over to make good on the promise of a good time.

After some flirting and innuendos, Sarah said, "Well, are you going to come over or what?"

"Yeah! Here I come!" I said. I wasn't sure how I was going to get there because we still lived in West Oakland, and I didn't have the 40 cents it took to get on the bus. Asking Mom was out of the question, and James was out playing a gig. I decided to walk.

All those years of traversing the streets of Mexico City with Inspiration at ridiculous speeds for hours at a time made walking 40 or 50 blocks a breeze, especially with the fantasy about what was waiting for me. I used the same technique, a very fast-paced walk that resembled a mild jog.

It took me about an hour. When I got to Russell and Telegraph, I found them standing on the corner, smoking cigarettes and waiting for me. We walked half a block up Russell to Leila's house. Her mom was gone, and we had the house to ourselves. We went straight to Leila's room and the three of us stripped down to our underwear. Following Sarah's lead, we got under the covers. I was very nervous inside, "like a long tailed cat in a room full of rocking chairs," but I used my skills to hide it.

The lights were dim and Prince's *1999* album played softly in the background. A pair of candles burned on the windowsill at the head of the bed. My nervousness subsided a little, but the thing that made me most nervous was the fact that I had no pubic hair. The shame of that alone had almost prevented me from going to meet them altogether.

Now that I was under the covers, I felt a little bit safer. I lay between them, not knowing exactly what to do. I decided to be the first to take off my underwear and they followed suit. We were all lying on our backs, so I decided to turn my head to kiss Leila, then turned it to kiss Sarah. Back and forth I kissed them. Each kiss became longer and more sensual.

Finally, I rolled onto Leila and humped and grinded on her while kissing her deeply. She frustratedly guided me into her. I was amazed at the warm, soft, slippery sensation. Ten seconds later, I was having another sensation, this one a thousand times greater than the one before it. My eyes rrolled back in my head, and my body began convulsing uncontrollably. Time stood still again, and Leila smiled at me.

Sarah beckoned me with her eyes as Prince sang "International Lover." Every drop of pain and sorrow I had ever known faded into the emptiness as big as the Milky Way. I felt and knew true peace in that moment. Unconditional true love was mine.

I let out a loud moan, time caught back up, and I was again aware of myself. I continued to stroke up and down, in and out, but the intensity was waning fast. I stopped and lay on top of Sarah for a couple of seconds then rolled back between them. As I did, I didn't understand why the feeling had gone. And my dick was limp.

I began to panic. What was wrong with me? A deep fear grew in the pit of my stomach, a horrible hollow feeling worse than any fear of physical harm I had known. It was fear that had nothing to do with anyone else. I thought my dick was broken. I was crippled with fear, lying between the two of them, forcing out fake laughs at their anecdotes. My masterful ability to conceal how I was feeling was in full swing.

"Oh my god! My dick is broken. I will never be able to fuck again," I thought. I was so embarrassed and sure that they were going to tell everyone. While I was busy beating myself up, Leila got up.

Sarah said, "Now it's my turn!" As we started kissing, it was just what I needed to get out of my head. Her soft lips and smooth skin felt good. Being in bed with her alone gave me a stronger sense of confidence. I was more attracted to her than Leila and having this time alone with her was bringing back my sexual excitement. It was the biggest "Aha!" moment I had ever had.

"That's how it works!" I thought, as I got hard again. Joy and happiness returned, and a great sense of relief came over me. I had sex with each of them that night before trekking back across Berkeley and Oakland. Sara asked me to walk her home, which made my trip even longer, added to the fact that my

virgin dick was painfully sore. It was a bittersweet walk home. I felt proud and triumphant about myself and wanted to brag to the world about my conquests, but I knew that no one would believe me, so I cherished it as my own private coming-of-age.

I finished the school year at Willard with D's in every class with the exception of PE. And, in every class, it was not the work I did or the curriculum that I completed, it was my ability to communicate and articulate clearly and powerfully to my teachers that allowed me to even pass.

Years later, I ran into my history teacher, Mr. Williams. He was a nice man who made me feel good about coming to class. He told me that none of the staff could figure me out, that I obviously had a high IQ but failed miserably on every exam. He told me my test scores were the lowest in the state. I shared with him the tragedy of my childhood, and he was stunned. I saw deep sympathy in his eyes.

That summer, I got a job through the City of Berkeley Youth Program at Cazadero Music Camp, washing dishes. While there, I met two very influential people: Josh Jones and Stan Franks. Josh Jones was a master percussionist and a good friend of my brother, Pio. Stan Franks was rivaled by few in his musical ability, having played with The Grateful Dead, along with many other world-renowned musicians after Jerry Garcia died. By meeting them and getting to know them, I learned that men could achieve great things through practice and diligence. I also met lots of kids, rich and poor, black, Asian, Latino and white, artists and musicians.

It was a really great summer, and I looked forward to having some money saved after camp was over. I was excited to begin the 9th grade at Berkeley High School, and, although I had made many new friends, my secret continued to haunt me. Jaci's method of dealing with the abuse was to pretend like it never happened. Isabella's method was all about talking about it. Pio was a rock star.

A week before school started, I went to my hidden cash box where all my savings were. My $350 was gone! Jaci had been coming into my room late at night. He'd wake me up to borrow money, promising to take me to concerts and to do other fun things. He'd promised to pay me back. I didn't know he was developing an addiction, but I was sure he was the thief. When I told my mom I thought Jaci stole my money, she told me she had taken it. She was unapologetic and told me that she used it to pay bills. When I expressed my hurt and anger, she screamed and bullied me out of my feelings.

Never once did she express any wrongdoing or show any care. Isabella was living across town at the time and happened to be over that day. When Isabella tried to defend me, Mom slapped her face so hard that Isabella let out a cry. Then Mom slammed her on the ground and pinned her down, grabbed her hair violently, and pressed her head onto the floor. When I tried to pull her off,

Mom yelled at me with a violent snarl, "Get the fuck back!"

After Isabella stopped trying to fight back, and only when her body was completely limp, showing complete and utter submission, and she was saying, "Okay, okay," did Mom get up and storm into her room. Mom slammed the door so hard the dishes fell in the kitchen. I felt so sorry for Isabella. I could see she was physically and emotionally hurt.

I began to get glimpses of my mother as the cold, calculating, manipulating sociopath that she really was – the true extent of which I would not fully grasp for years to come.

Now, having my "own room" meant nothing. I felt so violated, like my existence meant nothing. Once more, I'd been betrayed again by the one person who was supposed to love me. I took this betrayal as more evidence of the fact that I was unlovable and unworthy. I took off for a week or so, couch surfing and hanging out elsewhere.

While I was hanging out, Blaine and I decided to steal our school clothes, which he didn't need to do. His mom bought him a new wardrobe for the year, but he liked the excitement of stealing. Meanwhile, I stayed mad at Mom for months and tried to avoid her as much as possible. James always helped me out when he could, giving me money for lunch and being a kind, loving person. But, he always went along with whatever Mom said.

Mom stopped buying groceries and sometimes wouldn't pay the utility bill, so the lights would often be off while she and James ate takeout from Spenger's Seafood Grotto by candlelight. When the lights got turned back on, she would make sure and let me know what a struggle it was to keep the electricity on and pay all the bills, even though she didn't work.

If I complained about there being no food in the house, she would scream and bully me out of my feelings again, telling me to go to Blaine's house because they had plenty of money. And if I asked for some of her takeout food, she would get even madder at me.

Finally, Isabella told me I could move in with her, to which I happily and eagerly agreed. In exchange, I would babysit Liliah sometimes and help clean. Isabella had a cute, one-bedroom apartment on University Ave above a massage parlor. This was a very critical time in my development, and, had Isabella not been there, my life most definitely would have taken a dramatic turn for the worse.

The male figures who were in my life showing me "how to be a man" were predominantly pimps, thugs, drug dealers, womanizers, thieves, and players. I was beginning to hate women. All of the women I had ever known had betrayed me on some level, whether it was Inspiration or any woman. I hated Isabella for leaving me, Grandma and Jackie for not protecting me, and, worst of all, my mother, who I loved so much and wished she'd just love me back, but who was a horror of a mother.

Isabella began to make right all of the wrongs I had known from the female species. She showed me through love, kindness, gentleness, trust, tenderness, and encouraging words that I was loved and that not all women were traitorous, conniving, lying Jezebels who would be willing to sell me out for their whimsical needs. Sometimes, I would wake up in the middle of the night and Isabella would be holding me and rocking me back and forth.

When I'd ask her what happened, she told me that everything was okay and that I was just having a nightmare. I didn't remember the dreams, but I woke up to her holding me on many, many occasions. But, like any teenage boy, I was unaware of the help she was providing.

High school was a great time for me. I was very popular and liked. Socially, I got along with most everyone. I was intellectually more advanced than my peers but academically way behind. So, they put me in all remedial classes, which was a horrible blow to my social status. I learned that, based on my age, I was a year behind where I was supposed to be in school. So, I began lying about what grade I was in, even though lots of kids knew I had just come from Willard. There were about 3,000 kids enrolled at Berkeley High, so it wasn't too hard to get away with lying about my grade. Also, because I was ashamed about my remedial classes, I cut school often and hung out across the street at Provo Park. That was the hangout for all the cool people, "the legends," who were really the dropouts or the 20-somethings who'd never moved on.

I started hanging out with Lion and Tamm. Lion was a wild and funny black and white kid, and Tamm was the blond heartthrob. Both had spent time in the streets and had learned to fend for themselves at an early age like me. Lion was three years older than me and Tamm was four years older. Lion's mom had nursed me back to health once when I was an infant. Our families were as close as dysfunctional, biracial, hippie, revolutionary, cult-following, drug-taking families could be. Lion and Tamm had become friends during my long absence.

Tamm was born on the East Coast but moved to Berkeley early enough to be considered a Berkeley boy. He was friends with all of my siblings while I was gone and had heard stories about me. So, when we finally met, we became instant friends. The two of us were like brothers, but Lion more than Tamm, because of the nature of his personality and our history. Tamm, having had a troubled relationship with his mother and an absent father and no siblings in his life, was a very self-centered, cold product of the streets. He was the most ambitious person I had ever met. Everything came down to dollars and cents with him. His knack for making money and working an angle was unparalleled by anyone I'd ever known, and I immediately wanted to emulate him.

Lion's family life was tragic, like so many other biracial kids in our town, specifically black and white kids whose black fathers had experienced and internalized the Jim Crow racism of their time. It was a unique period in the early 70s, with hippies, free love, Black Panthers, and the Civil Rights Movement. White women eagerly rebelled against their racist parents and slept with black men, and black men eagerly enjoyed the forbidden fruit. So, when so many of these white women had their babies, most of the time there wasn't a father around who gave a fuck about being a father. And so many of us mixed kids grew up fatherless.

So, after the Summer of Love became the winter of fatherless children, Lion and I and a lot of our friends were a product of it.

Lion masked his pain with the brilliance of comedy, but just below the surface of a funny one-liner lived a cold-blooded warrior. He was the kind of guy you wanted to have on your side in a fight.

They both called me "Lil Bali" and our friendships grew. Like so many kids from the streets, our tragedies created a strong bond between us. Tamm, in his endless pursuit of wealth and building a cocaine business, would eventually help teach me mathematics.

I navigated through school, my social landscape, and my dysfunctional home life. I struggled with undiagnosed PTSD, nightmares, and depression. My fear of black males who resembled Om was transferred to all who held positions of authority, including cops, teachers, and bus drivers. An unrealized hatred for women manifested in the relationships I had with girls. I was always lying, cheating, manipulating, and callously showing indifference to their feelings whenever I felt like it gave me an advantage.

I also avoided certain death on many, many occasions. Once, I was at a house party in Oakland. I was having a good time while simultaneously looking over my shoulder so as to not get robbed. I was dancing to the Houdini song "The Freaks Come Out at Night" when a fight broke out on the dance floor. I was very small, and party experience had taught me that, when there's a fight, get close to the nearest exit.

As I made my way out while trying to catch a glimpse of what was going on, someone shouted, "He's got a gun! He's got a gun!" Everyone came running towards the door, which was now only a few feet away from me. As the crowd pushed outside and people scattered in different directions, I began looking for my friend, Tony, who had brought me. Tony was one of the Berkeley boys, a notorious fighter whom many called friend. Just then, I was bumped violently by a guy running faster than anyone else.

When he reached a clearing in the street, he turned and pulled out a small revolver.

Standing 10–15 feet directly in front of me, he turned back in my direction, drew, pointed aimlessly, and began firing.

Time played its usual trick by slowing to a near-standstill, and I watched an explosion of fire protrude from the barrel directly in front of my eyes. The sound of two rapid-fire explosions caused the crowd to simultaneously duck and drop their heads like a choreographed dance. I noticed in my peripheral vision that, one after another, a person fell to the ground on either side of me. It was as though some force guided those bullets away from me as I looked down the barrel of that gun.

The explosion created a flash, which illuminated the gunman's face. His expression was not one of anger or malice, but of fear. His Jhery curl had dripped oil on his forehead and his cheeks were flushed. His tight eyes clashed with his African features, and his dark clothes and black Members only jacket helped him blend into the night as the flashes subsided.

It was pandemonium in the streets. Two people were shot, and I was standing there, between them, in shock. Tony came out of nowhere, swooped me up into his arms like I was a rag doll, and carried me away from the scene.

We didn't wait for the police. We jumped in to Tony's silver Nissan Coupe and drove back to Berkeley, both of us amazed I was still alive.

Tamm was now moving large quantities of cocaine, and he needed someone to handle the smaller qualities. He recruited Lion and me for the job. He knew we were trustworthy, and, unlike so many other guys my age, I wasn't doing drugs and really didn't enjoy drinking that much.

The first time I touched cocaine, Tamm brought over a kilo to break up into smaller amounts. Isabella was gone, and Liliah was watching *Punky Brewster*. Tamm and I went into the small walk-in closet to hide from Liliah. We first had to smash the plaster of Paris cast that it was in. Then, we got a Sullivan grocery bag and broke the hard, white brick into it. After several attempts, it finally exploded into a giant, white cloud that left residue all over our faces and the clothes that hung above our heads.

Because my introduction to this substance was on such a large scale, I never appreciated the street value of 1/16 or why people acted so irrationally over the crumbs I would throw away. Tamm paid me $400 a week to sell as much blow as I could. Our customers were only people we knew, never strangers. There were no computers or cell phones to instant message on. Beepers had just come out, so whenever I needed to "re-up" I would page him from any of the public phone booths across North Berkeley.

He got so many calls from me that it got to the point where he had each booth's number memorized. So, instead of calling back, he'd just show up at the phone booth ten minutes after the page with a scale and a minimum of a pound in the trunk to service whatever the quantity was.

This was more money than any grocery store bagger job I could get. I was able to buy new shoes and socks and clothes and hats. I actually felt good when

I showed up for school. I figured out that by proctoring in English, math, and history, I could use those lessons to cheat my way out of the remedial classes. When it looked like I knew the curriculum, then the teachers bumped me up to standard classes where my social status wasn't hindered by my academic ignorance.

That lasted me a semester. Then I transferred to East Campus, a division of Berkeley High for kids with ADD and other issues. Because I was making such good money and my peer group was not these high school kids, I began to care less and less about graduating and all things school-related.

Blaine was especially jealous of my new status and wealth, and, although we were still friends, we didn't hang out as much. Hippo was not as jealous, but I did sense resentment in him, more because we weren't hanging out as much. I was intent on owning a 70s BMW 2002. In the meantime, going to frat parties, taking trips to Santa Cruz and other nearby party towns made me feel good.

Lion and Tamm showed me that life didn't have to always be heavy and deep. I could be silly and crazy and wild, and that was okay. To have fun was the purpose of life. And it was actually very therapeutic for me.

Pio was at the height of his popularity as the front man for his band. They were the Bay Area's premier band, and they toured with the Red Hot Chili Peppers and other greats. Going to see them play was always exciting, especially since the band's star was my brother, and I was always on "the list."

At the end of each week, I would count all the money collected, take out my $400, and hand Tamm a stack of cash in the thousands. Although Isabella was doing drugs, she tried to convince me that what I was doing was morally wrong. I disagreed and began plotting my departure. It took several months, and the process strained our relationship. In her appeal to my better judgment, she used Jaci as an example of what negative effects drugs had on the world and on people. He had recently kicked her door down and forced his way into our apartment to beat me up. He had become a violent alcoholic, and anytime he saw me in public, he humiliated me to the best of his ability by bullying me, punching me, pinning me down, and verbally degrading me. It was as though he was jealous that I had become independent and had created the reputation of being a "D" boy, a drug dealer.

We got into an argument on the phone that night, and, the next thing I knew, he was kicking down the door. After that ass-kicking, I hated him but could do nothing to retaliate physically. So, I began a campaign of slander against him.

Inside, I still couldn't understand why he acted like he hated me. After all, he was the one who left me in Mexico. I had all the right in the world to be upset. Yet, I was willing to move on from it. I understood why he left me, but my understanding and compassion only seemed to make him hate me more. Now I was going to express my pain and anger at him.

So began a 25-year dysfunctional love-hate relationship with my brother Jaci.

The impact and aftershock of Mom's inability to love us and treat us with the most fundamental parental care and her outright indignant, self-righteous, hypocritical, and sociopathic stance were now reverberating through all of our lives. It was as though a bomb had been dropped on our family, and we were all crawling out of the impact crater, burning and smoldering.

All of my siblings and I were suffering, and, although some in our community recognized and sympathized with our plight, none was qualified to handle our collective or separate torment. I dealt with the suffering by attempting to let it go, with a shrug-of-the-shoulders attitude. I just wanted to be happy and to have fun, and I was willing to forgive my family and just move on. But, at that time, I didn't understand the complexities of surviving such an event.

Although my technique got me out of my teens and into my twenties, the scar tissue that remained required a kind of emotional, spiritual, psychoanalytical, and metaphysical surgery that I eventually found through deep introspection, books, seminars, and a little therapy. But, more about that later.

At this time, I was young and focused on the important issue of my life – girls. I began a crusade of womanizing. I wanted to have as many girls as possible, and I was willing to lie, cheat, beg, borrow, and steal to get my way. Isabella gave me insights into the minds of teenage girls, unwittingly helping me cultivate my misogyny along with all the street hustlers and gangsters. Not to mention the fact that my first formidable "father" figure was a sadistic, maniacal, sex-addicted pedophile who beat and tortured his women and me.

It was no wonder I had become the boy all parents warned their daughters about. I never hit any of my girlfriends. I didn't need to or want to. I didn't go after the women with malice with the intention of hurting them. Inside, I wanted them to love me, but I couldn't trust them. I was stuck in this horribly dysfunctional paradigm I could not see beyond.

We were moving pounds and pounds of cocaine every week. Lion got into a motorcycle accident and collected a $25,000 settlement with which he bought a Porsche 911. Tamm had a 1970 Cadillac Coupe Deville convertible. He could barely see over the steering wheel. He customized it with white sheepskin, four 15-inch speakers in the trunk, and then lined the trunk with mirrors and a disco strobe light.

Here was this little 19-year-old white kid driving around in this giant car with music so loud you could hear it coming three blocks away, dealing kilos of cocaine with a ragtag crew of misfits, riding along thinking they were inconspicuous drug dealers. Those were great times. We had so much fun with parties, girls, trips, money, and eating out. I was having the time of my life trying to make up for all those years of hell, and, truth be told, I did a pretty good job.

Inside, though, I was still troubled, and I had told only my crew about what had happened to me. That experience set me apart from everyone I knew, including my siblings. No matter how many girls I used or how many parties I went to, I always knew there was something else deeper and of a spiritual nature out there for me in the world. That knowledge and curiosity led me on a journey of self-discovery and introspection.

I saw first-hand the effects of what drug abuse can and will do to all of its victims. Crack was sweeping across the nation. It was an epidemic. My friends were being systematically slaughtered by its deadly effect. I tried to justify my dealing as being different because I didn't sell crack; I sold cocaine. And I convinced myself that crack dealers were somehow lower and more deserving of punishment. As the hurt, heartbreak, and death of people I knew became more and more evident, my higher self dug at me to reevaluate what my actions were helping to promote.

The dope game was changing and becoming more and more dangerous. Not only were the users dying, but now, dealers were either being killed or sent to prison. We worried that someone would fold under pressure or that we would be killed out of jealousy, most likely by someone we knew.

Finally, Tamm decided he wanted out, so the gradual walk away from "The Game" began. But not before Lion and some friends would be robbed at gunpoint and nearly killed. The same force that saved me from those two bullets in Oakland was now propelling me to change my life and my actions. But there would be more escapes from death before I realized this.

ELEVEN

Self-Discovery

I n 1996, the "party" was in full swing. I bounced around from one restaurant to another, working just hard enough not to get fired until there was a party I just couldn't miss. My appetite for fun, sex, and dancing most often included drugs. Ecstacy had become my drug of choice, which was followed by hours and hours of dancing at 24-hour parties, which led to casual sex with random women.

Tamm, along with Lion, Hippo, and Blaine, were always there with me, sharing in the fun, sometimes with the women. Isabella continued to be a beacon of hope for my emotional health, although she moved to Fort Bragg, California, and we didn't see each other that often.

Jaci's addiction made him sicker and more demented than he ever had been as a child. He continued to bully and mistreat me and all my friends, then wondered why none of us liked him. Pio was enjoying mild fame as a lead singer in one of his bands, and Mom was just beginning to reap what she had sown: James was leaving her in the twilight of her life for a younger woman, and I saw life's poetic justice unfolding.

I was unknowingly fighting seasonal depression and severe post-traumatic stress. Beneath the partying, dancing, and womanizing was a deep self-hatred and destructive dialogue that was going on between my ears. I was turning away from the shame and trying to dodge the pain with women, drugs, and partying.

I had decided all those years ago that I wasn't good enough, wasn't lovable, and that I was stupid. Now my battle with acne also made me ugly. I thought I could fill my emptiness with the things that helped me forget. I ran to the arms of women, concluding that their willingness to go to bed with me meant

I was lovable, handsome, and smart. My promiscuity was matched only by my stupidity. The emptiness and loneliness was hidden deep within me, and my self-destructive behavior was mitigated only by that sense of spirituality and connectedness that I'd found that night in Cuernavaca.

And, although I would not have been able to admit this at the time, I now know that I walked away from the travesty of my cult experience with a deeper, broader understanding of life and of the human condition. I wanted to know the meaning of life. I wanted to understand God and the purpose of it all. These were questions my friends seemed blissfully unaware of.

I could not cry. I knew instinctively there was a river of tears in me, but I couldn't get in touch with that part of myself long enough to produce any tears. There was only one thing that could bring me to tears, and I had discovered it once while I was sick at Mom's house: watching couples figure skating on the *Wild World of Sports*. The beauty and graceful moves executed in unison with smiles and poise touched me deeply. In the solitude of my room at my mom's house, or wherever I found myself alone on Saturday mornings, that graceful dance of joy briefly opened my broken heart. Yet, in my depression, I felt there was no hope for me. Coming down off the drugs brought me back to the reality of my PTSD and my self-hatred.

I was now alone, with no money, no job, and a depleted appetite for the company of women or friends. For months, I scraped by eating junk food. I stayed home every day, trying to write and practicing the conga drums. Those years I was being starved had created an eating disorder in me. I would unconsciously not eat all day, and then realize I was very hungry, and, many times, I'd just eat something sweet like candy or grab some junk food.

Little by little, I was beginning to understand that I didn't have anyone to rebel against. The women in the cult did not represent women as a whole. The pimp and player mentality was quickly losing its appeal, although I still went out looking for love and got my self-worth by having casual sex with women.

My intimate friend Samira made me a mixtape of her favorite songs. My favorite was a song by Tracy Chapman called, "Remember the Tin Man." At that moment, this song affected me profoundly; it opened my heart to the terrible truth of how deeply sad I felt.

One evening, I sat on my couch in my dimly lit living room with a pistol in my lap and contemplated the very real fact that I wanted to end it all in that moment. Then I heard the pulling of guitar strings in an old mysterious gypsy folk-blues melody sadly beckoning me to listen.

"*Who stole your heart?*
The smile from your face?
The innocence, the light from your eyes?"

That song allowed me to shed the first authentic, heart-healing cry of my life; it reconnected me with that inner strength I'd found in myself all those years ago. It empowered me to consciously begin the journey of my healing.

My desire for spiritual and intellectual stimulation led me to a sociology and psychology course that I dropped out of after failing to produce papers when they were due. The three scattered years of formal education I'd received had only helped fuel my shame and self-hatred. I quickly learned that the 5th, 8th, and 9th grades where I'd cheated to barely pass had not prepared me academically for what my intellect was capable of comprehending. So, I did what I knew to do to adapt to my environment and use the tools available. I did things like sneak into lectures at Cal on religion, philosophy, sociology, and psychology. I sought therapy from different therapists but quickly realized I was neither willing nor able to pay for their work. I began reading books, and, although my reading comprehension level was low, I was feeding my mind and developing myself emotionally.

I lost another waiter job at a restaurant called Gertrude Stein's and didn't know how I was going to pay my rent. Lion told me there was a job opening at a car dealership he worked at with Tamm and an old friend of Pio's named Mike. Mike was more than willing to hire me because of my relation to Pio, his old crime buddy.

Lion told me a person could make as much as $1,500 by selling one car. I was shocked and jumped at the opportunity. None of my closest friends had graduated high school, so I thought, if they could do it, so could I. But, inside, I was afraid I couldn't do it. After two weeks – the time it took to get the weed and drugs out of my system in combination with "Eliminate," a blood-cleaning drink that tasted worse than its name – I was ready to start my new job.

Mike's nickname to his old street pals was "Bones." Bones liked me and assured me I could handle the job. He had become very successful and was now the general sales manager, so I had someone at the top to help me. Tamm was a "closer" and team leader who helped the rookies complete the sales. Tamm had been in that business for a couple of years and also became very successful.

Tamm, Lion, and I were still very close, and, although very, very different, our broken homes and lonely childhoods created a bond we share to this day. I heard once that "your friends are God's way of apologizing for your family." I liked that saying and had a love for my friends I could not find in my family.

My first car sale was to a little old lady and her husband. I had no idea what I was doing. Tamm did all the paperwork, I just followed his instructions: "Go do this." "Go get that." About an hour after I met Mr. and Mrs. Rodriguez, they were driving home in a brand new Chrysler Sebring under the misguided notion that they had purchased a 6-cylinder.

When Mr. Rodriguez tried to verify he was purchasing a-6 cylinder, Tamm replied with his convincing, golden boy smile, "It has 16 valves."

I made $750 on that smile and only had a small bit of reservation about the morally and ethically compromising transaction. I was hooked and didn't care about the lies I would learn to tell to make my sales. After all, this was a legitimate business where people wore a suit and tie.

I now had a job that I couldn't be fired from. I was making $30,000 annually and continued to party, do drugs, and chase women. I was able to get my own apartment in Oakland in a highrise. I had a driver's license, car insurance, and a checking account – things that were not only impossible in my family and community, but purposely discouraged.

There was always a cloud of despair close by. The nagging hurt in my heart was no longer being anesthetized in the arms of women. The party and the fun were no longer working on silencing the pain. I found more books: *The Peaceful Warrior, The Celestine Prophecy, Dianetics* … Then an old girlfriend told me about a training called "The Landmark Forum," a revised and updated edition of the works of Werner Erhards' EST training. It took her some time to convince me to go to a seminar.

She and I had been close, and I liked the person she had become. It seemed to have opened and broadened her understanding of life. I still had major PTSD around groups like AA, or religions and cults like Scientology or the Jehovah's Witnesses. I stayed clear of all of them, with the exception of going to the Kingdom Hall when I wanted to spend time with my younger siblings. It was easy to placate my dad's incessant religious pitch for the sake of developing those relationships.

But when she told me the cost was $300, I laughed and said, "Hell no!" She told me that it was so powerful she would pay for me with the agreement that, if I got something out of it, I would pay for someone else. I agreed.

I don't know whether I was born with or learned through my cult experience the desire to learn about the human condition and myself, but my curiosity was piqued. I told myself to leave all my preconceived notions at the door, to go with an open mind. She was right! That seminar series gave me a language to articulate and communicate the depth of my sadness and hurt more effectively, and, more importantly, it gave me the tools that allowed me to begin to let it go.

I was turned on and moved so powerfully by this training that I uncovered my greatest fear – facing Om. I walked away from Landmark a different man. It was revolutionary to be able to look at my past and not be compelled to make excuses for where I was in my life right now. I learned to be accountable for my actions of both the past and of the future – to own the things I did wrong and to face and accept the wrongs that were done to me.

After I finished the Advanced Course at Landmark, I had developed an ability to access my inner strength on demand. I no longer had to access my strength through a traumatic experience or by a dire emotional state.

Nor was it some magical euphoria brought on by chanting. The training allowed me to take a hard introspective look at my life experience and to become aware of the fact that I had the ability to choose how I was going to interpret my life and all its complexities.

I was now aware of the meaning I had given to my mother's abandonment of me at six years old. I'd let it mean that I wasn't good enough and that I was unlovable. It meant she didn't love me, and that Jaci and Isabella didn't love me. But a little boy of six is not qualified to make that assessment.

In reality, my mother did love me. My brother and sister did love me. Mom was just simply not fit to be a mother. She had been molested by her stepfather as a young girl and had grown up in a time when child abuse was definitely not in the collective vernacular or consciousness. She'd had all her front teeth knocked out by an abusive, violent, evil husband, and had turned to drugs, sex, and mysticism as an escape. It's no wonder she failed as a mother.

I was able to see her as a woman, as a plain ordinary human being with no special qualities or gifts. I felt sorry for her. I felt free for the first time – and drugs, women, or alcohol had never brought me to this feeling. I found forgiveness, one of the greatest tools available to child abuse victims. I found compassion for all human suffering, self-love, and love for humanity. Integrity, authenticity, and accountability had all become infused in who I was and who I aspired to be – although the application proved far more challenging than perceiving it intellectually.

I was three years into my career as a car salesman, and, with my newfound value system, I needed a new approach. I applied my new virtues and they exploded my sales each month. I became a #1 salesman, earning $13,000 in one month, my best month in the car business.

I went back to all the women I could find whom I had hurt through my lies and manipulation and tried to make ammends. Some openly and graciously accepted my apology, others were indifferent, and others told me to get lost. Seeing their unwillingness to accept my apologies was a valuable lesson.

I decided to quit selling cars because lying to customers put me out of integrity.

Integrity was the intended genesis of all my future behavior. I got a job working for one of the Landmark staff member's private companies. He ran a job placement company for computer programmers. It was now 1999 and the Internet was huge and only getting bigger. I knew nothing about how to navigate it, so taking a job in the computer field was ambitious to say the least.

I remember one call I made in an attempt to place a systems administrator (sys admin). The person on the other end gave me his email address "joe_blow@xyz.com." I spelled out the word "underscore" and didn't know why I lost the placement until my boss told me.

To add to my challenge as a headhunter, almost everyone I talked to was from India and I could not understand their super-strong East Indian accents. Their accents also reminded me of the Krishnas and Om and this further triggered my PTSD. After six months, I quit.

As luck, fate, or destiny would have it, Bones and the crew found a dealership where Bones would be the GM and run the store. He asked me to join him. I decided I knew enough about selling cars that I did not have to lie, that I could develop and grow as a salesman and keep my integrity intact. *Who cares what an underscore is anyway?*

Understanding high-minded virtue is very different than being virtuous. So, although I was practicing these new ways of being, I was still, on a subconscious level, suffering from PTSD. I eventually reconnected to my higher self and began to practice high-minded thinking again. I learned that just because I was in a new place of forgiveness and understanding didn't mean the rest of the world was (as was evidenced from my past behavior in which I'd hurt those people and didn't receive forgiveness).

I learned there are two parts of my being: my higher self that believes in love, compassion, forgiveness, helping others, being humble, being kind; and my lower self that holds onto anger, jealousy, revenge, hate, selfishness, bitterness, dishonesty, and violence.

As I began to recognize these two aspects of myself and gain insight into recovering from child abuse and navigating through PTSD, I saw that fear and pain had paralyzed me. I began to fully comprehend that the decisions I made about myself as a child had crippled me as an adult.

I wanted desperately to transform, to become a better man, a better human being, to crush my self-limiting beliefs. I decided that, in order for me to achieve these goals, I would have to face my fears. My biggest, most debilitating fear was the fear of the one person who had haunted me in terrifying nightmares, which had been plaguing me since childhood; that was Om.

First, I found my mother. At least one of my siblings would know how to get in touch with her. We'd all developed a love/hate relationship with her: hating her for what she had done to us and all the sickness and dysfunction it created, and loving her or "using her" for what she was worth at the time, like having a place to lay our heads for a night. Each of us took turns over the years visiting her.

While Jaci stood by her, Pio lambasted her with every breath, and Isabella would decide each of them was justified in their given position. Then it would be Isabella's turn, then mine. On this particular occasion, Mom was subletting a small house in Emeryville, not far from me. This time, she hadn't spoken to any of us in several months and was very happy to see me. I had always been the most agreeable of all her children, the one least likely to throw a temper tantrum. I found her still sad, lonely, depressed, and heartbroken that James had abandoned her for a younger woman.

I told her of my newfound understanding of love, compassion, and forgiveness, and how I forgave her for her mistakes and how I wanted a functioning, healthy relationship with her. She cried in shame, and, for that single moment in our lives, she owned her bad decisions and admitted her horrible mistakes. I had prepared myself by letting go of any expectations of her response, which allowed me the emotional space to hear her without getting emotionally charged by her reaction.

She tried to explain why she did it, what compelled her, what was going on in her life and mind, but the more she tried to explain, the less authentic she sounded. It became the rehearsed version that she must have told to all her friends, but, more importantly, what she had convinced herself of. I listened from a detached place, which was very empowering, and it created more evidence to myself that I was "over it."

I left her house that night feeling a great sense of closure like I had never experienced before. Feeling powerful and unstoppable, armed with a new outlook and a new technique, I was ready to face Om.

Something told me to take the time to go to the Department of Motor Vehicles and to take care of a registration issue that had just come to my attention. Well, I wasn't in the habit of handling issues like that. However, on this particular day, in a city I didn't live in, I decided to take care of it early.

As I approached the massive line of irritated, grumpy people, I noticed a tall man wearing a tennis jacket and shorts with a large, light brown Afro. He was standing two people ahead of me. His golden light skin told me he was mixed. The combination of skin, clothes, and hair grabbed my attention.

The man stood there, head and shoulders over the person behind him. With his arms folded in front of him, his keys and paperwork dangled from his right hand, which held onto his left elbow as he slowly swayed back and forth. On one of his bigger sways, I saw the profile of his face: a scruffy, patchy beard covered a handsome, chiseled cheek. I leaned to get a better look, without drawing too much attention, as I prepared myself for an encounter with an old rival. It was Freedom.

I was now committed to making contact. When our eyes met, I was close enough for a handshake, a gesture that was extremely foreign to our old relationship and equally awkward now. Our hands met in an unenthusiastic way.

He said, "Hey Jabali." The disconnected Freedom I once knew stood before me unchanged, other than his deep voice and now nine-inch height advantage. He spoke in the same slow, thoughtful way. I asked him how he was doing and his answer gave me déjà vu. He said, "Perfect," the standard Om Lover cult response to that question.

I saw in front of me a young boy born into a life of lies and half-truths that he wore sadly on his face. He remained blissfully unaware of his and his father's morally reprehensible conduct. Still brainwashed and believing that he was heir to the Kingdom of the Lord, I decided not to engage in small talk and went straight to the question I felt compelled to ask, "Where is Om? How can I get in touch with him?"

His eyes lit up, assuming I inquired because I wanted to return, then his look shifted to one of suspicion. I waited for his slow, thoughtful response, "You can find ME down at the San Pablo Park Tennis Courts, and I'll give him the message that you are requesting to visit him."

I told him it was nice to see him and that I would catch him at the park, knowing better than to ask what day or time, because, of course, time didn't exist. I left the DMV without my registration, a little shocked at the sequence of events, but determined to face my greatest fear.

During that time, I had been cultivating the relationship with my biological father and all my siblings. I stopped by my dad's house periodically, knowing that every conversation would end up with him talking about Jehovah. I didn't have the courage to tell him that he was also the victim of cult brainwashing. I knew if I did, it would jeopardize my relationship with Audrey, the baby, Cesely, the forgotten middle child, Javan, the beloved son, and Arran, my first "little" brother. I got tremendous healing from my visits with them. I loved them, and they loved me.

I was eventually able to tell my father how it broke my heart to have him put out his hand for a shake instead of hugging me after not having seen me for six years. His reason only solidified what I had always suspected, he was just a simple man. He didn't know what it took to be a father to me.

Since I was practicing love, compassion, and forgiveness, I chose to forgive him, too. We began to develop a father-son relationship and that helped the healing process, although I still loathed his "God talk." Unable to fathom the depth of my religion-triggered PTSD, he continued to try to convince me of Jehovah's Plan, and I strung him along for sake of the love I got from my siblings.

Judy, his wife, was always loving and kind, a real genuine Christian woman who had converted from Judaism. Her Hebrew genes stood out like most Eastern European American-born Jews. Passing on bits and pieces of Jewish culture and heritage to her four kids, I made fun of them and called them "Hebros." My joke was they didn't know whether to steal or buy wholesale.

Being with them felt like I belonged to a family that was "normal" in the sense that the parents worked for a living, insisted on their children going to school, prepared dinner at night, had no fear of the electricity being turned off, and offered a clean home environment with an open policy on food consumption. This gave me great hope that, genetically, I was capable of doing the same.

I worked on myself internally, emotionally, mentally, and intellectually as much as I could while partying and continuing my pursuit of love and acceptance in the arms of women. Knowing is different than doing.

On a weekday in early July 1999, I was leaving my dad's house, having just used my personal key to let myself in to grab a quick therapeutic bite to eat while everyone was out. I drove past Martin Luther King Park with no particular place to go when I noticed a very large, old, yellow school bus parked at the tennis courts. It stood out because of its unusual faded coloring and the fact that it had parking blocks underneath its tires. It was an instantly recognizable scene to me.

My heart stopped and I felt the lump of salami in my stomach. This is it. I knew instinctively it was the Om lovers. As I drove past, I tried to look through the front windshield, but it was covered with tapestry.

I decided to park around the corner so that they wouldn't be able to associate me with my car. I passed the tennis courts and turned right onto Martin Luther King Drive, drove down a block, and found a parking spot. I made my way back towards the bus, a little nervous, but committed to face the man who had destroyed my family and nearly destroyed me.

I tried to think of what I was going to say, but I drew only blanks. Somehow my feet continued to carry me toward uncertainty as if being pulled by some unseen force. I didn't want to do it, yet there was no stopping me. Flashes of my childhood raced before my mind's eye. The joys and pains of my time with them, before them, and after them looped over and over in my mind. I knew he was armed, and I knew there was a chance violence could erupt. I didn't know if I was walking to my death. Yet, I was committed. When I got to the tennis courts, through the fence, I could see a woman at the front door of the bus. It looked like Harmony, but I wasn't sure. She was cleaning up some trash from the street. My eyes were fixed on the figure and my heart began to thump more noticeably against my chest. I had not yet been spotted or identified.

I took a deep breath and turned the corner, putting myself in direct view of the person cleaning. It was Harmony. I could tell by the way she bent over, keeping her back straight, her big hips now even bigger. I gained quite a bit of distance on her before she noticed me. Looking up, her face slowly changed from the pleasant smile one might give a stranger to the slow shock of recognition. Her neck jerked back into a curious, yet slightly scared position.

She said my name, "Jabali?!?" as though she was not sure if I was there to do her harm. In an instant, she gathered her fear and turned it into a fake and transparent series of pleasantries. "How have you been? Nice to see you! It's been so long."

It never occurred to me that, in my pursuit of healing and growth, I would have to forgive her as well. The state I was in at the moment allowed me to recognize that there was more work for me to do within myself about her specifically. However, it would require instant compartmentalization. I smiled a half-smile and asked if Om was there.

She said, "Just a second," and turned and darted onto the bus, closing the door firmly behind her. I waited, still in a mild trance and state of shock about what was happening and what might happen next. A few minutes later, she returned. Her frumpy gray and blue outfit was just what she wanted it to be, nondescript. She opened the door and leaned out, beckoning me with a smile.

I put one foot on the bus and knew there was no going back. The tapestry hung just behind the driver's seat, blocking everything beyond it. I slid past her as she shut the door with the giant swiveling door handle that protruded from the bus dashboard.

"Just a sec," she said before I could brush by the tapestry. The smell of sandalwood, frankincense, and myrrh mixed with dried fruit, incense, musk, body odor, and weed was exactly the same as I'd first smelled when they came into my life so many years before.

Om sat upright on a makeshift bed, back straight with his legs spread wide like I had seen him a million times before. The long aisle that led to him seemed a hundred yards long. Most of the windows on the bus were covered except for the one that was open next to him. The dim lighting made it difficult to see his face.

As I got closer, everything in my peripheral vision became clouded and the sounds of Harmony behind me faded into silence. With every step closer, I saw that the once strong, vibrant "God" I'd known had morphed into an old, shriveled, gray-haired man. Although his posture looked good, I was shocked to see what was looking back at me.

"Hello, Jabali!" he said with the same big smile I once knew.

I nodded my head and responded, "Hello." I was now face-to-face with the person who had been haunting my dreams for almost 20 years. Here was the person who scared me, lied to me, and betrayed me, who destroyed and ruined my family. He was the scumbag, lowlife pedophile who molested my sister and sadistically beat me, starved me, confined me to weeks at a time in a closet, and abused my brother.

He sat before me without a care in the world. I measured his physical attributes and quickly assessed I might beat him in a fight, but I was scared. I knew he was sitting on that nickel-plated Colt .45 and that it was loaded, cocked, and waiting.

The sun's brightness crashed through the window, bringing with it wafts of fresh air. His face was old and his silver beard matched the head that once carried a large black Afro.

"How's your mother?"

"She's fine," I said abruptly, not wanting to give the impression I was there to catch up or give him the space to ask about anyone else. I wanted to begin speaking by telling him why I was there. This required a clearing of my thoughts.

"Your actions, with regard to me and my family, caused great, great harm to all of us. Specifically, the beatings, verbal, physical, and mental abuse that you perpetrated against me have caused enormous suffering in my life."

I tried initially to be very articulate, choosing words slowly and carefully. On some level, I guess I was trying to impress him. But when I realized that there was still an air of teacher/student, master/disciple dynamic happening, I immediately broke away from being linguistic and said, "You failed! You failed as a father ... as a teacher ... you fucked my sister, a child ... you beat me sadistically!"

He interrupted me. Inside, I was glad he did because it helped me fight back the cracking in my voice that would quickly be followed by the tears that had not yet made their way up from the bottom of my heart.

He told me, "Lisa chose me!"

Isabella was known as "Lisa" when she was a kid. That statement shocked me out of my pattern of thinking. It reverberated through my skull and gave me the clarity to realize that this person in front of me, this old man sitting in the back of an old, smelly, run-down bus, whose bones were weak and whose eyes held only the empty gaze of a once fast-talking, two-bit conman, was only a self-deluded charlatan who had the audacity to call himself the Lord of All.

I saw this sad, ugly example of a man, far removed from reality and any ethical or moral code of conduct. I calmly stood up, shook my head, and before I could say another word he said, "I'm sorry for slapping you."

And with that, I turned and walked off the bus, passing Harmony who ruffled through a bag as she pretended to be busy. I looked at her and saw a sad, broken woman who had given two children up and who had kept the death of another a secret from doctors and police – a child born in Mexico with no birth certificate, with no proof of her existence. I looked at them through the eyes of a grown man, and saw the closing of a chapter in the story of my life.

I walked away from the bus feeling numb. I rehearsed in my mind the things I might have said. Ultimately, I was proud of myself and the dignity I had exhibited. I came back to a place of forgiveness on the walk back to my car. That forgiveness was a gift to myself, a freedom from the burden of hurt and anger and pain and sadness that had plagued my life up until that moment.

But the process of forgiveness is a journey with many peaks and valleys and sometimes perilous cliffs, the fear of which, at times, drove me to relapse into self-hatred, anger, shame, or fear. But now, I was committed to transforming my life and to using love, compassion, and forgiveness as my foundation.

Our team of car salesmen had now grown into an efficient, professional group. We went around to different dealerships and shattered their previous records. Bones was the head, followed by Tamm, Julie, John, Jason, Lion, Steve, myself, and a few others.

I was making a good living for myself and felt that I had found a deeper and wiser approach to life through an unreligious, intellectual application of observations, which were distinctions based on a platform of love, compassion, and forgiveness.

Simultaneously, I was still also attracted to having fun with ecstacy, weed, acid, mushrooms, and women, which of course, slowed my healing, growth, and recovery process. My "higher self" often took a back seat to my "lower self," and the struggle continued. I was having a record month at a dealership in Burlingame, California. I upgraded my car and enjoyed the usual sex, drugs, and rave 'n' roll lifestyle I had built.

I was ambitious and hungry to earn more money. I was looking forward to beating the previous month's record when Bones told us we were leaving that dealership. He told us he was going to buy a dealership in Modesto, California.

We were all shocked. I, most of all, was disappointed. I felt like I had just gotten my groove on and was ready to really get serious about my career. I thought I was going to write a book and tell the world my story. It seemed to me that moving to Modesto was going to change all of that.

We waited the four months it took to close the deal in April of 2000, and I officially moved to Modesto, into a nice, one-bedroom apartment within a block of the "new" dealership.

Bones was officially an owner. His having dropped out of high school and surviving a life on the streets to have reached this accomplishment was inspiring for me to witness. Bones had a large heart and he often helped me with "loans," rarely asking to be paid back. He could also be ruthless and cutthroat. I grew to care for him like I did all my friends from the streets.

We all had a very specific bond, a chemistry born of hardship, drug addiction, crimes, and heartbreak. We were a wild pack of handsome, charming, cunning, and sometimes dangerous, wild cards who loved each other and found in one another what all humans want – a sense of belonging and camaraderie, loyalty, and significance. Out of our collective pain was about to grow success beyond what I ever thought myself capable of.

I had revisited Landmark Education several times and the impact on me was consistently profound. As I practiced love, compassion, and forgiveness, the idea of anything being possible for me was uplifting and inspirational.

I began listening to different self-help teachers. My favorite at that time was Brian Tracy. His book, *The Psychology of Selling*, gave me even more tools to apply to my salesmanship. I experienced my best month in the car business – 30 sales in one month. That was also the year I began writing the first draft of this book. Brian Tracy helped me believe in myself and apply a practical approach to what seemed like an un-climbable mountain. I was learning and growing as a man, but I was still partying and drinking and doing drugs regularly. I was happy, and I enjoyed my life. My girlfriend at the time, Airol, had two kids, and I loved them. I'd had many relationships with women with kids, and although my friends always made fun of me for it, it didn't bother me.

Lion called me "Rent-a-Dad." I always loved kids and knew how to relate to them. My own childhood having been what it was, I somehow lived vicariously through their innocence and found a sense of joy in their happiness. Airol got pregnant, and it was the first time I had ever been faced with the possibility of being a father.

Even though Airol wasn't my ideal partner, if she had chosen to keep it, I would have supported her. Instead, I took her to the clinic and walked past the abortion protestors with their gross and graphic posters of aborted fetuses.

I was very, very sad about the abortion, and I broke up with Airol shortly after. In my quest for transformation, I decided to stop drinking, smoking, and doing drugs for an entire year. I felt a need to prove to myself that I was in control of my life and of all my decisions. December 31st, 2001 was my last night to "party" for a whole year. In the first week of 2002, I wrote out my goals for the year.

As a young boy, I often had dreams that were so vivid and so powerful I would wake up shocked at how realistic they felt. Often within a week or two, I would find myself in the exact same circumstance as the dream, and I could foretell what was about to happen. The moments often lasted about 10 seconds before they actually occurred. This happened on many, many occasions during my time with the "Lovers" and long afterwards.

There were two occasions that stood out that I will never forget. The first was while I was living with Isabella on University Ave in Berkeley. I was about 17. In those days, and most all days since returning home, sleep was a very valued commodity. I often slept for 12–18 hours at a time. Those kinds of hours don't work when you're supposed to be going to school in the morning. Isabella somehow knew that my sleep was better for me than school (sometimes!).

I had such a problem getting up in the mornings that I had to devise different tricks or methods to ensure that I would get up. One trick I used was to put the alarm clock on the other side of the room so I couldn't roll over and turn it off. This alarm clock was not digital; it was an old-school clock, the kind your grandmother had on her nightstand. But, I turned around and went back to sleep. That didn't work.

I thought I would put a bowl of cold water next to it, so when I went to turn it off, I would lean over and splash water on my face to help me wake up. That worked twice. The third time, I wanted to drop the alarm clock in the water, but turned it off, avoided the bowl, and went back to bed.

Another idea I had was to pull the small, 12" black and white TV set, with the coat hanger as an antenna and the vice grips as the dial, over on my niece Liliah's tea set chair. I'd set the alarm clock on top of the TV set, and, when it went off, I'd turn it off, then immediately turn on the TV, hoping to hold my attention past those few short but critical moments between being asleep and being awake.

One morning I was having one of those vivid dreams. It was of me, Tamm, and Lion. We were driving very fast in Tamm's little 1978 320i BMW. We were in a large field of green grass. He stopped the car and we all got out to shuck and jive while Lion had to pee. There was a very large chain link fence that seemed like it went on forever. We all put our hands above our heads and held onto the fence as we looked out into the endless green field.

But, as we looked out across the field, a giant 747 airplane came barreling in. It tipped from one side to the other, its wings almost making contact with the ground, back and forth. Then finally it was too close to the ground, and one of the wings made contact before the wheels did, and in an instant, it slammed into the ground. The fuselage exploded, lighting up everything around it in a huge orange and red ball of fire. I leaped forward out of the dream, sat up straight, and gasped for air, completely shocked to be awake in my bed.

I looked around in amazement, realizing it was close to the time I needed to get up. I reached over and turned on the TV. As the screen came into view as I lay back in bed, there was a special news bulletin. A news crew was filming the exact plane crash I just saw in my dream – from the exact vantage point.

Behind the chain link fence in the big grass field, the news anchor said, "Just in … a 747 has crashed in Bolivia." I jumped out of bed, terrified and confused, shocked and amazed. I ran into the living room where Isabella slept, yelling, "Oh my God! Isabella! Isabella!"

I was in shock for weeks. I tried telling friends, but no one believed me. There were dozens and dozens of other dreams that showed me events that would eventually come true, some less intense and others even more jarring.

The most shocking of them all was a couple of years after I moved out of Isabella's apartment. I was living with Lion in the home his mother owned. She had moved away and let Lion take care of it. Lion sublet a couple of the rooms to our friends and it became a party/crash pad.

Blaine had a girlfriend named Rachel that he'd met somewhere along the way and brought her over to hang out and meet "the crew." During one of the many Saturday night pre-party gatherings, Lion figured out that Rachel was not loyal to Blaine and convinced her to have sex with him in the bathroom. I didn't find out until a couple of days later when she showed up at the door to see Lion. I was surprised, but not shocked, because we often shared, stole, or borrowed each other's girlfriends.

After she and Lion had sex, which took only five minutes, we all went up to the lookout to hang out and smoke. Rachel drove a small, two-door silver Honda hatchback with tinted windows. It was impressive to me because I didn't own a car, and any girl that did, according to the unwritten rule amongst us Berkeley boys, was a keeper.

Rachel had long, straight blond hair that fell over her shoulders. She stood about 5'2" and had a plain but cute face. Knowing she had no loyalty to Blaine and that she wasn't loyal to Lion, I knew I could potentially convince her to have sex with me. We spent several hours at the lookout and drove around Berkeley before she had to go home. I convinced her to drop Lion off first so she could take me over to my godmother Jackie's house, which was on the way to Rachel's house. On our drive, she told me that it was actually me she thought the cutest of our crew. She said Blaine was mean and Lion was too aggressive.

I accepted that I was a better choice. She said she liked me, not just because I was cute, but also because it was easy to talk to me. Rachel and I started secretly seeing each other and stopped going over to Lion's house. She would pick me up around the corner and we'd have sex in her car or go out to eat. She even flew me down to San Diego to visit her at school. That was the last time we hung out, though. We both realized it was over, and we never spoke again.

A few months later I had a dream that I was driving up a street in North Oakland in Rachel's silver Honda Civic with the tinted windows. In my dream, I thought it was strange that I would be driving her car after our breakup in San Diego, but I shrugged the thought away and began speeding through the tree-lined neighborhood.

Shifting up into fifth gear, then downshifting at the corners as I ran stop sign after stop sign, I turned the corner of a nicely shaded street, the length of two or three regular city blocks. It was a sunny day and the weeping willows were casting their lovely shade on everything beneath them, while the sun glistened atop them with a bright green glow.

On the left side of the street, about halfway up the block, was a big truck that had a large cab behind the driver's seat. Attached to it was a wood chipper. I was far enough away from it to see a group of feet under it. I gained speed, hearing the sound of the gears screaming for third. The closer I got to the truck, the angle changed and I could no longer see the feet, but my instinct told me there was a small tree-trimming crew behind the truck, out of sight.

I quickly shifted up into third as the tachometer pushed into five thousand RPMs. The engine was at its peak as I pressed the accelerator. I was just thinking about how my speed would impress a bunch of dudes, when out from behind the truck came one of the workers. There was just enough time for me to see the smile on his face leave him before I hit him.

I looked into the eyes of the victim; he was a thin, Latino man wearing a blue bandana on his head like a pirate. His goatee was nicely manicured. The smile from whatever conversation he had just had transformed into a look of terror. Blood splatter covered my windshield. I was shocked out of bed with a force so strong I was standing upright when I realized it was dream.

I stood there in a kind of sleep trance, astonished by the realness of the dream. It was reminiscent of my other dreams that came true, but I felt assured that this was just a dream and was going to stay just a dream because it had been months since I'd seen Rachel in San Diego, and I knew I would never see her again. I felt at ease and went back to sleep.

That summer, I was hanging out at the lookout with all the usual Berkeley folks, smoking weed, drinking beer, and plotting where to go for the next party. The sun was setting beautifully behind San Francisco, the night was balmy, the air smelled like the warm eucalyptus that covered the Berkeley hills. Grizzly Peak was packed with locals and some tourists who had stumbled upon this gorgeous view as they followed their maps through Tilden Park.

The local bikers also shared this lookout with us. These guys weren't the Hell's Angels type of bikers; they were racers. I was throwing a football back and forth in the road with a friend named Keith. Whenever either of us saw a car coming around the sharp bend, the other would scream "Car!"

As Keith threw the ball and I caught it, I simultaneously screamed, "Car!" Keith stepped out of the way and the car drove slowly past him, the driver looking like they were interested in the crew. As I stared, the color, make, and model jumped out at me. It was Rachel's silver Honda. I stopped and waited until her eyes met mine. She smiled as I stood waiting for her to notice me. She pulled up to me, still smiling, and asked where she should park. We spent the next few days together, enjoying the short time she was in town.

One morning, I asked to borrow her car while she spent the day with her mom. She reluctantly agreed on the condition that I pick her up from her mom's house later that day. I agreed and happily hit the streets. I spent the day looking for my friends in the usual places. With a few beepers but no cell phones then, looking for friends was challenging. I found some on Telegraph, some at Town & Country, some at Provo Park, and some at Lookout.

Before I knew it, the day had passed, and I had only a little while left before I had to pick up Rachel. I found myself speeding across town. Suddenly, there I was in the same car, in the same neighborhood, on the same street, with the same weeping willows, and the same chipper truck as in my dream. As this dawned on me, I saw the feet underneath the truck. I zoomed up the street, knowing he was going to pop out from behind the truck. I immediately downshifted and approached the truck cautiously. As in my dream, the same man, with the same smile and same blue bandana, stepped out, his laughter quickly changing to surprise and then shock. Equally shocking to him, I'm sure, was the look on my face as if I might be looking into the face of God or death. I slowly drove on, completely amazed at what had just happened.

That experience and others like it forced my young mind to stretch beyond what I could see, hear, or touch.

As I reviewed my goals, I wanted to understand this ability/phenomenon. I decided to get a book on psychic phenomena as part of my goals. The book I found was titled *Psychics for Beginners*. It described a way of setting up and achieving goals that was very different from the Brian Tracy way.

Brian Tracy's method was working very well for me up until that point. His method, in part, instructed me to write out my top 10 goals, then write out 20 different ways of achieving each one. It was a very painstaking exercise, but it was also effective. In fact, it started the writing of this book, and it led me to start reading the psychics book, because Brian Tracy encourages reading every day.

The psychics book instructed the reader to draw a circle on a blank piece of paper and divide the circle into eight different sections. At the top of each section, I was to draw a picture of my top eight goals, putting one in each section.

After drawing them, I was to write how I intended to achieve the goals in as much detail as possible, using the amount of space available in each section. Then, at the top of the page, I was to write the date and add: "With harm to no one, goal bowl for Jabali Ornelas Smith."

Each night before I went to bed, I read each goal out loud, then closed my eyes, repeated the affirmation, and visualized each goal in my mind's eye. I repeated this process for 30 consecutive days.

My goals (in no particular order):

- Earn 70k in car business
- Buy a house in Modesto
- Become a finance manager
- Write my life story
- Go to Rio de Janeiro and hang glide
- Buy an old American classic car
- Meet a loving, kind, beautiful, tender, sweet, loving, crazy woman
- Become a black belt in tae kwon do

Choosing not to drink or smoke or do drugs was very instrumental in my success. My new choice gave me clarity, energy, and freed me from hangovers, missed work, missed opportunities, bad decisions, and regret.

It's difficult to attribute one particular action or decision to my success, but, after those 30 days of meditation and visualization, the very next day, the most amazing, uncanny series of events began to unfold.

First, I had been arriving at work early so I could listen to Brian Tracy CDs at our car lot. Like most dealerships, there were several rows of cars that were parked in front of the main building. I decided to do an inventory check. After checking several cars for their price, miles, and condition I looked up and saw a 1966 convertible Cadillac Coupe de Ville driving by. I hurriedly whistled and flagged the guy down.

He made a U-turn and pulled into our driveway. The 1960 V8 convertible was immaculate, in pristine condition, and looked brand new. It featured a money-green exterior and a 1960s green leather interior. I asked the guy if he wanted to sell it.

"As a matter of fact," he said, "I was on my way to Pep Boys to get a For Sale sign!"

I was blown away. I asked him how much he wanted to sell it for, hoping it would be in my price range. "$7,000" he said, firmly.

My heart sank into my stomach, I had $3,500 to my name, but blurted out, "Would you take $5,000?" He scoffed. Being at a dealership didn't help.

"How about $6K?" He began to sell me on why it was worth more than $7K: only 100,000 miles, two owners, no accidents, and a brand new white electric top. I was sold. But the car wasn't, because I didn't have the money.

I wanted to win him over, earn his trust with great rapport, so I asked him questions unrelated to the car. I learned in selling that most people, given the opportunity, love to talk about themselves. My natural curiosity and genuine interest in people helped create that rapport that is so important in "making friends and influencing people," which was, coincidentally, the title of an audio book I had recently listened to by Earl Nightingale.

Talking for a while, I asked him to give me until the end of the week, so I could get my banking in order. He hesitated, so, before he could say anything, I offered him a $500 deposit to show my commitment. He agreed to not put it on the market until the following week. I ran over to my apartment and got my checkbook.

Although I instinctively know it's important to test drive any car you're planning on buying, the dealership was about to open, and I had a 9 a.m. appointment. I wrote out a simple contract and scheduled a test drive later that day.

I didn't know where I was going to get the $3,500 by next week, but I convinced myself Bones would surely lend me the money for such an awesome deal. Having just proved myself as the top salesman with 30 deals, I was sure I was good for the money. I knew I had money on the books in commission, but I wouldn't get that payment until the 15th. I was so excited. I didn't know how, but I knew was going to get that car.

Bones, in his predictable yet unpredictable, generous yet cold-blooded way, said, "Hell no! I'm not going to lend you $3,500 so you can disappear next month in a fucking Cadillac! Show me some consistency and maybe!"

I argued humbly that I had already earned it, but to no avail. I was hurt and a little down, but I wanted that car!

He flippantly said, "Go to the credit union and get a loan for the money!"

Bang! I was filled with renewed hope. I sold my 9 a.m. appointment, then went straight downtown to one of the credit unions to whom I referred my clients.

The credit union would lend me only $3,000 dollars. As luck, chance, co-incidence, fate, or destiny would have it, I found myself in Berkeley visiting Jackie, where I bumped into Pio. He had just come off tour and had $500 cash in his pocket. In an unexpected act of trust and generosity, Pio lent me the cash.

Wow! A week later I drove up to work in my new, drop-top Caddy.

Through the studying techniques I learned at Landmark, listening to Brian Tracy, reading books like *The 7 Habits of Highly Successful People*, Napoleon Hill's *Think and Grow Rich*, *The Richest Man in Babylon*, Anthony Robbins' *Unleash the Giant Within*, and Robert Kiyosaki's *Rich Dad Poor Dad*, and many others, I discovered that I could take pride in being a salesman. I could help people instead of harm them.

It was challenging to transform, but I was trying to live and work based on my newly cultivated inner principles, rather than from a need for outward gratification. I found great success. I tried dating, but my commitment to remain sober kept me away from the clubs and the bar scene. I decided to be celibate for the rest of the year.

I blossomed at work and continued my routine of visualizing my goals before I went to sleep. Every night, as the book suggested, I declared: "From the infinite source, with harm to no one, goal bowl for Jabali Ornelas Smith."

Another component and reality of being sober was that I was very present to my pain and hurt and anger. With no place to go for escape, I was forced to look at it and deal with it. One morning, while in the shower, I heard myself saying to myself, *"You stupid, dumb, ignorant, worthless piece of shit, you will never amount to anything. You didn't even graduate from high school. It's no wonder your mom gave you away. You will never make it."*

I witnessed myself saying these horrible destructive things to myself from the outside looking in. It was a very penetrating and shocking observation of what was going on in my mind. I had been totally unaware of it. Now, in an instant, I was keenly aware that this was going on in my head.

My whole life, if anyone would have ever said anything half as bad to me, I would have done my best to cause them great bodily harm. Yet, here I was saying and believing this poison.

I decided, in that moment, to create a mantra that I would chant every time I caught myself indulging in any form of self-destructive inner dialogue. I love myself, I love myself, I love myself. I said it over and over and over. Sometimes I would even physically hug myself while I said it. I still say it to this day, and it is how I put myself to sleep when I am suffering from insomnia.

A month after buying the Cadillac, I got a promotion to finance manager. This automatically put me in the tax bracket of my financial goal. I continued to go to work early and stay late. According to Brian Tracy, eight hours of work is for survival, every hour beyond that is for success.

The dealership was growing in leaps and bounds. We were one of the number one dealerships in California, and number two or three in the entire nation. I was making more money than I had ever made in my life. Bones then bought into part ownership of a private jet that we often flew to Las Vegas for wild, lavish parties at the best hotels and restaurants in town. One night, I watched Bones win $200,000 on the craps table.

In my new tax bracket, I began shopping for a home. That was an unbelievable experience; I was living a successful life. I was happy. I was healing. After looking at several homes, I finally found one I liked. It was a cute, bungalow-style, stucco mixed with red brick. A small, white fence bordered the pathway that led up to the front door through the front yard. A medium-sized tree shaded the small rose bushes that lined the fence. A red chimney poked out from the top of the house.

The seller was a sweet, middle-aged woman. Her husband stayed in the background. When I arrived to view the house, her two German shepherds greeted me at the door without barking. The woman was shocked that they took to me instantly. She said I was the only person that they didn't bark at. She gave me the tour, continually bringing up how much her dogs liked me.

There was a beautiful koi pond that featured a fountain. The sound of water falling over rocks into a small pool quietly filled the area. Next to the pond stood an apple tree and an apricot tree. The backyard was split by a curved pathway that matched the front yard. At the end was a large trellis that was covered with beautiful blue morning glory flowers. To the left was a small green lawn that held a fruiting peach tree with giant peaches.

She was very proud of them and insisted that I have one. She carefully surveyed which one would be the best and plucked it for me. She insisted that I eat it, but not before she rinsed it, confirming, "You do like peaches, don't you?"

"I love them," I replied.

She walked over to several large planter boxes that lined the corner of the lawn where the hose was still dripping onto a tomato plant. After rinsing the peach, she handed it to me and watched in eager anticipation for my reaction.

I bit into its soft, sweet, juicy meat. I couldn't help but moan at the succulent, delicious flavor. It sent messages of sweet goodness throughout my body.

She nodded knowingly as my face and body registered this gift from Mother Earth. She told me how to care for the trees and the fish in the pond. She explained all the intricacies of the house while continuously reminding me about how her dogs bark at everyone, and how confused she was about the fact that they were silent.

We both had forgotten about the real estate agent who had brought me there. After the tour, she walked us to the car, thanked me for my interest, and said goodbye.

The next day, my agent told me that the woman really, really liked me and wanted to sell me her home. But, there was a problem. Her list price was $200,000 and I was capped at $185,000. Over the next couple of days, she decided to lower the price to meet my cap, only because her dogs liked me so much.

I was now on my way to being a homeowner. I was a manager and I was earning $70,000+ dollars annually. I had a drop-top Cadillac and a 1998 Audi A6. I was actually doing it! Making it! Thriving.

I felt like I was done with the hurt and pain. I was done blaming my family and the world for the wrongs that were done to me. I was living proof that one's past does not equal one's future.

I started working on my black belt from a sister school of the master I knew in Berkeley, which I found coincidentally in Modesto. All of my psychic goals were coming true, and there was no denying it. I began training three days a week in tae kwon do, committed to getting a black belt.

When I could, I would drive out to Berkeley to continue my drum lessons with Josh Jones. I wanted to create an environment in Modesto that would replace the cultural diversity, intellectualism, political awareness, and diverse spiritual influences that I enjoyed whenever I walked down any street in Berkeley. Modesto seemed void of these very important components.

With my new position as finance manager, it was difficult for me to find the time to drive out to Berkeley, so Josh referred me to his friend Carlos Carro, an amazing Cuban percussionist. I began taking lessons from him. Carlos was a kind man and loving father with two children and a lovely wife. Although I was getting some diversity, it was hard to adjust. I was very happy with where I was in my life; it was clear that, statistically, I should have been dead, hooked on drugs, or in jail.

Bones married the receptionist and had a wonderful wedding in Jamaica. We all thought it would never last and that she just married him for his money. I can happily say we were all wrong, and they are still together as I write these words. Stephanie turned out to be a loving wife and a caring mother.

Stephanie was friends with a woman named Jeanette Durrani, who was a supplemental insurance agent at the dealership. Jeanette was a beautiful woman of mixed Pakistani and Cuban heritage with beautiful chiseled features, an infectious smile, and medium-length, silky black hair.

Jeanette was the mother of two amazingly sweet children: Ruben, nine, and Vanessa, six. They had different fathers, and it was easy for me to relate to their situation. Jeanette loved her kids very much, and I was drawn to her because I saw an unwavering love for her children that touched me.

Jeanette and I would laugh and laugh for hours together. We went on trips and began to fall in love. She was kind, grateful, tender, loving, and beautiful – and, honestly, yes, a little crazy. I saw a dysfunction in her and her family that was similar to mine. Jeanette's mother had four children with four different fathers; they were poor and struggled as fatherless children often do.

Jeanette and I had many similarities that allowed us to bond very quickly. We understood hunger and shame, sibling anarchy and hatred. We chose different paths than our brothers and sisters, and our choices were working out much better. Jeanette heard the stories of the long journey I'd traveled to get to the place where I was when we met. She saw my strength, resilience, and conviction, and the outcome of my choices.

It was on one of our trips on Bones' private jet that Aché was conceived. When Jeanette got pregnant, I was ecstatic. I felt like I knew I was ready – ready to be an honest, loving, good, faithful man. The days of lying and cheating, being selfish and being a player were over. I was ready for fatherhood, and I picked Jeanette because I knew, if anything happened to me, she would love and protect our child until her very last breath.

The thrill, joy, and excitement of being a father was overwhelming. I began a very strange and intense sympathetic pregnancy. I knew instinctively that a woman's emotional, psychological, and spiritual health was directly related to her unborn child. So I tried my best to facilitate the best environment for her that I could.

She and the kids moved in, and I was on my way to being a father. However, in the six months leading up to the pregnancy, Jeanette and I found many reasons to argue. The strong mother and independent woman who I fell in love with was still dealing with the emotional trauma of her childhood. She hadn't done a lot of the soul searching, emotional, spiritual, and psychological work that is required for anyone who suffers as a child if they want to have harmony and peace.

Part of her was really damaged, and all of her past hurts and fears were exploding onto the peace, love, compassion, and forgiveness I had developed for myself. Because I had done so much work on myself, I had developed a surplus of compassion and love, but the "crazy" part of what I had asked the universe for was also manifesting.

The illness didn't show up overnight. It was a slow manifestation of over 20 years of unaddressed childhood trauma from not having had a father and from all of her mother's mistakes. I was putting up with behavior that would have driven me away in the past because I had become a different person. I had built a reservoir of patience, and I was practicing forgiveness. Although I was not anywhere near perfect, I was intentionally being the bigger person.

The day we told Ruben and Vanessa that we were going to have a baby and move in together, Vanessa asked Jeanette and me, with the innocence of a child, "Can we call you Daddy now?" to which Jeanette abruptly said, "No," causing a long awkward silence. She finished with, "Jabali is fine."

That stunned and hurt me tremendously. Here I was, taking in this woman and her two kids with our baby on the way, and she didn't want them to call me Dad. That spoke loudly to me, but I didn't say anything. After all, I wasn't their dad. But I was about to be a dad, and I was committed to being the best dad in the world. I was committed to raising my child with love, kindness, sensitivity, strength, discipline, and wisdom – a child who would never doubt being loved, never question his or her value, or feel that their voice wasn't heard. I wanted with all of my heart to raise this child together as a family, as a mother and father, siblings and all.

Ruben and Vanessa enrolled in school, and I continued to successfully do my job as finance manager. Jeanette was successfully doing her job, too, working hard even though she was pregnant. In the midst of my instant family, becoming a stepfather of two, having a loyal lover, being a manager, a homeowner, and soon-to-be biological father, I had no time for myself. I had no time to continue to cultivate all the aspects of myself that had brought me to this better place in my life.

The age-old saying "If you don't use it, you lose it" was beginning to come true. Jeanette was very demanding, and, if I wasn't doing what she wanted when she wanted it, that was great cause for a potential fight. She would raise her voice almost to a scream when things were not to her liking.

I tried to be mindful of the baby inside, but often found myself trying to prove my point, which led to an escalation of her screaming. We wound up in loud and abusive arguments. I demanded that I continue continue practicing martial arts (between the fights and disagreements). I experienced some joy and happiness, but, overall, this wasn't what I envisioned my life to be.

My year of abstinence from drugs and alcohol was over, and I happily began drinking again and doing drugs recreationally behind Jeanette's back. Between the love we felt and the pain of our relationship, we were still doing okay. Then on January 21st, 2004 at 5:27 a.m., all of the joy and happiness that the universe allows one man to feel came zooming magically into my world. Jeanette gave birth in 30 minutes. My son, Aché Durrani Smith, was born.

Months earlier, I had decided to finally change my last name from Ornelas to Smith. The Ornelas family had long since been obliterated and fragmented. All that remained from the impact crater of the cult landing on our family were scars and faded memories of much pain. The Ornelas name represented too much hurt, too many lies, betrayal, and pain. I felt like Ornelas was a curse that I would not to pass on to my son. Because I had mended my relationship with my father, I wanted my son to be a Smith. After all, that was his blood, his genetic lineage. Aché's middle name belonged to his grandfather, Jeanette's father, who was of Pakistani aristocracy, another bloodline I felt should be represented in my son's name.

The name Aché means "blessed" or "amen" in the West African Yoruba language. During the slave trade, as the Dutch, French, Portuguese, and Spanish ships landed in Southern and Central America and the Caribbean Islands, the name and language migrated through many cultures of the indigenous peoples. The meaning changed ever so slightly to "breath of God" or "keep the faith."

I first heard this name many years ago at age 14, when Pio took me to a *bembe* – a musical and religious ceremony practiced by the descendants of the African slaves, practices that are often called Santeria, Candomblé, or Vodun. They splintered among the many mixed cultures across Dominican, Cuban, Haitian, Puerto Rican, and Brazilian landscapes, all influenced by African religion and music.

The ceremony took place in the basement of a two-story home. The upstairs was off-limits to the guests, many of whom wore all white with different-colored beads strung around their necks. The women wore white headdresses.

We walked along a path on the side of the house. Pio was greeted by many of the people there. He was very popular. He crossed his arms in front of his chest, holding onto his opposite shoulder. He leaned in and touched each opposite shoulder to the others as he introduced me. I could tell the same greeting was not required of me. They were all very happy to meet me and were full of smiles.

I could hear drumming and singing coming from inside. We entered a small door on the side of the house that led into the basement. It had been turned into living quarters with a kitchenette. The whole space was packed with people. In the very back of the room was a sliding glass door and, in front of it, were several conga players.

There was one main singer and several backup singers. The drummers were called congeros, the singers, soneros, and the backup singers, coro. The music was powerful. The energy in the room was electrifying. To the right of the musicians, the room opened up to reveal another, larger room that ran the length of the entire house.

As we made our way through the crowd, the music came to a sudden stop.

The rustling of the crowd reminded me of the sounds of Mexico when I used to ride the subway with Inspiration. Although largely unintelligible, I could make out they were speaking some kind of Spanish. But this wasn't Mexican Spanish, which I had grown to understand. This was Cuban Spanish, which had a large African influence and overtone. I could only make out a few words.

As we made our way to the back, Pio continued to greet people. The musicians were all moving around. Some got up and joined the rest of the room while others positioned themselves in the circle of drummers. One man dressed in all white was barking orders and gesturing to people in Afro-Spanish. I couldn't tell if he was angry because, in-between his barking, he would smile knowingly. His dark brown skin contrasted with his big white teeth that matched his white garments.

After a few minutes of mingling and being introduced to people, the musicians began playing again with distinct precision. There were some additional instruments that were to become the focal point this time.

Three people sat with batá drums across their laps. Batá drums have skin on both ends and are played with the left hand on the left end of the drum, which is the smaller side in diameter, while the right hand plays the larger, lower-pitched, right end of the drum. The lead drum is called okónkolo, the second drum is called the itótele, followed by the iyá.

I was moved by the very complicated patterns that I heard. Combined with the beautiful vocals singing in amazing harmony, I was instantly in love with the music. There was a similar feeling to the old drum circle on the Berkeley campus, but this was much, much deeper and more spiritual. I don't remember the name of the song, but the rhythmic, beautiful repetition of the word "aché" compelled me to commit it to memory. I decided in that moment that my firstborn would be named Aché.

Now a father of a beautiful, healthy baby boy, all of the hurt, pain, sadness, depression, and anger that I was methodically and diligently working to transform into love, compassion, and forgiveness, had an innocent, pure, vulnerable, trusting vessel. This little body with these little eyes was here to receive my very best. I was, and will be, to my very last breath, committed to my son. His birth provided far more healing to my future than I could have possibly imagined. I thought that I was done with the work, that because I had achieved all the goals on my list and I had faced and forgiven Om, Mom, Jaci, Isabella, Pio, my father, and everyone else, that I was free.

But, through my struggles with Jeanette, I discovered that the journey to healing was really in its infancy. I learned that forgiveness is a process that requires persistent attention and exercise – that it's not a destination. It's a constant, ever-changing disposition that first begins with forgiveness of oneself.

Jeanette had inadvertently become one of my greatest teachers. Through our tumultuous relationship, I was faced with putting the ideas and the sentiments I'd learned into practice in the real world. And I failed over and over. But that is real life. Falling down and getting back up. It is part of the journey.

I remained committed with the strength I found all those years ago in a closet in Mexico. Why? Because it was worth it! I was worth it. My son was worth it. The price for those failures was my romantic relationship with Jeanette. It ended with my son crying in the middle of one of our shouting matches. Like so many times when I face extreme stress, the world momentarily froze, then picked up in extreme slow motion. The sound of her screaming voice was muted, her mouth froze with the words still forming in the back of her throat.

I saw the worry and fear begin to gather and form on Aché's face. He had never, until this moment, seen or experienced any animosity between her and me. And the pain of this experience swelled up, taking the form of tears in his eyes, and the sound of pain from his heart.

The scene was still muted and frozen as I contemplated the effect of my behavior on his fragile innocence. I saw the shouting and arguing as affecting his worldview later in life, subconsciously scarring and affecting his emotional and psychological well-being.

As the sound of his pain sliced piercingly through our screaming voices, I discovered the following resolutions:

1. I will never expose him to the arguing and pain of my inadequacies again.
2. I will put his emotional and psychological and spiritual well-being before my own, until he is capable of protecting himself.
3. Because I had no control over Jeanette, I was leaving her.
4. He would never see us fight again.
5. It is better that he knows us individually as a happy father and a happy mother apart, than as an unhappy mommy and daddy together.

I felt it was early enough in his life for him to acclimate to us being apart, as opposed to trying to figure out and understand why Daddy and Mommy were breaking up later on. I saw his vulnerability and his complete dependence on me in a glaring and raw new light.

In that moment, I felt Jeanette was completely incompetent as a mother. Later, she proved me to be wrong. His cry finally landed on my ears, causing a primal cringe in every fiber of my being. I calmly walked over to him, demonstrating by my body language that he was safe. I picked him up and consoled him, speaking softly, with reassuring words of love and safety into his ear.

The breakup was hard on me emotionally. Although I knew we could not reconcile, my heart still longed to raise my son in a home with a loving mother and father, living harmoniously. I was deeply hurt and heartbroken, but my pride, ego, and defense mechanism would not allow me to admit it.

Jeanette and I agreed on a 50/50 split of our son's time. Despite her anger, we agreed to put our differences aside for his sake. I consciously decided that his emotional well-being would always take precedence over my personal issues. I wanted her to be happy so that my son had a happy mom.

I sold my house and moved back to Berkeley. I loved being back in Berkeley. But depleted and still in denial about my pain, I reverted back to the old coping mechanisms of women, ecstacy, and dancing.

I began studying secret societies and conspiracy theories – things like who killed JFK?, UFOs, the 9/11 truth movement (as it was developing), government black-ops projects, and groups like the Council on Foreign Relations and the Bilderberger group.

I read book after book: *The Creature from Jekyll Island, Confessions of an Economic Hitman* ... I discovered an entire subculture through the Internet that I never knew existed, things that I had only heard about through fringe radio talk shows like the Art Bell show. It was all at my fingertips and just a click away.

If I wasn't at a party, I was down the Internet rabbit hole, learning about who was "really" running the world. Some stories were obviously made up by loonies, and some were factual and provable with evidence that was compelling. Whether the stories were about reptilians disguised as humans running the world or the Federal Reserve Bank being a secret government agency, I couldn't get enough.

On the weeks I had Aché, I didn't do drugs or go out chasing women. His innocence, sweetness, beautiful eyes, and curly locks gave me a great sense of purpose. He was my compass back out of the rabbit hole.

Jeanette refused to make the trip from Modesto to Berkeley, so I drove the considerable distance there and back most of the time. I didn't want to work, even though I was burning through all my savings and proceeds from the selling of my house. I decided to begin a marijuan- growing operation. Lots of my friends were doing it, and it was just about to become legal in California, if you grew under 70 plants.

I was obviously planning to grow three times that amount. My friends and I built the entire operation in the basement of the house I was renting. It was enough to gross about $10,000 a month, provided everything went just right.

Still, beneath the surface of my masquerade, I was hurting but unable to access a remedy or ask for help. I had slipped back into the hypnotized state of denial, avoidance, and self-pity.

Eventually I partied my way through all of my savings. The crash of 2008 was to me just more evidence that the Illuminati plan was unfolding, and my life was unraveling with it. I was able to grow a few crops before my landlord wanted his house back. I had recently been involved in a car accident where my BMW was destroyed. Luckily, it happened when Aché was with his mother.

I used my past success and reputation to move in with my brother, Javan. He was living in a small two-bedroom apartment, and he was kind enough to let me stay in his extra bedroom. I was very good at hiding my inner turmoil while he was busy trying to hold together his failing marriage.

I then turned to my younger sister, Audrey, for her generosity – all the while partying while Aché was gone. I had no overhead except for my phone bill, and I could make some money on marijuana deals from connections made through the grow operation.

My life was unraveling faster and faster. But no one could tell. I always dressed nicely and had an outward appearance of happiness. But I was now at the last of what my prior success afforded me. There was no one left to borrow from and no more couches for me to surf. I had to get a job. Although I vowed never to go back, I went back to the car business and sold Toyotas in Berkeley.

With nowhere to go, I turned to Mom. She had been working as a caregiver and was now living in a tiny, one-bedroom cottage, nestled behind a large communal hippie co-op. I was troubled and repulsed by the smell of cat shit left behind by the 15 cats that lived on the property, but I had seen worse.

The bungalow was 600 square feet. The living room was almost filled by a small, secondhand couch against the right wall. Just beyond the living room was a small kitchen. The living room rug's filth, hidden in its brown color was from years of wear and tear. To the left was a small bedroom where Mom's mattress sat frameless, and, to the left of that was the bathroom. A bookshelf was squeezed in the living room to hold Mom's books. On top was a small color TV. I could barely stand being in the place, but desperation forced me. I was thankful that Mom was letting me crash, but my bitterness and heartbreak were still poisoning me.

I slept on the floor because the couch was too small. The dust and funk from the floor made my eyes itch every morning. I had to clean up each day just to maintain some sense of sanity.

When Aché came to visit, we slept together on the floor. The joy of being with my son made the dust and dirt almost bearable. Yet, seeing his face pressed against the filthy floor demanded that I rise above my current circumstance. I had reached my bottom and knew, in the back of my mind, that the only place to go was up.

I decided I needed a book that would snap me out of this funk. I had been able to continue to pay my storage fees from miscellaneous weed transactions. I thought about getting some of my books from storage, but the task was too daunting. I decided to go to Moe's books on Telegraph, directly across from the Med. I wandered around until I found myself in the metaphysics section, scanning the shelves, not knowing what I was looking for.

A bright, reddish-pink book caught my eye. It was nestled between a series of dark-colored books on witchcraft and the occult, a subject I had zero interest in. The title read *The Law of Mind in Action*, by Fenwicke Holmes. I glanced through a couple of pages before stopping. The words on the pages were so powerful, I had to sit down and read more. It was as though I had been taken directly to it. The words on these pages were, in essence, the same as what led me to create all of the items on my psychic goal bowl list back in Modesto.

I had to have this book, but I didn't have a penny in my pocket. From its pages, I was reminded of my connectedness to the universe, to the infinite source, to the metaphysical and the non-local reality. I decided I had to steal it, with the promise to myself and to the universe that I would return it, or bring back the $5.99 when I had the money.

Fenwicke Holmes's words reconnected me with strength, courage, and determination, all of which had fallen dormant inside of me. I drew on a power that lives in all human beings, but requires exercise, like the muscles in our body. I realized, if I didn't exercise these particular muscles, they would atrophy.

I believe in spirituality and that having a sense of power greater than myself is an important step in the healing process. Connecting to that power recharged my inner strength. I understood that I create my reality and determine how my life will be. I define myself. My past does not dictate my future. I am the director of my life. I am the star in the story of my life – the hero, the protagonist, the architect of my future. These simple truths began to rekindle my passion and commitment to live a powerful and fulfilled life. But I had to change my circumstances by taking action.

I went for a run through Berkeley. I got up early every day and began training in martial arts again. Selling cars was not fulfilling, so I quit and got a job selling private security contracts for a security company a friend of mine started. It involved posting unarmed guards at hotels, shopping centers, and banks. I started to play drums again every night before I went to sleep, and every morning when I woke up, I read from my book.

I wrote down my new goals for the next 12 months. I was slowly rekindling. But, as the universe works in mysterious ways, I was again faced with a tremendous hardship and a blow to my psychological, spiritual, and emotional healing.

It was years earlier, while I was in Modesto, that Pio had told our family secret to a local reporter who worked for the Berkeley Express. In it, he told his version of what happened to our family. He told me he would be doing the interview, and I had reservations about him telling the story in which he had been only a very small participant. But, at the time, I was focusing on my goal bowl and felt far removed from it all, so I did not object.

The reporter also spoke to Isabella, which gave the article legitimacy. But, overall, it had a negative effect on the Ornelas family. Pio did not have the experience of living with the cult and his account of what happened and what life was like under the tyranny of the cult's pernicious rule was gleaned from stories he'd heard from me.

Jaci was very angry about it and threatened to physically harm Pio. The entire town was shocked. I was getting calls from all over the country asking, *"Is it true?"* I often had to set the story straight, and it caused considerable scandal in our town. To me, it cheapened and sensationalized my pain. I was living in Modesto at the time, and I was hurt and angry at Pio for outing us in what I saw as such a tawdry way.

Now, on the verge of creating a new life again, I was shocked to hear that a man from the East Coast, named William, had found Pio after doing a Google search on Om that had led to the East Bay Express. He asked Pio to help him get his two sisters away from Om and the cult.

The cult had recently recruited his two sisters, both in their twenties. Pio and William began a correspondence via email. Pio then asked me if I would help William. I was happy to help, and he and I began a correspondence.

I gave him insight into how the cult traveled, and places they frequented and what dangers I felt they posed, specifically, to the well-being of his two sisters. This correspondence went on for a few weeks, and, eventually, I received an email from William in which he shared with me a correspondence from someone who was advocating his sister's affiliation with Om and the cult.

It was sent to him from one of his sister's email addresses. This person was advocating for the cult and stating that the cult leader was a benevolent, loving, gentle human being who would never cause harm to his sisters. The writer reiterated that he had nothing to worry about, that they had direct experience with the cult, and that they stood by all of their decisions with regard to the cult. It was signed by Marilyn Ornelas – my mother.

It was a devastating letter to read. I was still living with her but did not let her know about my correspondence with William, nor that I had read her letter releasing Om of all responsibility and guilt for what he had done to me and her two other children. I kept my mouth closed, trying to use all that I had learned in order to not lash out.

That same week, I happened to be on a bike ride in the Berkeley Hills and ran into an old friend, who was looking for a housemate. Her children's father had just passed away on Christmas Day, and she needed someone to rent a room and help support her during this hard time.

It was a perfect match on many levels. My son was gifted with two new brothers to grow up with, which would help his developmental process, as well as that of her two boys, and my being there would provide them with a positive male role model in their lives. I could help her with the boys, and I could help her as a kind of life coach to empower her to remember the things she already knew but had forgotten. This was a chance to start over in a new environment so that I could reignite the magic I had lost over the last three or four years.

The letter from my mother was the final straw. I could not in good conscience, and while acting in my own best self-interest and self-love, continue to be in a relationship with this woman I called Mom.

It was now utterly and unmistakably a relationship that had to die in its entirety. I didn't tell her I knew about the email. I simply waited until she was out for the day and grabbed what little belongings I had and left. Crawling out of the impact crater of my childhood, I had developed a coping mechanism, which allowed me to analyze and process immense amounts of pain that were completely hidden from friends and family and enemies. From behind an impenetrable wall, I forged this strength out of necessity and self-preservation. Meanwhile, I continued my journey of love, compassion, and forgiveness.

Each day, I read from my new book. Each day, I found a new insight into how I could become a better father, brother, and friend, and learned more about how to achieve my goals. One of my daily incantations became: *"I am receptive to the highest wisdom today, so that I can only see that which is best for me and others. I now choose this course of love, compassion, and forgiveness. Circumstances have no power over me. I am master of my fate. I am free to will and to do. I feel the God power acting in me. I breathe the finer forces. My firm will is a magnet that draws to me my good and attracts and holds friends for me. I have a courageous soul. I am open to the highest truth and I show only the greatest wisdom in my affairs. I play my part today with all the power of a mind conscious of His infinite strength and filled with divine love and wisdom. I have the will to win. I can, I will, because I say it is so."*

Declaring my power to heal and to ask from a place of love, compassion, and forgiveness meant I had to first love myself enough to end my codependent relationship with my mother. I had to forgive myself for the mistakes I'd made over the past years, mistakes with Jeanette and with my finances. Admitting to myself that I had given up and forgiving myself for that, I needed to exercise compassion for myself and grant myself permission to make mistakes.

When I started out in life, everything I loved was taken from me. My ability to detach from people and things is a skill that was cultivated out of necessity; it made cutting Mom out of my life all the more easy. The journey back to a much better financial state was no easy task. Then, the emotional impact of my mother's ultimate and final betrayal required an immense amount of time and work in which I listened to my inner dialogue. Along with reading from my new book, I began using EFT (Emotional Freedom Technique), which proved to be incredibly effective.

EFT tapping is a method of healing done through positive affirmations, stated sometimes in the negative first, then in the positive, while tapping the pressure points, or acupuncture points, on the body. Those pressure points are in the head and chest area, between the eyebrows, on the temples, under the eye socket, between the nose and top lip, the chin, clavicle, and the ribs below the heart. There are others, but I found these to be the most effective. I would say an incantation like, *"I know I've had a hard life, and I know it sometimes feels like there's no hope, but I choose to love, honor, and respect myself every day. All of the circumstances of my past have no power over me. I have the ability to overcome all the challenges I face ..."* I said this over and over and over. I did it in the morning and at night.

I found a gentleman named Brad Yates on YouTube, and, because he was the exact opposite of where I thought I could get help, I chose his methods of EFT. Thank you, Brad Yates.

I heard sometime later from Pio that William eventually committed suicide in relation to his sisters' involvement with the cult.

Now, I was healing, but I wasn't out of the darkness yet. On one morning walk to Peet's Coffee & Tea, I was rehearsing my day's incantation, hoping to have some kind of breakthrough. I got to the coffee shop, and, across from the whistling espresso machine and coffee room chatter, there was Mom. Seeing her was not too shocking. After all, it was Peet's, and that's where my whole family went for coffee.

She had already spotted me and was smiling at me. As I walked in, I was mildly unnerved, but what stabbed my heart with the force of a freight train was the orange scarf drapedproudly around her neck. Orange was the newly adopted color of the cult.

I almost made an about-face, but, in that instant, I thought, *"I'm not going to run or disrupt my routine because of her or because of anyone. I'm going to get my tea and be on my way."* The look on my face was not welcoming, and, as the line to order shortened, she came up to me and said, "You look like you have something to say to me."

To which I responded, "Yes! I do. Why don't I meet you outside after I make my tea?"

She agreed, and, in the few minutes it took for me to add the right amount of honey and milk, I decided I was going to tell her all of the things I had held back and never said.

I felt surprisingly calm, and the butterflies that usually accompanied me into battle were not there. A clear and decisive diatribe was being formulated. I calmly collected my tea, cleaned up after myself, and went out to finally confront this person I knew as Mom. I could feel a turbulence of emotion building from deep within, but I knew I could not lose my cool. I could not and would not come to an emotional breakdown, neither through anger or sadness. The things I had to say were severe and harsh, and I did not want to make a scene on the corner of Vine and Walnut. I suggested we cross the street to a less populated section of the block.

She knew I had a lot to say, so she waited expectantly, unaware of the barrage of merciless words that would soon be landing like an asteroid that had traversed the vastness of space to finally make its resting place on an unsuspecting planet.

When we reached the corner I began. "You have proven to be a disgusting, immoral, and reprehensible human being. You have the nerve and the audacity to smile and ask me how I am doing as you wear his color, representing your allegiance to him. After everything he did to your children. He destroyed our family. You destroyed our family."

My adrenaline began pumping with every word. "The suffering and the pain created three drug addicts and a dysfunctional, self-hating womanizer. Your selfishness has no bounds. You have been a self-serving narcissist betraying your children, for what? So you could collect our welfare money while we were being molested and abused."

She cut in with, "It was only $35 a month."

I raised my voice. "That is a bald-faced lie and you know it. You gave your 13-year-old daughter to a pedophile. You knowingly and willingly served her up as a piece of human life to be raped repeatedly in front of her little brothers while you and James partied, and we suffered. Do you have any idea what that did to our psychology, to our development, to our hearts? Do you see Jaci's addiction destroying his life and also destroying any chance for us to be loving brothers?

"We hate each other. You created that hate. I am appalled and disgusted by you. You didn't want to be under the rule of that sick, maniacal, evil scumbag, but you forced us to. Now you walk around with his colors around your neck? But, because you didn't go, you weren't put through the starving and beatings and daily humiliation of watching your brother and sister unjustly and cruelly treated. No, you got to smoke your cigarettes, drink your coffee, and fuck your boyfriend. All paid for by the state money you should have been spending feeding and raising your children."

She tried to interject, but I didn't stop. "But you know all of this. I knew all of this, and I was willing to forgive you, as incredible as that sounds. I worked diligently on that forgiveness for years, and what have you done? You have taken advantage of me, of your children, of your friends, of your community. You are the most selfish, narcissistic, dissociative, sociopathic bitch I have ever met."

"How?" she squeezed in.

"How? Mom! I read the letter you wrote to William releasing Om of any wrongdoing. Telling him Om is good and loving. You jeopardized his sisters' safety and well-being. I never want to see you again. You will never see or speak to Aché again."

In a dejected manner, she rolled her eyes sheepishly.

"You have betrayed my love, my trust for the last time. Goodbye! Never contact me again." I walked away feeling like a huge weight had been lifted from my shoulders, like the healing of a festering wound.

I thought about my commitment to love, compassion, and forgiveness. Was this an abandonment of my declaration? Could I forgive her for all of this and everything else, or was I a hypocrite?

I contemplated and reviewed my life. The multilayered, multifaceted complexity of healing while coping with PTSD proved to be an overwhelming and sometimes burdensome obligation to myself. But I knew it would be worth it for me, for my son, for my family, and for my community.

I had to map out my life step by step. I had to create a game plan, a course of action that would get me the specific measurable results I wanted, needed, and deserved. I knew I had to become a new kind of person. I was out to transform myself – again.

***

Fall down, get back up! The journey of self-discovery brought me through the fire of darkness, isolation, shame, and loneliness, which was the "fall down." For me, that was followed by "get up" – the self-reflection or personal inventory, the commitment to recovery – my dedication to focus on love, compassion, forgiveness, healing, and wellness. I wanted to understand how and why my mother and so many of the people in my community failed to protect me and all the other children of my childhood from the evil that men do. How could they knowingly and willingly allow their children to be exploited and abused?

After studying, analyzing, talking, and meditating on what happened, I've come to believe that it was a combination of many different factors, including selfishness, drugs, naiveté, and multigenerational PTSD. Undiagnosed and untreated mental health disorders, negligence, denial, and apathy also contributed to the abuse. The social and political climate of the era created the perfect storm for me to disappear and not have a single person call the police or report to Child Protective Services that a six-year-old boy was gone.

Cults have been around longer than organized religion and will continue to exist as long as humans seek the answers to our origin. They permeate every culture and society and their impact on society is grossly underestimated. They range from the Om Lovers to Jim Jones and the People's Temple, Children of God, the Source Family, the Symbionese Liberation Army, Europe's Solar Temple Cult, Japan's Aum Shin Rikyo Cult, and Heaven's Gate, all the way up to the larger cults like Scientology, the Jehovah's Witnesses, and the Mormon Church. They all inject an insidious poison into the lives of a vulnerable, unsuspecting public, disguised as the truth. Many are innocent victims, others are willing participants in the abuse, and still others were victims of child abuse who unwittingly continue to repeat the abuse as a result of their trauma. Some are just simple, ordinary people looking for hope, while others are just bad people.

According to Dr. Margaret Singer in *Cults in Our Midst*, an estimated 5,000 economic, political, and religious groups operate in the United States at any given time, with 2.5 million members. Over the last ten years, cults have used tactics of coercive mind control to negatively impact an estimated 20 million victims. Worldwide figures are even greater.

According to Dr. Paul Martin, cult expert and director of the Wellspring Retreat & Resource Center in Ohio, the cult problem is so prevalent that the chances of a family member joining a cult are greater than a family member catching chickenpox, four times greater than contracting AIDS, 90 times greater than contracting measles, and 45,000 times greater than contracting polio.

Dr. Martin says, "Compared to other social or medical problems, the havoc created by destructive cultism is the most understudied, neglected, and ignored mental health and social problem in the world ... If the symptoms exhibited in former cult members were attributed to a virus, it would be considered a worldwide epidemic."

When I did a search online, I discovered that one in three girls, and one in five boys, are sexually molested before the age of 12. There are more than three million reports of child abuse made every year. Between four to five children die every day from abuse or neglect. Forty to fifty percent of athletes experience abuse; sexual abuse in sports affects 8% of all athletes. Eighty percent of 21-year-olds who were abused as children meet the criteria for at least one psychological disorder.

These are just a few of the startling statistics on the subject, and these are only the reported ones. My experience was never reported, nor are those of the countless other survivors of child abuse who live, work, and play with you and your children. Or, maybe you are one. Studies show children who experience abuse are more likely to contract sexually transmitted diseases earlier in life, and/or develop drug and alcohol addiction, depression, and mental/behavioral health issues. Kaiser Permanente and the CDC did a study on childhood trauma called the Adverse Childhood Experiences Study, or ACES.

The term ACES describes abuse, neglect, and other types of experiences that occur to individuals under the age of 18. The study examined the relationship between these experiences during childhood and reduced health and well-being later in life. Participants in the study reflected a cross section of middle-class Americans and varied by gender, age, race, and education. For the sake of space, I will not provide an in-depth description of the methodology of the study, but rather give you its conclusions. Adults who scored one or higher on the ACE test had a significantly higher rate of obesity, drug addiction, sexually transmitted diseases, unemployment, incarceration, depression, anxiety, suicide attempts, diabetes, alcoholism, strokes, and cancer. People who had a score of seven or higher had a life expectancy 20 years less than people who scored zero. My score was nine out of ten.

Child abuse victims also have a higher likelihood of being sexually exploited and trafficked. Trafficking is the recruitment, harboring, transportation, provision, or obtaining of a person for labor or services, through the use of force, fraud, or coercion for the purpose of subjection to involuntary servitude, peonage, and debt bondage of slavery. In many cases, child abuse is committed by someone close, like a family member, coach, religious leader, extended relative, or friend of the family.

The impact this phenomenon has on our society is reported on daily in the nightly news, although it might not be directly identified as the reason for a crime, violence, prostitution, or death. But there are other equally deadly and sinister forces that exist in the shadows of our society that are a clear and present danger! A pandemic. It is, in fact, the root of why I believe this issue continues to plague our world: Apathy, denial, and silence all play a part. Turning a blind eye to child abuse makes all of us complicit.

Refusing to report child abuse due to some irrational moral or ethical misguidance makes us culpable. When people say, *"Not in my Church, not at my school, not on my team, not my family member,"* they are directly contributing to a cultural denial that protects predators. This is a cancer that continues to ruin the lives of our children and destroys the very essence of what makes us human.

Victims are kept locked in a prison of silence. This deafening silence from victims is perpetuated by the stigma that surrounds the issue, along with the embarrassment, shame, judgment, and fear of retaliation and ridicule by the perpetrator.

The journey of healing is arduous and challenging. Many victims never find the road that leads to healing. The lack of adequate support from family members, teachers, doctors, social services, police, and judges hinders healing. There is also the trauma of the experience itself, which can lead to an array of self-destructive behaviors triggered by PTSD. PTSD is an anxiety disorder that develops in reaction to physical injury or severe mental or emotional distress. A trigger is an emotional or physical sensation that brings up past or dormant memories. PTSD is multigenerational.

Many victims of child abuse become sexual predators. Others grow up and abuse their own children, continuing the cycle of abuse. Yet others are able to find help or have a natural ability and inclination towards resilience.

Abuse is a self-perpetuating illness that requires a drastic interruption. There are many paths to the road to health and wellness for adult survivors, including remembering, mourning, healing through cognitive therapy, counseling, group workshops, Alcoholics Anonymous (AA), and many, many others. There are also many organizations designed to help children, such as Seneca, Children International, and Youth Uprising.

I believe going from victim to survivor and on to a thriving life is possible for all of us. How do we interrupt the phenomenon and provide the tools to heal? How do we live with and manage PTSD? How do we go from victim to survivor to thriver?

Here are some approaches from an external, social, and environmental standpoint:

1. Starting with prenatal care, strongly integrate Child Protective Services (CPS) with doctors and nurses and provide families with counseling.
2. Provide more in-depth training for social workers to offer high-quality support.
3. When needed, remove the child from the home and ensure the child is placed preferably with family members or a qualified foster or adoptive-care parent.
4. Implement an education system which is trauma-informed and focuses on resilience-building from preschool through high school.

There are many other avenues to healing and wellness for children. I found through dance, music, yoga, theater, and martial arts, along with cognitive, art, and music therapies, that children can develop a sense of self-love, self-expression, freedom, and power, and that they can create an optimistic future vision. That's why I created the Well Child Foundation, (wellchildfoundation.com).

Through these arts, our children can build a future they design. My vision is to heal and empower children, to inspire a new generation of young people to discover their inner strength and to instill in them the ability and desire to live healthy, happy, and successful lives. I hope that, in some way, these words also help adult survivors to find the strength and inspiration to heal.

LOVE

Love is the most powerful force in the universe. Hatred, anger, jealousy, spite, and revenge all pale in comparison to love. All of those negative emotions require fuel. They are fueled by an experience or an indoctrination that is brought on or taught by some external force. If you're born into a white-supremacist household, you grow up hating non-whites. If you're a victim of a crime, you hate your perpetrator. If you belong to a certain religious faith and want to annihilate others of an opposing faith, it's because that's what you were taught. If you're from a particular country or from a different side of town in the same city of that country, you learn to hate the people who don't share your geographical location. If you have a favorite sports team and your team loses to the competition, an interaction can end in violence and even death.

All of these behaviors are learned. I am not saying that certain circumstances do not warrant anger and outrage, but that they are all driven by external forces. When there is no fuel for hate, it dissipates.

Love does not require an external force or fuel for its existence. The best example of this is the unconditional love a parent feels for his or her child. No matter what that child does, it will not result in the disintegration of a parent's love (except in cases of certain mental illnesses). Siblings may rival, but their love can exist permanently if we can strip away all the hurt that is created by the environment. Love is an unseen force that exists at all times without the need for an external fuel. It is the love of sunlight that makes the flowers grow. Love can also be developed, nurtured, and grown, as is witnessed by what expands between two people who care for each other, or by what is cultivated when a reverence for life is fostered.

Self-love and cultivating love for others is where we gain access to the unlimited source of what I believe drives the expanding universe. By acknowledging the inherent value in the smallest forms of life, we maturate our own self-worth, which allows us to expand and cultivate our self-love.

We can examine our personal experiences and put them into a clearer perspective. Although adverse childhood experiences prove that certain experiences can lead to certain outcomes, I think that's only part of the equation. I assert that we are not solely the products of our experiences, the environment, and genetic predisposition, but that we are the creators of our future through choice.

I choose, therefore I am. Most adults who have experienced childhood trauma live their lives from a decision that was created in or around the time of the traumatic event. *"My father sexually abuses me, therefore ..."*

"My mother abandoned me, therefore I must be unlovable" was the line I made up about myself. We are unqualified to make such observations about

the world at such a young age, yet we convince ourselves of this fabrication and go about our lives gathering more evidence to support it. *"God (Richard Thorne) beats me, ridicules me, and tortures me, therefore I must be unlovable." "My brother and sister left me behind, therefore I am of no value."*

The truth is, rather, that those were events that took place in my childhood. They were just that – events. What I did with those events, in my child's mind, was to create "meaning" about the events, which led to all of the destructive behavior I engaged in during my teen and adult life. Finding reasons to hate myself, like the acne pock marks that made me feel ugly, provided more evidence. I didn't have anyone to help me or take care of me, and that was additional evidence to my mind. It all intensified my self-loathing.

So often we find ourselves making excuses about the condition of our lives. *"If my boss wasn't such a jerk." "I'm like this because I was never given the opportunity." "My family was like this."* All of these are self-perpetuating lies. We are the products of all the choices we've made after the traumatic events occurred.

None of those decisions I made about myself were true. I *am* lovable, I *do* have value, I *am* handsome and deserving of joy, happiness, and peace. When I discovered that I could choose to actively love myself, I began to slowly open the door to create a new way of being. It required me to remind myself daily and exercise a diligent, focused, intentional practice of self-love. I began to understand that I was worthy of love, despite the events of my childhood. But I also learned that I would have to create and foster and pursue my cultivation of love daily.

Discovering that my past did not equal my future and that I was more than a product of my experiences was instrumental in my healing. I had to take 100% responsibility for my life without exception. As I recovered from the trauma of my childhood, exploring and cultivating self-love was the first step on the journey to emotional wellness and healing.

Next, I began to expand that love to others, to animals and plants. Ultimately, a love of life grew inside of me. It requires constant attention and intention. My decisions are crafted out of love. I cross-reference my choices with this love. Is drinking and driving an act of self-love? No! I don't drive drunk. I realize I can correct my behavior by using love as the measure for my conduct. When I am able to base all or most of my decisions from this place of love as my barometer, I see an enormous jump in my productivity at work, in my personal relationships, and in my general life experiences. I find myself doing far less risky behaviors.

I decided to stop drinking and smoking and doing drugs for a year at a time. I ate healthier foods, not because I had to, but because I chose to out of honoring this love.

As long as I generate my life from this place, I cannot make a bad decision.

My life has blossomed, my relationships have flourished, my self-concept has changed, and my health has improved. This inner transformation was not some blissful Utopian state of mind brought on by positive thinking. I still get mad, and I still react to triggers in my environment, but I have learned that, if I take the time to evaluate my choices and use self-love as the platform, I will not just survive, but thrive. Love is life's greatest experience.

FORGIVENESS

Forgiveness is the next ingredient in my recipe for healing and wellness. The first place forgiveness begins is within. This was very, very difficult for me. It was counterintuitive. I secretly blamed, hated, and loathed myself and everyone else for what happened to me. I say secretly because I didn't consciously know I blamed myself, and I was afraid to voice my true feelings out of fear of some kind of punishment born out of my PTSD. I didn't feel safe, so I carried this hatred in me for many years.

The good thing about negative feelings and emotions is that they can be unlearned. One of the most powerful tools for overcoming feelings of negativity and destructive behavior is forgiveness. The inability to forgive is at the root of unhappiness. It's like a quiet cancer that secretly grows inside and consumes your spirit. I've been witness to its power in the lives of my closest friends. It can be unrelenting and all-consuming, if we let it.

The inability to forgive ourselves is the number one cause for grief, resentment, anger, and turmoil. If we are going to heal, if we are going to set an example for our children, we must find forgiveness. We must forgive ourselves for EVERYTHING we have ever done that was not congruent with our inner spirit.

There is a second piece to achieving forgiveness – repentance. Repentance is a commitment to never under any circumstance repeat that thing for which we seek forgiveness. Accepting that we are not perfect, that we will make mistakes, yet will stand committed to that truth, will allow for forgiveness.

Then, we must forgive EVERYONE else. EVERYONE who has ever hurt us in the past. We must commit to health, wellness, and to living a happy, loving, peaceful life above all else in order to take on the mighty endeavor of forgiving others.

The first place to look in forgiving others is toward our parents. The lines of communication are not always open with our parents; in some cases, many years may have passed since your last conversation. If you have to, write them a letter. Maybe your parents have passed on. Still, writing a letter to them can be very cathartic. In it, forgive them for all of their mistakes. Then, make a list of every person who has hurt you in the past and begin forgiving them. The hardest people for me to forgive, even more than William Brumfield, AKA Richard Thorne or Om, were the women in his cult, especially Harmony and Perfection, who I still run into on occasion to this day.

Next, move on to your family members, like your brothers, sisters, cousins, or maybe "that one uncle." Sometimes they have hurt us more than our parents. Next, our lovers, spouses, and friends. You could even go as far as to forgive the criminals in our society and our leaders, who may often be one and the same.

These were the steps I had to take in order to take control of my life and begin the healing process. I knew in order for my son to get the best version of me, I had to flush out the poison and replace it with love, forgiveness, and compassion.

COMPASSION

My earliest memory of feeling compassion, although I did not know its name, was when I was trying to help little Prosperity when she was tied to that bed all those years ago with her horrible skin disease. I don't know if that incident germinated a seed that lay dormant in my being or if it was learned. Maybe I learned it from Isabella, who set an example of tenderness for me before the Om lovers came. That experience brought me face-to-face with my vulnerability, and I understood the hurt and abandonment Prosperity felt.

I have since found compassion to be, along with love, one of the most powerful tools for navigating the landscape of my humanity. Knowing and living through so much of my own pain and seeing so much child abuse in those early days, I learned that each of us walks a separate path, and, on it, we must each face some kind of pain, sorrow, loneliness, or fear. But love, compassion, safety, happiness, and connection are the inalienable rights of all children as the building blocks for life. Unfortunately, many do not have those elements in their lives.

From behind my prison of silence, I saw the hurt, pain, and suffering in the faces of so many. It gave me an understanding that behind the eyes of every human being is a story of tragedy or triumph, of joy or pain, of good or evil.

We all require the gift of compassion. Compassion for ourselves is the start. Then we can apply a gentleness and reverence for our own innocence. But before we can give it to ourselves, we must receive it from our parents in conjunction with other family members, friends, teachers, and community members. Then and only then can we offer it to others. Compassion cannot be a convenience; it must be a state of mind.

Looking back at all the turmoil, pain, and suffering that my family endured, as well as the struggles of the pimps, hustlers, drug dealers, and prostitutes I knew from my life on the streets, I believe if they had the blessing of more compassion from their parents and childhood caregivers, they would have had a better chance of living happier, more well-adjusted and successful lives.

It seems that most people want to blame their parents, their teachers, the government, the weather, any and everything around them. They're unable to own where they are in life and why they are there. There's a saying, "Don't judge another unless you've walked a mile in his or her shoes." I believe we all must take full, 100% responsibility for our actions and where we are in life and for the kind of life we are living. What we have and where we are in life is because of the choices we've made after the trauma, right up until this very moment.

We cannot blame anyone for our unhappiness or the circumstances that we find ourselves in. No one is responsible for where we are in life except us as individuals. With a commitment to developing wellness and cultivating ourselves with rigorous self-reflection, naked accountability, and by granting ourselves compassion for our mistakes and awarding it to others, we can, with love, find the road to health and wellness.

There's an ancient Greek fable about a traveler who stops to ask an old man which road is the way to Mount Olympus, and the old man replies, "If you really want to get to Mount Olympus, every step you take must be in that direction." That old man was Socrates. Love finds its greatest expression in giving, manifested through compassion and forgiveness.

FINAL WORDS

We all have the ability to make our way out of the darkness. We can turn our lives around with the decision and commitment to do so. Choice and freewill are our greatest gifts. Let us create and expand who we are, and how we relate to ourselves, our families, communities, and society. It's not too late to have a wonderful life and to share that wonderment with the less fortunate. A kind word, a loving gesture, or an act of kindness to a stranger can change the trajectory of their life. I know because it happened to me.

I believe it is my duty, and our duty as a society, and for humanity as a whole, to break the chain of apathy, silence, and shame. And not just for child abuse, molestation, and human trafficking, but for all forms of abuse. I hope that by having shared my story that I have helped other people who have suffered in silence to find their voice, or perhaps, you to find yours. May it be a voice of confidence, a voice of joy, a voice of self-expression.